THE OBSERVER'S
SOVIET AIRCRAFT
DIRECTORY

COMPILED BY
WILLIAM GREEN
AND GORDON SWANBOROUGH

FREDERICK WARNE & CO LTD London
FREDERICK WARNE & CO INC New York

Published by Frederick Warne & Co Ltd 1975

© *Pilot Press Ltd 1975*

LIBRARY OF CONGRESS
CATALOG CARD NO 73—89832

ISBN 0 7232 1529 4

Printed in Great Britain by
William Clowes & Sons, Limited
London, Beccles and Colchester
51.874

Introduction

On 24 April 1946, the Soviet aircraft industry flew for the first time prototypes of turbojet-driven fighters of original design. Powered by sequestrated German engines, these fighters were crude and relatively ineffectual by comparison with their western contemporaries, but unremarkable in concept or performance though they may have been, they represented the first Soviet step in overhauling the commanding lead in combat aircraft capability enjoyed by the West.

All but three decades have since elapsed; nearly 30 years during which the Soviet Union has pursued a massive campaign to achieve aviation technological parity if not supremacy. Emphasis has been placed on the development of military aircraft systems and as major programmes have translated from the experimental, through the production, to the service phase, there have been numerous occasions when western complacency has been shaken profoundly; when western concern has resulted from evidence of the progressively accelerating growth of Soviet expertise. The writing on the wall was first seen when the MiG-15—a warplane that could out-climb and out-manœuvre the best of its western opponents—made its début in Korean skies barely five years after the first Soviet jet fighters had flown as prototypes. Soviet combat aircraft design capability was again demonstrated forcibly some eight years later with the MiG-21, which is still, today, recognised internationally as being numbered, if not among the most sophisticated or advanced, certainly among the most efficaceous air superiority weapons in service.

More recent Soviet technological progress in military aviation hardware is to be seen in the service introduction during the early 'seventies of a fighter undeniably capable of Mach 3·0 speeds and a service ceiling of the order of 80,000 feet, and advanced variable-geometry medium- and deep-penetration strike aircraft and a strategic bomber; these markedly reducing the qualitative advantages which, hitherto enjoyed by western combat aircraft, have served in some measure to balance massive Soviet quantitative superiority. The tempo of quality improvement has been particularly noteworthy of late in the equipment of the tactical elements of the Soviet Air Forces and the Warsaw Pact countries deployed along the western periphery of the USSR, dictating upward re-assessment of NATO projections of Soviet tactical capabilities over the remainder of the decade, giving, at a time when western defences are being eroded by dissension and economic difficulties, rise to widespread concern.

In the sphere of commercial aircraft development, the Soviet aircraft industry has consistently lagged behind the West in certain respects—the shortcomings of modern Soviet airliners were underlined during 1974 by the dissatisfaction of Egypt's national carrier, Egyptair, with its newly-acquired fleet of Tu-154s, this airline's chairman stating at the time that Egyptair had 'no intention to fly the aircraft any longer unless repeatedly requested modifications be made to fuel, electrical and fire-extinguishing systems.' Nevertheless, shortcomings or no, Aeroflot *did* introduce on its routes the world's second commercial jet transport in 1956, and the world's first airliner powered by turbofan engines in 1962, and on the last day of 1968, the Soviet aircraft industry flew what was, by a hair's breadth, the world's *first* supersonic commercial airliner.

There can be no doubt that Soviet expertise *still* lags behind that of the West in some critical areas, but what gaps remain are being closed fast. According to estimates arrived at by the Central Intelligence Agency, the Soviet Union and the USA are devoting roughly equal amounts of their resources to military procurement, but the former is spending the equivalent of 25 per cent more on research and development. Intelligence appraisals of Soviet aircraft production suggest that 1,800–2,000 military aircraft are being manufactured annually—an imposing quantity indeed.

The *Observer's Soviet Aircraft Directory* has two main purposes. First and foremost, it attempts to provide as comprehensive a reference to current Soviet aircraft as is possible within the obvious limitations imposed by characteristic Soviet reluctance to reveal detailed facts and equal reluctance on the part of western intelligence agencies to reveal the extent of what information they have gleaned. Some operational background is provided for these aircraft by a general outline of the organisation of the Soviet Air Forces today and an historical survey of the national airline, Aeroflot, the latter having been contributed by John Stroud, internationally recognized as an airline historian.

The secondary purpose of the *Observer's Soviet Aircraft Directory* is to trace, by means of the western system of assigning reporting names to Soviet aircraft, the development of aircraft in the USSR in all the various categories over the past quarter-century plus, and to explain the cryptic appellations assigned their aircraft by the Soviet design bureaux and the Government agencies.

The illustrative content of the book includes 356 individual line drawings, which, prepared by Dennis I. Punnett and the copyright of Pilot Press Limited, are the result of many years' research and believed to be the most accurate yet prepared depicting Soviet aircraft, plus 320 carefully selected photographs. Credits for photographs supplied by individual sources appear on page 256.

Contents

DESIGNATING SOVIET AIRCRAFT

Over the past score-and-ten years, confusion in the West concerning the designations applied to Soviet aircraft, and particularly to those aircraft employed by the Soviet armed forces, has increased steadily. When hostilities in Europe terminated in 1945, aircraft development in the Soviet Union was already becoming something of an enigma to the western nations. With the onset of the cold war and the progressive worsening of relations between the Soviet *bloc* and the Soviet Union's erstwhile western allies, the gathering of intelligence concerning military aviation development on the far side of what had come to be called the 'iron curtain' was transformed from an activity of casual interest in the West to one acknowledged to be of vital importance.

Apart from vague generalities disseminated for purposes of propaganda, no *official* information was forthcoming from the Soviet Union, and although the newer progeny of the Soviet aircraft design bureaux were glimpsed fleetingly from time to time, they could rarely be tied to a precise designation. But

it is axiomatic that an essential requirement in air intelligence is the ability to attach a designation to an aircraft when its existence becomes known, and as few official Soviet designations percolated through the security mesh of the 'iron curtain', a system of designating Soviet aircraft had to be evolved in the West for reporting purposes.

The Lavochkin La-150 (above right), the first prototype of which is illustrated, was referred to for identification purposes in the West as the 'Type 8', and the Tupolev Tu-73 (below), forerunner of the Tu-14, was allocated the designation 'Type 12'

In an attempt to meet this requirement, a system of *Type* numbers was conceived. The original intention was to utilize a *Type* number for each new Soviet aircraft as it was sighted, the precise designation of the aircraft being applied when it became known with certainty. The *Type* numbers were thus restricted to aircraft not fully identified, the arrangement being a compromise between a reporting system and an intelligence system. However, intelligence is a cat-and-mouse affair, western agencies soon concluding that it would be inadvisable to reveal to their Soviet opposite numbers how much they had or had not discovered. The *Type* numbers were therefore retained even after the Soviet designation of the aircraft concerned had been ascertained.

The *Type* numbers were applied indiscriminately, no attempt being made to indicate the function or status of the aircraft, and within a short space of time 40 had been issued, but the system was proven ineffective when it was discovered that, in some cases, several different *Type* numbers had been allocated to one aircraft type, and in 1954 the system was abandoned. The principal *Type* numbers issued were as follows, the actual Soviet service designations or, in cases where the aircraft failed to attain service status, the design bureau designations being included in parentheses:

Type 1	(Yak-15)	Type 26	(Yak-17)
Type 2	(MiG-9)	Type 27	(Il-28)
Type 7	(Yak-19)	Type 28	(Yak-23)
Type 8	(La-150)	Type 29	(MiG-15UTI)
Type 9	(Tu-77)	Type 30	(Tu-14UTB)
Type 10	(Il-22)	Type 31	(Tu-85)
Type 12	(Tu-73)	Type 32	(Mi-1)
Type 14	(MiG-15)	Type 35	(Mi-14)
Type 15	(La-15)	Type 36	(Mi-4)
Type 16	(Yak-17UTI)	Type 37	(M-4)
Type 20	(MiG-15)	Type 39	(Tu-16)
Type 21	(La-15)	Type 40	(Tu-20)

With the *Type* number system proven unsatisfactory, it was obvious that a standardised system of colloquial names that could be applied to *all* Soviet aircraft types was desirable, overcoming language difficulties in translation, transliteration and pronunciation. Thus, in 1954, the Air Standards Co-ordinating Committee (which involves the USA, the UK, Canada, Australia and New Zealand) proposed to the North Atlantic Treaty Organization (NATO) what appeared to be an ideal reporting system in which a name was applied to every Soviet aircraft type believed to be in service or intended for service, irrespective of whether or not the actual Soviet designation was known. It was agreed to adopt this proposal and all Soviet aircraft to which *Type* numbers had been allocated under the earlier system and which were known to have been superseded or to have failed to advance further than experimental status were omitted from the list of 55 appellations compiled, and it was proposed to add to the list as new Soviet aircraft were reported. A number of obsolete aircraft that it was believed might still be in use in the Soviet Union or could have been passed to the Soviet 'satellites' received names under the new system which thus included several US wartime Lend-Lease types.

THE NATO SYSTEM

The new identification system adopted by NATO in 1954 employed a simple key: the names allocated to bombers and attack aircraft commenced with the letter 'B' (indicating *Bomber*), those for fighters and fighter-bombers commenced with the letter 'F' (indicating *Fighter*), transport aircraft, both civil and military, were given names commencing with 'C' (indicating *Cargo*), and the names of miscellaneous fixed-wing aircraft (e.g., trainers, flying boats, cargo gliders) began with the letter 'M' (indicating *Miscellaneous*). To differentiate between airscrew-driven and turbojet-driven aircraft, the former were allocated names possessing only one syllable while names for the latter possessed two syllables. All rotorcraft, both piston-engined and turboshaft-powered, were given names commencing with the letter 'H' (indicating *Helicopter*), and in this instance the number of syllables had no meaning. To indicate a variant of a basic type a suffix letter was appended to the name (e.g., *Flagon-A*, *Flagon-B*), and the system was intended to include any new aircraft of foreign design and manufacture that should enter Soviet service with the course of time.

Although sound in essence, with the passage of years this naming system has not proved infallible. For instance, when, in 1959, NATO became aware of the existence of the prototypes of the Tu-28 two-seat multi-purpose aircraft as a result of a clandestine USAF photographic reconnaissance of an experimental test establishment within the Soviet Union, the size of the aircraft led to the belief that it was essentially a bomber and the appellation *Blinder* was bestowed on the type. It was only as a result of the air display held on 9 July 1961, at Tushino, near Moscow, when the multi-purpose role of the aircraft with emphasis on the intercept task became manifestly obvious, that the name was changed to *Fiddler*, the name *Blinder* being simultaneously transferred to the Tu-22 bomber which made its public début at the same time over Tushino, and the existence of which had previously remained unknown in the West.

At times names have been allocated to aircraft whose development had, in fact, already been abandoned in the Soviet Union, cases in point being provided by the *Brawny* (Il-40), the *Blowlamp* (Il-54), and the *Boot* (Tu-91), these providing one of the more humorous aspects of air intelligence. This trio was shown briefly to a western delegation headed by the then C-in-C of the USAF, General Nathan F. Twining, at Kubinka airfield, near Moscow, in 1956, and it is to be wondered if there was not a twinkle in the eye of the Soviet host who assured the delegates that these were among the latest Soviet combat aircraft. Accordingly, identification names were allocated to them. Many years were to elapse before it was to be revealed that the three aircraft types had completed their flight test programmes and their further development had been abandoned *prior* to the delegation's visit. Soviet reluctance to reveal the service designations of their military aircraft at this time is illustrated by an incident that occurred during the visit of the western dele-

This first generation Soviet jet fighter, the Yak-19, appeared in 1947, and was referred to in the West as the Type 7

gation to Kubinka. While passing an example of the Myasishchev-designed M-4 heavy bomber, a member of the delegation asked an accompanying V-VS General the designation of the aircraft, the Soviet officer replying enigmatically, ' That is the bomber that you call *Bison* !'

At other times, names have been allocated only to be promptly changed when it became obvious that their use could lead to confusion, examples being provided by the Il-28 which was initially named *Butcher*, only to be rechristened *Beagle* when the similarity of the earlier appellation to *Badger* (Tu-16) was seen, and the Yak-28 originally dubbed *Brassard* but renamed *Brewer* when it was pointed

The Yak-28 tactical aircraft was assigned suffix letters for pro-gressive versions, illustrated being the Yak-28I (Brewer–C)

out by NATO Headquarters in Paris that the original name could be confused with *Broussard*, the name of the then widely-used Holste M.H.1521M light utility transport.

Despite such incidents as those cited, the naming system adopted by NATO *has* proved effective, although with the passage of 20 years a *lot* of new Soviet aircraft have made appearances, and as the list of identification names has grown to its present total of 122, the ingenuity of the Air Standards Co-ordinating Committee (ASCC) responsible for conceiving and allocating names as soon as new Soviet aircraft appear has been increasingly taxed until some of the names bestowed have ranged from the mildly amusing to the almost hilarious.

THE SOVIET SYSTEM

There is a growing tendency in the West to use the official Soviet designations where they are known, or are *believed* to be known, but there is some confusion between Soviet

service designations and Soviet *design bureau* designations, further zest being added to the game by Soviet insistence on using mystifying combinations of letters and figures for standard aircraft types adapted for record-breaking pur-poses. An example of the confusion existing in the West between Soviet service and design bureau designations is provided by the turboprop-driven heavy strategic bomber dubbed *Bear*, this frequently being referred to as the Tu-95, which was the design bureau designation and *not* the service designation which is Tu-20. Conversely, the *Badger* and *Blinder* are usually referred to as the Tu-16 and Tu-22, these being service designations, the respective design bureau designations for these types being Tu-88 and Tu-105.

Compounding the confusion are instances of official Soviet service designations being used in conjunction with the suffix letters appended to reporting names (e.g., the MiG-21MF or *Fishbed-J* being referred to as the 'MiG-21J'). The previously-mentioned cryptic nomenclature for record-breaking purposes, first instituted some 17 years ago, is totally unrelated to either service or design bureau designa-tions (e.g., the MiG-25 interceptor and reconnaissance air-craft dubbed *Foxbat* by NATO has established a number of speed and altitude records as the Ye-266), and was presum-ably originally adopted to avoid providing the western intelligence agencies gratuitously with the true designations of more-or-less secret aircraft and power plants when making formal declarations concerning the details of the new records to the Fédération Aéronautique Internationale.

The basis of the official Soviet system for designating air-craft adopted by the armed forces has remained unchanged since its introduction in 1940 in place of the system indicating the role of the aircraft but affording no indication of design origin. The current system utilizes an abbreviation indicat-ing the leader(s) of the OKB (*Opytno-Konstruktorskoye Byuro*, or Experimental Design Bureau) responsible for the design (or the original leader, now deceased or retired, whose name is commemorated in the appellation of the OKB, e.g., 'Design Bureau named after S. V. Ilyushin' which has been headed by Genrikh Novozhilov since Ilyushin's retirement). This is followed by a number which, in theory, is applied when the aircraft successfully completes State Acceptance Trials or is ordered into production, odd numbers being applied to fighters (e.g., MiG-19, MiG-21, MiG-23) and even numbers to all other types (e.g., Tu-12, Tu-14, Tu-16), but as with everything else in the Soviet Union, there are apparently inexplicable if infrequent exceptions to this rule, an example being the use of the Yak-11 designation for a basic trainer (this being accounted for by the fact that this type had been designed as a *fighter*-trainer).

Again, the advent of multi-purpose aircraft, the basic design of which is intended to fulfil more than one principal role, has added complexity to the situation. An outstanding case in point is provided by the second and third generation derivatives of the Yak-25 all-weather interceptor. Design development of this aircraft led to the Yak-25R tactical reconnaissance aircraft, the suffix letter 'R' indicating *Razvedchik* or 'Reconnaissance Aircraft'. This, in turn, was evolved into the aerodynamically refined Yak-27 produced in substantial numbers for the tactical reconnaissance role as the Yak-27R (see page 241) and in limited numbers for the all-weather intercept task as the Yak-27P. The suffix letter 'P' indicated *Perekhvatchik* or 'Interceptor', a term used in the Soviet Union over the past two decades in the all-weather intercept connotation and (with the Yak-27P being the exception proving the rule) signifying the *addition* of suitable radar to a basic design created primarily for another role (e.g., MiG-17P and MiG-19P which were essentially clear-weather interceptors adapted for the limited all-weather intercept task). In the case of the Yak-27P, the suffix letter indicating a specialized role was applied despite the fact that the role indicated was that for which the aircraft concerned was specifically *intended*. A further derivative, the Yak-28, was developed primarily as a tactical attack bomber to succeed the Il-28, and featuring further aerodynamic refinement, an internal weapons bay, a revised undercarriage and more powerful engines, was adopted for the V-VS, but an all-weather interceptor variant evolved simultaneously and also adopted for the V-VS, retained the even number' bomber designation to which was added the letter 'P'.

The suffix letter of the Yak-28P designation indicated an interceptor variant (seen below) of the basic Yak-28 design

Service numbers are issued in the sequence in which aircraft from a particular OKB are accepted, but the application of a service designation does not necessarily mean that the aircraft concerned *will* attain production or service status, as later evaluation, the superiority of a competitive type, or changes in official requirements, may still lead to its eventual abandonment, this accounting for gaps in the numerical sequences of service designations of aircraft of an individual OKB that actually achieve service.

The OKB abbreviations that have been used or are currently in use as prefixes for both Soviet commercial and service aircraft designations are as follows:

Examples of the use of suffix letters are provided by the Su-7U (above) and the MiG-17PFU (below)

Oleg K. Antonov	**An**
A. A. Arkhangel'sky	**Ar**
Georgi M. Beriev	**Be**
Ivan P. Bratukhin	**B**
Ivor Chetverikov	**Che**
V. K. Gribovsky	**G**
Sergei V. Ilyushin	**Il**
Nikolai N. Kamov*	**Ka**
Semyon A. Lavochkin*	**La**
Artem Mikoyan* and	
Mikhail Gurevich*†	**Mig**
Mikhail L. Mil*	**Mi**
Vladimir M. Myasishchev	**M**
Vladimir M. Petlyakov*	**Pe**
Nikolai N. Polikarpov*	**Po**
Vladimir Shavrov	**Sh**
A. I. Shcherbakov	**Shche**
Pavel O. Sukhoi	**Su**
V. P. Tsybin	**Ts**
Andrei N. Tupolev*	**Tu**
Aleksandr S. Yakovlev	**Yak**
V. G. Yermolayev*	**Yer**

Aircraft possessing purely civil application normally retain their design bureau designations when they enter service.

*Deceased.
†MiG prefix retained by Artem Mikoyan's OKB after death of his co-designer Mikhail Gurevich. This OKB is now known as the 'Design Bureau named after A. I. Mikoyan and M. I. Gurevich'.

Another current example of the use of the suffix letter 'U' to indicate an instructional or training adaptation of a combat aircraft is provided by the Tupolev Tu-22U (above), assigned the ASCC designation Blinder-D (see pages 219–221)

There have been instances when confusion has arisen from the service début of one type (e.g., the MiG-25) prior to that of another to which an earlier type number has been allocated (e.g., MiG-23), resulting in the temporary transposition of these designations in western publications.

It should be mentioned that the previously-described system of designating aircraft is not generally employed by the Soviet armed forces, which utilize a classified system of their own; a coded system that, it may be presumed, identifies the sub-variant of an individual aircraft type or its specific equipment standard. Some fighters, for example, are assigned the letter 'K', which it is assumed signifies the aircraft category, this letter being followed by three numerals to complete the designation.

THE USE OF SUFFIX LETTERS

The practice common in the West of employing suffix letters in alphabetical sequence to indicate developments or modifications of a basic aircraft design is not used in the Soviet Union other than for commercial transports, and even then no consistent method is followed. A rarely-used Soviet method of signifying a major change in a basic aircraft type is the application of *bis*, *ter*, etcetera (e.g., MiG-15bis), these being among the many Latin words absorbed into the Soviet vocabulary and roughly equivalent to 'Mark Two', 'Mark Three', etc., but variants are normally indicated by one or more suffix letters which, apart from the commercial transports previously mentioned, indicate either a modified role or function, or provision for new or modified equipment or power plant, an exception being the application of 'M' (**M**) which simply means *Modifikatsirovanny* or 'Modified' (e.g., Su-7BM) without giving any indication of what the modification is.

Conversion trainer derivatives of standard service combat aircraft have received, in the case of fighters, the letters 'UTI' (УТИ) appended to the basic designation, this usually being added as a suffix (e.g., MiG-15UTI) but sometimes being employed as a prefix (e.g., UTI-MiG-15), and indicating *Uchebno-Trenirovochny Istrebitel*, literally 'Instructional Training Fighter'. In so far as bombers are concerned, a similar practice was initially employed with conversion training models, the letters 'UTB' (УТБ) being added to the designation (e.g., Tu-14UTB) to indicate *Uchebno-Treniro-*

vochny Bombardirovshchik, or 'Instructional Training Bomber', but these three-letter appendages have now been discarded in favour of the single letter 'U' (У) which is now employed almost exclusively as a suffix (e.g., MiG-23U, Su-7U, Tu-22U, etc). The use of the letter 'P' (П) indicating *Perekhvatchik* ('Interceptor') in the context of radar-directed all-weather interception has already been mentioned, and in the case of the all-weather variant of the MiG-21 day fighter this is used in conjunction with the letter 'F' (Ф) indicating *Forsirovanny*, literally 'Boosted'. When afterburners were first introduced in the Soviet Union, the letter 'F' was added to the designation of the aircraft to which they were applied (e.g., MiG-9F), but with the increasing use of afterburning this suffix letter came to mean any method of increasing the power of the basic aircraft, such as the installation of an uprated engine (e.g., MiG-21F). Thus, the MiG-17PF is an all-weather radar-equipped variant of the MiG-17F, which, in turn was an *afterburner*-equipped version of the basic MiG-17, and the MiG-21PF is an all-weather interceptor model of the MiG-21F but the 'F' suffix indicates that, by comparison with the original MiG-21 from which it is derived, it has an *uprated* engine.

Other suffix letters used to indicate changes in the basic function of a combat aircraft include 'T' (Т) to indicate *Torpedonosets* or 'Torpedo Carrier' (e.g., Il-28T), this being a naval term and the suffix, now obsolete, having been applied to torpedo-bombing versions of light tactical bombers supplied to the *Aviatsiya Voenno-morskovo Flota* (AV-MF), the Soviet naval air arm; 'R' (Р) for *Razvedchik* or 'Reconnaissance Aircraft' (e.g., MiG-15bisR, MiG-21R, Il-28R, Yak-28R), and 'B' (Б) indicating *Bombardirovschik* or 'Bomber'. This last-mentioned suffix letter is sometimes added to the designations of fighters to indicate that they have been optimised for the fighter-bomber role (e.g., MiG-23B, Su-7BM, the 'M' added to the latter designation indicating an unspecified modification).

Relatively infrequent use is made in the Soviet Union of suffix letters to indicate a design change. One example is provided by the MiG-19S, the 'S' signifying *Stabilizator*— the application of an all-moving slab-type tailplane. Another method of indicating a design change by use of suffix letters is provided by the MiG-21PF(SPS), the primary suffix signifying *Perekhvatchik Forsirovanny* and the additional letters in parentheses indicating the application of *sduva pogranichnovo sloya*, a boundary layer blowing system. An alternative style of signifying the application of SPS to earlier production MiG-21 variants was simply the addition of an 'S' to the basic suffix letters (e.g., MiG-21PFS, MiG-21US). With standardization of the SPS by the next basic production model of the fighter, the MiG-21PFM, the additional suffix was discarded.

There is considerably less consistency in the use of suffix letters by the design bureaux for purely commercial aircraft, or aircraft possessing both commercial and military roles, each bureau following its own system, and the same suffix letter sometimes having an entirely different meaning when applied to aircraft of different design origin. The letter 'P' (П) provides an admirable example of this. To differentiate between the military and commercial models of the Il-14 transport that were being manufactured in parallel, the Ilyushin bureau designated the latter Il-14P, the 'P' suffix indicating *Passazhirskii* or Passenger; when Aleksandr Yakovlev evolved a single-seat aerobatic variant of the Yak-18 two-seat trainer he designated the new model Yak-18P, but in this case the 'P' indicated *Pilotazhny* ('Aerobatic'), and the water bomber version of the An-2 utility transport is designated An-2P, the suffix letter now indicating *Protivopozharny*, or 'Fire Protection'.

It is by no means unknown for suffix letters applied to the variants of one basic aircraft type to indicate a role in one instance and a modification to the basic design in another. The Yak-18 is a case in point. The first variant of the basic production trainer, the Yak-18U, differed from its progenitor primarily in having a nosewheel undercarriage, and the 'U' (У) suffix was indicative of *Usovershenstvovanny* (Improved). This was followed by the Yak-18A with aerodynamic refinements and a more powerful AI-14R engine, the 'A' (**A**) indicating *Aerodynamichesky* and referring to the refinement of the basic design. The single-seat aerobatic Yak-18P already referred to followed, and a specially-developed version for the 1966 Aerobatic Championships received the designation Yak-18PM, the 'PM' (**ПМ**) signifying *Pilotazhno-Modifikatsirovanny* ('Aerobatic-Modified'), while a four-seater evolved in the same year by Sergei Yakovlev, the son of Aleksandr Yakovlev, is designated Yak-18T, the 'T' signifying *Transportny* ('Transport'). Another example is afforded by the An-2 which, for the night reconnaissance and artillery direction role, was dubbed An-2NRK (**HPK**) for *Nochnoi-Razvedchik-Korrektorovshchik* ('Night-Reconnaissance and Air Observation Post'), in basic float seaplane form is the An-2V, the 'V' (**B**) indicating *Vodyanoi* ('Water Floatplane'), and the modified agricultural variant introduced in 1964 is designated An-2M, the 'M' signifying *Modifikatsirovanny* ('Modified').

On occasions when an alphabetic sequence of letters *is* used to denote variants, the Cyrillic alphabet makes its contribution to western confusion accentuated by lack of uniformity. Whereas the Cyrillic **A** is the first letter of the alphabet and equivalent to the western 'A', the Cyrillic equivalent of the western 'B' is **Б**, and is *sometimes* omitted from the sequence of suffix letters in favour of the third letter of the Cyrillic alphabet which is 'V' (**B**), but its similarity to the western 'B' has led to the erroneous belief in the West that the An-24V and Tu-124V are, in fact, the 'An-24B' and 'Tu-124B'. Further confusion results from the inconsistency displayed. A standard version of the Il-18 *Moskva* (Moscow) medium-haul transport was the Il-18V (**B**), and the provisional designation for the next model, the Il-18D (**Д**), was, in fact, Il-18I (**И**) which was incorrectly rendered in the West as Il-18-I.

This by now almost unintelligible system is further complicated by the simultaneous use in certain instances of additional suffix letters indicating either a modified role *or* additional equipment. An illustration of this is furnished

by the An-24V short-haul airliner which has been developed as the An-24TV, a quick-change version with a convertible freight hold, the 'T' (**T**) preceding the basic 'V' (**B**) suffix indicating *Transportny*, stemming from the Soviet nomenclature for passenger/freight aircraft, and An-24RV fitted with an auxilliary turbojet in the starboard engine nacelle for use under hot-and-high conditions, the 'R' (**P**) indicating *Reaktivny* which, literally translated, means 'Reaction' and is the Soviet term most widely used for turbojet. Another suffix letter which may sometimes be applied to civil aircraft and military alike in the same connotation is 'D' (**Д**) to indicate *Dalny* or 'Long-range', an example being the Tu-114D, a transport adaptation of the Tu-20 bomber for high-speed ultra-long-range flights with priority governmental passengers or freight.

DESIGN BUREAU DESIGNATIONS

There is no uniformity among the individual Soviet aircraft design bureaux in the allocation of designations to their progeny. Whereas one bureau will use a continuous sequence of numbers which are applied to each new aircraft, irrespective of its role, another will employ designations which, in each case, are indicative of the role. In the former category are the several design bureaux which have been supervised by the late doyen of Soviet aircraft designers, Andrei N. Tupolev, these employing a continuous series of numbers commencing with ANT-1 of 1922 (the initials ANT having been superseded in 1947 by the abbreviation 'Tu' and thus conforming with the abbreviation used for official service designations since 1940), but a departure from this uniformity was made in 1957. The first turbine-powered commercial transport produced by the Tupolev bureaux under the supervision of A. A. Arkhangel'sky had been the Tu-104, and with the début of a second turbine-powered commercial transport, the Tu-114, it was decided that each succeeding aircraft in this category should adopt a new *second* digit in sequence. Thus, in 1960 the Tu-124 appeared, followed by the Tu-134 in 1962, and continuing with the Tu-144 and Tu-154.

The late Artem Mikoyan's design bureaux, primarily concerned with fighter development, usually allocate numbers to each new design in numerical sequence, these numbers having an 'I' (И) prefix indicating *Istrebitel* ('Fighter', or more literally 'Destroyer'). A third digit is indicative of a development in the basic design (e.g., variants of the basic **I-210**, **I-220** and **I-230** designs including the I-21**1**, I-22**5** and 1-23**1**) and usually a suffix letter or letters in parentheses. Such letters are indicative of a feature of the aircraft, an example being the 1-270 (Zh) rocket-driven target-defence interceptor, the 'Zh' (Ж) referring to the use of *Zhidkoye toplivo* (liquid fuel). However, with the I-310 (which entered production as the MiG-15) a parallel series of bureau designations was instituted, this prototype also being known as the Type 'S', a progressive development with the VK-1 engine (eventually to become the MiG-15bis) being known as the 'SD', while a variant with S-band *Izumrud* (Emerald) AI equipment was the 'SP'. Variations were signified by a numerical suffix (e.g., SP-5), and subsequent fighters included the 'SI' (MiG-17) and 'SM' (MiG-19).

Designs from the OKB of Pavel Sukhoi appear to follow the service system of designating aircraft, each successive fighter design receiving an odd number in sequence (e.g., Su-7, Su-9, Su-11), these duplicating designations issued to earlier Sukhoi designs emanating from the original Sukhoi OKB dispersed in 1949, a new OKB being established in 1953 after the death of Iosef Stalin.

Some Yakovlev design bureau designations have been duplicated by service designations later issued to entirely different designs (e.g., Yak-25, Yak-30), this bureau normally allocating a number in sequence to each *project* (e.g., the design bureau designation of the Yak-30 two-seat trainer of 1960 was Yak-104), but there have been several inexplicable aberrations in the system, as the helicopter completed in 1947 to compete with the Mi-1 received the design bureau designation Yak-100, a four-seat crew trainer tested in 1953 was assigned the designation Yak-200 while

The Type 'S' (above) and the Izumrud-equipped SP-5 (below)

A camera pack-equipped MiG-15bisR (below) of the Polish air arm

(Above top) The I-270(Zh) of 1946; (immediately above) the Yak-200 AV-MF crew trainer of 1953, and (below) the Yak-30 of 1948

the supersonic fighter evolved in the early 'fifties to meet the same requirements as those fulfilled by the MiG-19 was known as the Yak-1000! It is only rarely that the official service designation coincides with that of the design bureau, but an example of such a rarity is provided by the first post-war design by Oleg K. Antonov, the An-2 utility transport. However, whereas meteorological research and floatplane variants of the basic design saw service as the An-2ZA and An-2V, their respective design bureau designations were An-4 and An-6. The next design from this bureau to achieve production bore the design bureau designation An-8 and, logically, its service designation *should* have been An-4, but with predictable inconsistency, this twin-engined tactical transport entered V-VS service as the An-8!

Instituted in the Soviet Union over the past decade has been a system of indicating production standards of combat aircraft by numbers appended to the Soviet service designation (e.g., MiG-21PF-74, -76), and in certain cases the suffix letters are changed (e.g., the export versions of the MiG-21PF series which differ only in certain items of avionic equipment have been assigned the generic designation of MiG-21FL, the suffix letters signifying *Forsazh Lokator*). The practice of applying indigenous designations to Soviet combat aircraft manufactured under licence in Czechoslovakia and Poland* has now ceased, but suffix letters bearing no relationship to those used in the Soviet Union are frequently applied. For example, target-towing versions of the MiG-15 developed in Czechoslovakia have been designated MiG-15T and MiG-15bisT, while a Czechoslovak fighter-bomber

The MiG-15 manufactured under licence in Czechoslovakia and Poland was known as the S 102 and LIM-1 in the respective countries, the MiG-15bis being known as the S 103 and LIM-2, the MiG-15UTI as the CS 102 and SBLim-1, and the MiG-17 and MiG-17F as the LIM-5 and LIM-5P respectively. Some Polish SBLim-1 trainers were eventually fitted with the complete power plant, rear fuselage and tail unit of the obsolete LIM-2 fighter as the SBLim-2 trainer, and standard LIM-5Ps were progressively modified for the close support role by the addition of a large braking chute, the introduction of lugs beneath the fuselage for RATOG and the provision of additional weapons pylons, their designation being changed to LIM-6.

variant with bomb racks, JATO rockets and braking chute was designated MiG-15SB, the suffix letters indicating *Stihaci bombardovaci letoun.*

DESIGNATIONS FOR
RECORD-BREAKING AIRCRAFT

The combinations of letters and numbers applied to Soviet aircraft employed to establish new international records follow no apparent system, and would seem to be dictated by the whim of the design bureau responsible for the development of the aircraft concerned, and providing no obvious indication of the design origin. The use of the Cyrillic soft 'E' or 'Ye' is a common prefix for the numerical designations applied to all record-breaking aircraft emanating from the late Artem Mikoyan's design bureau, and apparently indicates *Yedinitsa* which may be literally translated as 'Single Unit', in other words, a 'one-off' aircraft. It was first applied to a Tu-104 which established a number of international records as the Tu-104Ye. The aircraft attributed to the Mikoyan bureaux that have established records confirmed by the Fédération Aéronautique Internationale are as follows:

Ye-33: Basically a MiG-21UTI, the Ye-33 established an altitude record of 79,842 ft (24 336 m) on 22 May 1965 when the pilot was Natalya Prokhanova, and a sustained altitude record of 62,402 ft (19 020 m) on 23 June 1965 with another woman pilot, Lydia Zaitseva. On 6–7 June 1974, S. Savitskaya of the Central Aero Club of the USSR established new time-to-altitude records in the Ye-33 by climbing to 9,842 ft (3 000 m) in 59·1 sec, to 19,685 ft (6 000 m) in 1 min 20·4 secs, to 29,528 ft (9 000 m) in 1 min 46·7 secs and to 39,370 ft (12 000 m) in 2 min 35·1 sec.

Ye-66: Basically a modified pre-production example of the MiG-21, the Ye-66 gained for the Soviet Union the world absolute speed record for the first time on 31 October 1959 with a speed of 1,484 mph (2 388 km/h) over a 15-25-km course, the pilot being Colonel Georgi Mosolov, and the

power plant being an R-37F (Tumansky R-11) of 13,120 lb (5 950 kg). On 16 September 1960, the same aircraft flown by Konstantin Kokkinaki established a 100-km closed-circuit speed record of 1,335 mph (2 148 km/h), equivalent to Mach 2·02, a maximum speed of 1,553 mph (2 499 km/h) or Mach 2·35, being reached on one section of the course.

Ye-66A: Embodying the results of an aerodynamic drag reduction programme, including a cockpit canopy of improved contour with a large fairing extending well aft over the spine to improve wave drag and provide a marginal performance improvement (this feature subsequently being adopted for the MiG-21PF), this MiG-21 augmented the thrust of the R-37F (R-11) turbojet with the 6,615-lb (3 000-kg) thrust liquid-fuel rocket motor referred to in the FAI documentation as a ZhRD Mk. U2, and on 28 April 1961 attained an altitude of 113,892 ft (34 714 m) in a zoom climb to establish a new international record, the pilot being Colonel Georgi Mosolov.

Ye-76: A MiG-21PF flown by woman pilot Marina Solovyeva established an FAI-recognized record as the Ye-76 on 16 September 1966 by covering a 500-km closed-circuit at an average speed of 1,281 mph (2 062 km/h). A month later, on 11 October, another woman pilot, Yevgenia Martova, averaged 559·4 mph (900,27 km/h) over a 2,000-km closed-circuit and, subsequently, 1,322·7 mph (2 128,7 km/h) over a 100-km closed-circuit while flying the Ye-76, and yet a third woman pilot, Lydia Zaitseva, flew this aircraft to establish a 1,000-km closed-circuit record at 806·64 mph (1 298,16 km/h) on 28 March 1967.

Ye-166: Adapted for high-speed aerodynamic and power plant research from an experimental fighter, the Ye-166 established a 100-km closed-circuit record of 1,492 mph (2 400 km/h) on 7 October 1961 with A. Fedotov at the controls. It subsequently established two FAI-recognized records by averaging 1,666 mph (2 681 km/h) over a 15-25-

km course on 7 July 1962 with Colonel Georgi Mosolov at the controls, attaining 1,865 mph (3 000 km/h) (Mach 3·01) during one run, and by reaching and sustaining an altitude of 74,376 ft (22 670 m) over a 15-25-km course on 11 September 1962, a speed of 1,553 mph (2 500 km/h) being maintained, and the pilot on this occasion being Pyotr Ostapenko. The power plant was stated to be a P.166 of 22,046 lb (10 000 kg).

Ye-266: The MiG-25 established a new 1,000-km closed-circuit speed record of 1,441 mph (2 320 km/h) with a 4,409-lb (2 000-kg) payload as the Ye-266 in April 1965 with Aleksandr Fedotov at the controls. On 5 October 1967, the same pilot and aircraft established a payload-to-altitude record by attaining 98,349 ft (29 997 m) with 4,409 lb (2 000 kg). On the same day, Mikhail Komarov flew the aircraft with a similar payload around a 500-km closed-circuit at an average speed of 1,852·61 mph (2 981,5 km/h), or Mach 2·76, while pulling 1·3 g in a 40-degree banked turn, and on 27 October 1967, Pyotr Ostapenko flew the Ye-266 with a 4,409-lb (2 000-kg) payload around a 1,000-km closed circuit at an average speed of 1,814·81 mph (2 920,67 km/h). A further series of international records was homologated by the FAI during 1973, Fedotov establishing a new 100-km closed-circuit record of 1,618·8 mph (2 605 km/h) on 8 April, and Ostapenko establishing a number of time-to-altitude records on 4 June, including an altitude of 82,021 ft (25 000 m) in 3 min 12·6 sec and 98,425 ft (30 000 m) in 4 min 3·86 sec. Seven weeks later, on 25 July 1973, A. Fedotov attained an altitude of 115,485 ft (35 200 m) with a 4,409-lb (2 000-kg) payload and reached a zoom climb altitude of 118,766 ft (36 200 m).

Record-breaking aircraft attributed to the OKB of Vladimir M. Myasishchev are as follows:

103-M: Referred to simply as the 103-M, a Myasishchev M-4 re-engined with turbojets referred to as four 28,660-lb (13 000 kg) D-15s, established seven speed-with-payload

The Ye-166 (above and below), which established FAI-recognized speed and sustained altitude records in 1961–62, possessed some commonality (e.g., wings and horizontal tail surfaces) with a twin-engined fighter revealed in 1961 and assigned the reporting name Flipper by the ASCC (see pages 72–73)

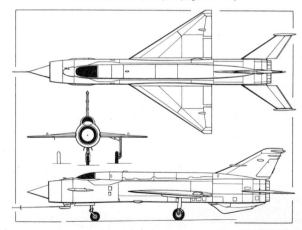

Responsible for a series of records between April 1965 and July 1973, the Ye-266 was the titanium MiG-25 (see pages 179–180)

records on 30 October 1959 piloted by Anatoli Lipko with a crew of seven. By carrying a 59,525-lb (27 000-kg) payload over a 1,000-km closed-circuit at an average speed of 629 mph (1 012 km/h), the aircraft established records for 1 000, 2 000, 5 000, 10 000, 15 000, 20 000, and 25 000 kg over a 1 000-km circuit.

201-M : Another M-4 derivative referred to as the 201-M, established a record on 16 September 1959 by carrying a 22,046-lb (10 000-kg) payload to an altitude of 50,253 ft (15 317 m), the pilots being Anatoli Lipko and Nikolai Gorianov. On 29 October 1959, the 201-M piloted by Boris Stepanov and Boris Yumachev established an altitude record of 43,048 ft (13 120 m) with payloads of 77,162,

88,185, 99,208, 110,231 and 121,254 lb (35 000, 40 000, 45 000, 50 000 and 55 000 kg). Like the 103-M, the 201-M was stated to be powered by four D-15 turbojets of 28,660 lb (13 000 kg).

Only one record-breaking aircraft had emanated from the Sukhoi OKB at the time of closing for press:

T-431 : A derivative of the Su-11 all-weather interceptor, the T-431 established an altitude record of 94,657 ft (28 850 m) on 14 July 1959 with Vladimir Ilyushin at the controls. No designation was announced for the turbojet which was stated to have a thrust of 19,840 lb (9 000 kg), and was undoubtedly a Lyulka AL-7F. Three years later, on 4 September 1962, again flown by Ilyushin, the T-431 raised the sustained altitude record to 69,456 ft (21 170 m) over a 15–25-km course. On this occasion the power plant was referred to as a TRD 31 of 22,046 lb (10 000 kg). On 25 September 1962, the T-431 raised the 500-km closed-circuit record to 1,452 mph (2 337 km), the pilot being Anatoli Koznov. The 1962 records were undoubtedly established by a later derivative of the Su-11 despite retention of the 'T-431' appellation.

One aircraft attributed to the Yakovlev OKB which has established world records has not been identified positively but is almost certainly a variant of the Yak-27:

RV : An aircraft referred to by the designation RV (*Rekord Vysoky* or 'Altitude Record') and flown by Vladimir Smirnov gained two payload-to-altitude records in July 1959 by lifting 2,205 lb (1 000 kg) to 67,113 ft (20 456 m), and 4,409 lb (2 000 kg) to 66,188 ft (20 174 m). The two power plants were stated to be of 37V type rated at 8,818 lb (4 000 kg), and were presumably boosted versions of the Tumansky RD-9. In the summer of 1967, the RV was used by a woman pilot, Marina Popovich, to establish a woman's international closed-circuit distance record of 1,559 miles (2 510 km).

ASSIGNED ASCC REPORTING NAMES

The following is a complete list of names allocated to Soviet aircraft by the Air Standards Co-ordinating Committee and adopted by NATO at the time of closing for press, together with the Soviet official and design bureau appellations where known, and some details of the development of the aircraft, their variants and competitive designs:

AIRSCREW-DRIVEN BOMBERS AND ATTACK AIRCRAFT

Bank: The reporting name *Bank* was applied to the North American B-25 Mitchell, 870 examples of which were assigned to the Soviet Union from 1941 onwards, 862 of these (including Mitchells of the B-25B, C, D, G and J sub-types) arriving at their destination. Of these, 733 were delivered over the Alaskan-Siberian ferry route, 124 were flown across the South Atlantic ferry route to Abadan where they were taken over by Soviet pilots, and five were shipped to Abadan by sea. Some B-25s remained flying in the Soviet Union on second-line tasks until the mid 'fifties.

Barge: Possessing the design bureau designation Tu-85, the heavy bomber on which the reporting name *Barge* was bestowed can lay claim to having been the largest post World War II aircraft built in the Soviet Union until the appearance of the An-22 *Antei*, the wing of the Tu-85 having a span of 183 ft 6¼ in (55,94 m) and a gross area of 2,947·56 sq ft (274,36 m²). Representing the first attempt to provide the Long-range Air Force, the *Aviatsiya Dal'nevo Deistviya* (ADD), with true intercontinental bombing capability, and utilizing technology derived from adapting the Boeing B-29 Superfortress for Soviet production as the Tu-4, the Tu-85 made its début in 1951. The Tu-85 was smaller and lighter than the Convair B-36, but possessed comparable range and load-carrying capabilities.

Powered by four 4,300 hp Dobrynin VD-4K 24-cylinder piston engines, the Tu-85 possessed a maximum loaded weight of 235,892 lb (107 000 kg), range with an 11,023-lb (5 000-kg) load being 7,455 miles (12 000 km) at an average cruise of 339 mph (545 km/h) at 32,810 ft (10 000 m).

Developed from specification to prototype testing within two years, the Tu-85 (Barge) could carry up to 44,092 lb (20 000 kg) of bombs for relatively short ranges and, in lightly loaded condition could attain 404 mph (650 km/h) at 32,810 ft (10 000 m)

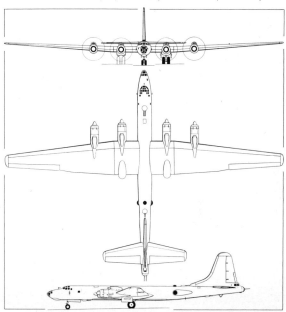

The Ilyushin Il-2m3 (Bark) was supplied with both unswept and swept wing outer panels and various armament combinations.

The crew had a complement of 16 members, and defensive armament consisted of a pair of 23-mm Nudelman-Rikhter NR-23 cannon in a tail barbette and in remotely-controlled forward and aft dorsal and forward and aft ventral barbettes. Performance did not justify series production, the ADD electing to await availability of the turboprop-driven Tu-95 and the contemporary turbojet-driven Myasishchev M-4 to fulfil its intercontinental requirements.

Bark: Despite the total obsolescence of the Il-2 by the time

the ASCC reporting name system was introduced in 1954, it was presumably assumed that, having been manufactured in larger numbers than any Soviet combat aircraft, 36,163 having been delivered when production terminated in 1945, this relatively primitive but effective attack machine *had* still to be in second-line V-VS service or with the air forces of the Soviet Union's satellites, and it accordingly received the appellation *Bark*.

Designed by Sergei Ilyushin to meet a requirement for a *Bronyirovanni Shturmovik* (literally 'Armoured Assaulter'), the first prototype, initially flown in the spring of 1939, was a two-seater powered by a 1,350 hp AM-35A 12-cylinder liquid-cooled engine, and as Ilyushin was working in the *Tsentralny Konstruktorskoye Byuro* (Central Design Bureau) of the GUAP it received the designation TsKB-55. Poor results obtained during State Acceptance Trials led to the redesign of the aircraft as a single-seater with a 1,600 hp AM-38 engine, the revised prototype flying as the TsKB-57 on 12 October 1940, and entering production almost immediately as the Il-2, 249 being completed in the first six months of 1941, and no fewer than 1,293 during the second six months. An improved version in which the 20-mm

The Tupolev Tu-85 (below) was the last Soviet piston-engined strategic bomber and was assigned the ASCC reporting name of Barge

Shpitalny-Vladimirov ShVAK cannon gave place to 23-mm Volkov-Yartsev VYa cannon of high muzzle velocity and firing armour-piercing shells, and the AM-38 was supplanted by an AM-38F offering 1,750 hp, passed State Acceptance Trials in July 1942, and was delivered as the Il-2m (*Modifikatsirovanny* or 'Modified'). This was, in turn, succeeded by the Il-2m3 providing accommodation for a second crew member with an aft-firing Berezin UB machine gun of 12·7-mm calibre on a flexible mount, combat trials being performed in January and February 1943.

During 1943, approximately one-third of all aircraft manufactured in the Soviet Union were Il-2s, and from May of that year, the VYa cannon were replaced by Nudelman-Suranov NS-37 cannon of 37-mm calibre. Variants included the Il-2T (*Torpedonosets*) torpedo-carrier for the shore-based Naval aviation elements, and the Il-2U (*Uchebny*) or U-Il-2 dual-control instructional aircraft. A potential successor was the Il-8 flown in April 1944, an aerodynamically refined *Shturmovik* of similar concept to the Il-2m3, and powered by a 2,000 hp AM-42, but this was abandoned in favour of a parallel development, the Il-10 (see *Beast*).

Bat: Perhaps the most successful of Soviet wartime bombers, the Tu-2 was designed to meet a 1938 requirement for a twin-engined three-seat bomber suitable for both level and diving attack. However, it did not begin to reach the V-VS in quantity until early 1944, a total of 1,111 having been delivered when hostilities terminated in Europe. Production and development continued in the immediate post-war years, being finally phased out in 1948 when the 2,527th example was completed, and the aircraft remained in service with the V-VS, the *Polskie Wojska Lotnicze*, various satellite air arms and the Sino-Communist air arm until the late 'fifties, being dubbed *Bat* by the ASCC.

The first prototype, the ANT-58, was flown on 29 January 1941, being followed in May by a second prototype, the ANT-59, which differed in having the crew complement increased from three to four. Both were powered by

Progressive developments of the World War II Tupolev Tu-2 (Bat) included the Tu-2R (above top) which was retrospectively designated Tu-6, the ANT-65 of 1946 (immediately above), and the ANT-63 two-seater of 1944 (below), the first prototype of which is shown

1,400 hp AM-37 12-cylinder liquid-cooled engines whose shortcomings led to yet a third prototype, the ANT-60 with 1,330 hp M-82 14-cylinder air-cooled radials. Flown on 15 December 1941, the ANT-60 was also a four-seater, and was the true prototype of the Tu-2, three pre-production examples of which were built for operational evaluation which began in the vicinity of Kalinin, north-west of Moscow, in September 1942. However, the State Defence Committee considered the Tu-2 overly complex, the result being the simplification of the structure and the hydraulic system, and with 1,850 hp M-82FN (*Forsirovanno-nyeposredstvenny* or 'Direct Boost') engines, the revised model flew as the ANT-61 on 26 August 1943, deliveries to operational units commencing early in 1944 as the Tu-2S (*Seriiny* or 'Series').

Several variants appeared during 1944–45, among the first of these being the Tu-2D (ANT-62), the 'D' suffix indicating *Dalny* ('Long Range'). Tested between 20 October 1944 and 1 March 1945, the Tu-2D was the 714th production Tu-2 airframe, and featured long-span wings and additional tankage doubling fuel capacity. The installation of vertical and oblique cameras resulted in the Tu-2R (*Razvedchik* or 'Reconnaissance Aircraft'); torpedo racks produced the Tu-2T (*Torpedonosets* or 'Torpedo Carrier') for the Soviet Navy, and the Tu-2Sh for the *Shturmovik* role was tested with a single 57-mm RShR cannon, and with paired 37-mm and 45-mm cannon. Early in 1944, a Tu-2 airframe was fitted with two 1,870 hp AM-39 12-cylinder liquid-cooled engines, attaining 401 mph (645 km/h) at 21,800 ft (6 650 m), a second airframe later receiving 2,000 hp AM-39F engines and a nose-mounted cannon armament as the Tu-1 two-seat fighter, the design bureau designation being ANT-63P (*Perekhvatchik* or 'Interceptor'). The ANT-64 was an experimental variant with 2,000 hp AM-42 engines, while the ANT-65 and ANT-67 were respectively versions with 2,200 hp AM-44TK engines with turbo-compressors driven by an auxiliary engine, and ACh-30BF diesels of 1,800 hp.

Post-war production of the Tu-2 concentrated on the version powered by the ASh-82FN (M-82FN), the photographic reconnaissance variant, the Tu-2R, being redesignated Tu-6 in V-VS service, and an improved long-range version flying on 24 May 1947 as the Tu-8 (ANT-69), while, with the usual lack of predictability of the Soviet system of designating aircraft, the ANT-68, a refined model with a redesigned, more angular glazed nose and 1,850 hp AM-39FNV engines first flown on 17 May 1945, received the designation Tu-10. Owing to the advent of turbojet-powered bombers, neither the Tu-8 nor Tu-10 attained series production. One post-war variant that *did* attain limited series production was the UTB (*Uchebno Trenirovochny Bombardirovshchik* or 'Instructional Training Bomber'), a structurally lightened derivative of the Tu-2 evolved by Pavel Sukhoi and powered by two 700 hp ASh-21 nine-cylinder radials.

Bear: Whereas little interest in the potentialities of the turboprop-driven intercontinental bomber was displayed in the West, development of such a warplane began in the Soviet Union in the late 'forties, and made its début in prototype form in 1954 as the Tu-95, being allocated the reporting name *Bear*. Accepted for service with the ADD as the Tu-20 (see page 215), this warplane is unique in being the only turboprop-driven bomber to have attained service, and is remarkable for its production longevity, manufacture reportedly continuing into the late 'sixties. With the appearance in 1961 of a version featuring a large duck-billed nose radome surmounted by an immense flight refuelling probe, and a modified weapons bay carrying an AS-3 *Kangaroo* stand-off missile semi-externally, the initial model with the glazed nose became *Bear-A*, the modified version becoming *Bear-B* to initiate a long series of suffix letters assigned to variants of *Bear* as they appeared in service (and described on pages 215–8). A high speed transport conversion of the bomber received the designation Tu-114D (*Dalny* or 'Long Range') but, retaining the basic bomber fuselage,

Although utilizing the basic Tu-20 bomber fuselage and thus having little commonality with the commercial Tu-114 (Cleat—see pages 40–41), the high-speed transport illustrated above was nevertheless assigned the designation Tu-114D

should not be confused with the commercial Tu-114 *Rossiya* (see *Cleat*).

Beast: In 1943, the Ilyushin OKB initiated the design of two new *Shturmoviki* as potential successors to the Il-2 (see *Bark*). These, the Il-8 and Il-10, performed State Acceptance Trials in the spring and early summer of 1944, the Il-8 being discarded and the Il-10 being ordered into production. Named *Beast* by the ASCC, the Il-10 was powered by a 2,000 hp AM-42 engine and fixed forward-firing armament initially comprised two 23-mm VYa cannon and two 7,62-mm ShKAS machine guns, this armament being retained until 1949 when the VYa was replaced by the Nudelman-Suranov NS-23 of similar calibre, some aircraft having four wing-mounted weapons of this type.

The Il-10 was too late to see much service during World War II, making its operational début in February 1945, but production continued in the Soviet Union until 1950, by which time 4,966 had been manufactured, variants including the more heavily armed Il-10M (*Modifikatsirovanny*) and

the dual control Il-10U (*Uchebny*) or U-Il-10. Production was transferred to Czechoslovakia under the Kosice Agreement (under which the Soviet Union agreed to re-equip the Czechoslovak armed forces) where, between 1950 and 1954, approximately 1,200 additional examples of the Il-10M and Il-10U were manufactured, the Czechoslovak designations

Czech-built Il-10M (Beast) attack aircraft. Some 1,200 of the Il-10s produced were of Czechoslovak manufacture

A total of 5,256 Il-4 (Bob) bombers followed 1,528 DB-3s from the assembly lines, production terminating in 1944

for the two variants being B 33 and CB 33 respectively. A number of the Czechoslovak-built Il-10s were delivered to the *Československé letectvo*, but the majority were exported. The Il-10 remained in service with the V-VS until 1957 and with the *Československé letectvo* until 1958, other recipients of *Beast* including the Bulgarian, Hungarian, Polish, North Korean and Sino-Communist air arms.

Bob: Another obsolete aircraft of World War II vintage to which a reporting name was applied by the ASCC was the Il-4, which provided the backbone of the wartime Soviet long-range bombing force and, in 1954, received the appellation *Bob*. Designed to meet a *Dalny Bombardirovshchik* ('Long Range Bomber') requirement conceived in 1933, the first prototype bore the *Tsentralny Konstruktorskoye Byuro* (Central Design Bureau) designation TsKB-26, and was flown in 1935, being looped over Red Square during the May Day Parade of 1936. Prior to this event, the ANT-37 designed by Pavel Sukhoi had been ordered into production to fulfil the long-range bomber requirement as the DB-2, but as a result of direct intervention by Iosef Stalin, the DB-2 was abandoned in favour of the Ilyushin design which was placed in production as the TsKB-30, the service designation being DB-3.

The DB-3 entered V-VS service in 1937, the initial production series being powered by two 765 hp M-85 14-cylinder air-cooled radials which, in 1938, were supplanted by 950 hp M-86 radials to result in the DB-3M (*Modifikatsirovanny* or 'Modified'). In June 1939, a third version successfully completed State Acceptance Trials, this being the DB-3F with a lengthened, aerodynamically refined fuselage nose, and M-87A engines capable of maintaining 950 hp to 16,420 ft, and by the beginning of 1940 this model had been delivered in some numbers to both the V-VS and the *Morskaya Aviatsiya* (Naval Aviation), serving as a torpedo-bomber with the latter arm, carrying a single 43-36 AN or AV 2,072-lb torpedo. With the replacement in 1940 of the letters indicating function in service designations by abbreviations of the OKB leaders' names, the DB-3F became the Il-4, and on the night of 7–8 August 1941, this aircraft gained the distinction of being the first Soviet bomber to attack Berlin when 15 Il-4s of the 1st Mine-Torpedo Regiment of the Baltic Fleet flew the 1,095 miles from Oezel Island (now Sarema Island), off the Estonian coast, to the German capital.

During the course of Il-4 production, the M-87A engine was progressively replaced by the M-88A and M-88B of 1,100 hp, the latter with a two-speed supercharger, and a number of metal structural components were supplanted by wooden components. Carrying three crew members and a defensive armament of two 7·62-mm ShKAS machine guns and a 12·7-mm Berezin UB, the Il-4 could lift up to 5,512 lb of bombs or mines over short ranges, and 2,204 lb over a 2,360-mile range. In 1943, the Ilyushin OKB was working on a more heavily armed, longer-ranging derivative of the Il-4 which received the designation Il-6, the crew complement being increased to six, defensive armament comprising five 20-mm ShVAK cannon, and the M-88B engines being supplanted by two 1,500 hp Charomsky ACh-30B diesel engines. The airframe was completed but was never flown owing to the non-delivery of the diesel power plants, and further development of the Il-4 terminated when the bomber was finally phased out in 1944, production of 1,528 DB-3s having been followed by the manufacture of 5,256 Il-4s.

Boot: Among aircraft shown to a western delegation led by Gen. Nathan F. Twining which visited Kubinka airfield near Moscow in the summer of 1956 was a turboprop-powered *Shturmovik* which, designed by a team initially led by Pavel O. Sukhoi and subsequently by V. A. Chizhevskii, was designated Tupolev Tu-91 and unofficially known to its test pilots both as *Tarzan* and as the *Bichok* (Young Steer). The Tu-91 was a side-by-side two-seater powered by a single Kuznetsov NK-6 (TV-2-F) turboprop and carried all armament externally. The Tu-91 was assigned the reporting name *Boot* by the ASCC, but development was discontinued with the decision by N. S. Khrushchov that no further work would be undertaken on specialized *shturmoviki*.

Box: Like the North American B-25 (see *Bank*), the Douglas A-20 was supplied to the Soviet Union in substantial numbers under the Lend-Lease programme, nearly half of all aircraft of this type manufactured being delivered to the V-VS. Of 3,125 A-20s allocated to the Soviet Union (including 151 DB-7Bs and DB-7Cs built against British contracts), a total of 2,908 actually reached Soviet hands, 50 being lost before leaving North America, 118 being lost at sea, 39 being lost on the South Atlantic ferry route, one being diverted, and seven being written off after arrival at Abadan. Variants included the A-20B, C, G, H and K, some being fitted with dorsal turrets of Soviet design after delivery. Most A-20s were withdrawn from V-VS service shortly after the termination of hostilities. Nevertheless, the type was given the reporting name *Box*.

Buck: Among the most successful of Soviet World War II aircraft was the Pe-2 three-seat light bomber christened *Buck* by the ASCC in 1954. This stemmed from a 1938 requirement for a two-seat high altitude fighter, a *Vysotny Istrebitel*, which materialized early in 1939 as the VI-100. Carrying a forward-firing armament of four 20-mm ShVAK cannon in the nose, the VI-100 featured cabin pressurization, escape chutes for the crew members, and was one of the first Soviet aircraft to make extensive use of electrics, but changed

requirements dictated the modification of the design as a *Pikiruyushchy Bombardirovshchik*, or 'Dive Bomber', and a second prototype flew as the PB-100 on 22 December 1939. The cabin pressurization equipment and TK-3 turbo-superchargers were removed, crew accommodation was revised, and powered by two 1,100 hp M-105R 12-cylinder liquid-cooled engines, the PB-100 successfully completed State Acceptance Trials and, in June 1940, entered production as the Pe-2, joining the V-VS during the summer of the following year.

Early in 1942, the inadequacy of the hand-held 7·62-mm ShKAS machine gun firing aft above the fuselage resulted in the hurried provision of a dorsal turret mounting a single 12·7-mm UB machine gun, the designation of the modified aircraft being Pe-2FT (the suffix letters indicating *Frontovoye Trebovaniye*, or 'Frontline Request'), and all first-line aircraft being modified in a similar fashion from June 1942. From

The Tu-91 (Boot) carried up to 6,614 lb (3 000 kg) of ordnance and had a max take-off weight of 30,865 lb (14 000 kg), optimum cruise being 404 mph (650 km/h). Max range was 1,490 mls (2 400 km)

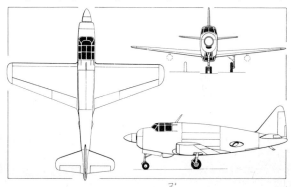

February 1943, the M-105R gave place to the 1,210 hp M-105PF which, together with some aerodynamic refinement, resulted in the Pe-2M (*Modifikatsirovanny*) with a 25 mph (40 km/h) increase in maximum speed. Variants included the Pe-2R (*Razvedchik* or 'Reconnaissance Aircraft') with vertical and oblique cameras for day and night photography, and auxiliary fuel tankage increasing range to 1,056 miles (1 700 km), and the Pe-2UT (*Uchebno-Trenirovochny*, or 'Instructional Training') with dual controls and tandem cockpits. A parallel development of the basic design was the Pe-3 multi-purpose fighter (not to be confused with the Pe-2VI) which, produced in relatively small numbers, differed from the Pe-2 primarily in having a fixed forward-firing armament of four 20-mm cannon and two 7,62-mm machine guns and built-in reconnaissance cameras.

Further development of the basic design was undertaken by Vladimir Myasishchev which resulted in the Pe-2VI (*Vysotny Istrebitel*, or 'High-altitude Fighter') which, flown

(Above left, top) The Petlyakov Pe-2 (Buck), of which 11, 427 examples were built, was further developed by Vladimir Myasishchev as the Pe-2VI fighter (immediately above left). The Tu-80 (illustrated below and by the general arrangement drawing opposite) was a derivative of the Tu-4 (Bull) with a 'wet' wing. Span and length were 142 ft $6\frac{2}{3}$ in (43,45 m) and 112 ft $7\frac{1}{8}$ in (34,32 m)

in 1944, featured cabin pressurization, a nose-mounted battery of four 20-mm ShVAK cannon, two 1,650 hp VK-107A engines, and a maximum speed of 408 mph (656 km/h) at 18,700 ft (5 700 m). A parallel development was the VB-109 (*Vysotny Bombardirovschik*, or 'High-altitude Bomber'), the sole prototype of which crashed in 1945. The Pe-2 was phased out of production in 1945, but remained in service with the V-VS until the late 'forties, production having totalled 11,427 aircraft. Both the Pe-2FT and Pe-2UT were delivered to the *Polskie Wojska Lotnicze* and the *Československé letectvo*, being designated B 32 and CB 32 with the latter air arm.

Bull: In July and November 1944, three USAAF B-29 Superfortresses, short of fuel after attacking Japanese targets, landed at Vladivostock. The aircraft were annexed by the Soviet Union and their crews interned at Tashkent, Siberia. When the USAAF personnel 'escaped' across the Soviet border to Teheran, representations by the US government failed to obtain release of their aircraft, the reason being revealed during the Aviation Day parade over Tushino airfield on 3 August 1947, when a Soviet copy of the B-29, designated Tu-4, made its début. At the time of their arrival at Vladivostock, the B-29s were undoubtedly the most advanced strategic bombers in the world, embodying advances in aerodynamics, structures and systems, and Andrei Tupolev was given the task of translating the bomber back to its production breakdown, and initiating production for the re-equipment of the ADD, the first of 20 pre-production Tu-4s flying in the late summer of 1946.

An engineering task of considerable magnitude and one unique in aviation history, reproduction of the B-29 introduced the Soviet aircraft industry to entirely new technological processes, but was effected in a relatively short time, deliveries of the Soviet copy to the ADD commencing as the Tu-4 at the beginning of 1948, and this subsequently receiving the reporting name *Bull*. Although externally almost indistinguishable from the B-29, the Tu-4 was,

according to Soviet figures, lighter than the US original, its ASh-73TKs were rated at 2,200 hp for take-off with a war emergency rating of 2,400 hp, and it was claimed to possess a higher service ceiling of 36,745 ft (11 200 m). Proposals existed to replace the Shvetsov piston engines with four

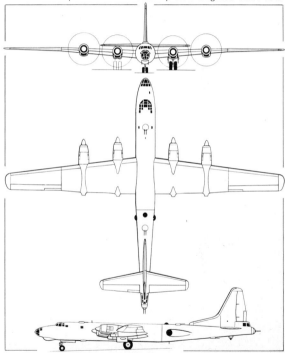

The Tupolev Tu-4 (above) served as standard strategic bomber equipment with the ADD from the late 'forties until the mid 'fifties, and was a Soviet copy of the Boeing B-29 Superfortress from which it was externally indistinguishable

Ivchenko TV-02 or Kuznetsov TV-4 turboprops, but no Tu-4 was, in fact, re-engined. The Tu-4 was progressively phased out of first-line ADD service with the availability of the Tu-16 from 1955, although a number adapted for the flight refuelling tanker role and polar transportation tasks remained in service until the early 'sixties, and a small number were supplied to the Sino-Communists. A development of the basic Tu-4, the Tu-80, differed primarily in having a lengthened, stepped fuselage nose, a revised wing structure with integral fuel tanks and redesigned vertical tail surfaces. The Tu-80 was overtaken by a later strategic bomber specification and progressed no further than prototype status, a fate shared by another derivative of the Tu-4 evolved to meet the same requirement, the DVB-202, which, featuring a shoulder-mounted wing, had been developed by a team led by Vladimir Myasishchev.

TURBOJET-DRIVEN BOMBERS AND ATTACK AIRCRAFT

Backfin: The aircraft on which the Air Standards Co-ordinating Committee bestowed the reporting name *Backfin* remained something of a mystery for a number of years.

Spurious reports widely published in the West ascribed to this type the designation 'Yak-42', and alleged that its service début was imminent in the late 'fifties. In fact, *Backfin*, which was of Tupolev origin and designated Tu-98, was a modified Tu-16 (*Badger*) airframe flown in 1955, and intended for experimental purposes rather than development as a combat aircraft. By comparison with the standard Tu-16, the prototype of which had flown three years earlier, the wing was lowered on the fuselage which was widened aft to accommodate two AL-7F turbojets mounted side by side, the air intakes being shoulder-mounted and carried above the wing. A similar arrangement was subsequently adopted for the Tu-28 (*Fiddler*).

Backfire: Unofficially reported to be designated Tupolev Tu-26 at the time of closing for press, this variable-geometry strategic bomber, assigned the reporting name *Backfire*, is believed to match the performance of the Rockwell B-1A in key areas and was being phased into service with the Long-range Aviation component of the V-VS at the beginning of 1974. Variants include the *Backfire-A* and *-B*, the former having housings at the extremities of the fixed portion of the wing accommodating the main bogies and the latter having a fuselage-mounted undercarriage (see pages 225–6).

Badger: Broadly comparable in both role and performance with the B-47 Stratojet, the Tu-16 (see page 212) long-range medium bomber entered service with the ADD as a successor to the Tu-4 in 1955, receiving the reporting name *Badger*. Developed as the *Samolet 'N'* and allocated the design bureau designation Tu-88, this bomber was evolved in competition with the Il-46 which, flown on 15 August 1952, resembled a scaled-up Il-28 (*Beagle*). Lower powered and lighter than the Tu-88, the Il-46 had two 11,020 lb (5 000 kg) s.t. Lyulka AL-5 turbojets, and empty and loaded weights of 54,156 and 92,594 lb (24 565 and 42 000 kg) respectively, attaining a maximum speed of 576 mph (928 km/h). The Tu-88, which also flew for the first time in 1952, was of rather more advanced concept, and its Mikulin-designed AM-3 turbojets were substantially more powerful than the AL-5s of the Il-46, production being initiated in 1953 as the Tu-16.

With the appearance of the version of the Tu-16 adapted to carry two air-breathing stand-off missiles of the AS-1 *Kennel* type, the original model became *Badger-A* and the missile-carrying variant was designated *Badger-B*, further suffix letters being added to the reporting name as further versions appeared. Between 1,500 and 2,000 Tu-16s are believed to have been built, and a substantial number of these remain in service with the AV-MF for maritime reconnaissance, electronic intelligence and anti-shipping tasks, some serving as flight refuelling tankers.

Beagle: Built in larger numbers than any Soviet bomber of post-war design, the Il-28, dubbed *Beagle* by the ASCC, was designed to meet a light tactical bomber requirement formulated in 1946, competitive designs being the Tu-72 and the Su-10, and prototype trials began on 8 August 1948, production commencing in the following year. The production Il-28 (see page 143) was initially powered by the 5,002 lb (2 270 kg) s.t. Klimov RD-45F, this subsequently giving place to the 5,592 lb (2 700 kg) s.t. Klimov VK-1. Production variants included the Il-28T (*Torpedonosets*)

torpedo-bomber for the Soviet Navy, the Il-28R (*Razved-chik*) tactical reconnaissance aircraft, and the Il-28U (*Uchebny*) conversion trainer with ventral radome deleted and second cockpit for trainee pilot (see *Mascot*). In February 1956, *Aeroflot* began operating several Il-28s over the Moscow–Sverdlovsk–Novosibirsk route to transport matrices of Moscow newspapers and, simultaneously, gain operating experience with turbojet-driven aircraft. For the civil Il-28 the designation Il-20 (originally applied in the late 'forties to an experimental *Shturmovik*) was resurrected.

The Il-46 (above and below) was a lower-powered and lighter competitor for the Tu-88 eventually produced as the Tu-16 (Badger)

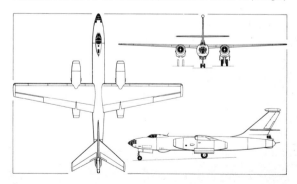

Bison: Evolved by Vladimir M. Myasishchev's design bureau in parallel with the Tu-20, the strategic heavy bomber named *Bison* by the ASCC and designated M-4 in V-VS service (see page 200) was responsible for establishing a number of FAI-recognized records as the 103-M and 201-M in 1959. Several versions of the M-4 have been manufactured, and the type is now used primarily by the AV-MF for long-range reconnaissance and 'ferret' missions with optical and non-optical sensors.

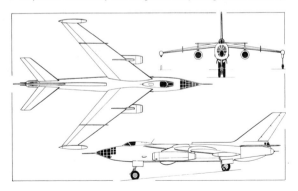

Despite the fact that it failed to achieve production status, the Il-54 (above and below) was assigned the reporting name Blowlamp

Blinder: Currently serving in substantial numbers with the V-VS, the Tu-22 (see page 219) was developed in the mid 'fifties as the *Samolet 'Yu'* (**IO**) with the design bureau designation Tu-105. The designation 'Tu-22' had been previously applied provisionally to the Tu-82, but when this 1949-vintage bomber failed to attain production status the designation lapsed until applied to the bomber now sporting the reporting name *Blinder*. The initial production version of the Tu-22 became the *Blinder-A* with the appearance of a developed model which, dubbed the *Blinder-B*, can carry a single AS-4 *Kitchen* stand-off missile semi-recessed in the weapons bay. Variants include the Tu-22R (*Blinder-C*), the Tu-22U (*Blinder-D*) and the Tu-22P interceptor.

Blowlamp: The Il-54, which received the appellation *Blowlamp* after having been seen at Kubinka in 1956 by a western delegation, aroused considerable speculation in the West. A three-seat light attack bomber evolved as a potential successor to the Il-28, the Il-54 was built in 1954 and was flown in 1955 with two Lyulka AL-7 turbojets with which it attained a maximum speed of 714 mph (1 150 km/h), this representing M=0·93 at the altitude flown, range and service ceiling being 1,490 miles (2 400 km) and 42,650 ft (13 000 m) respectively. It featured 55 degree leading-edge wing sweep, a widely-spaced 'bicycle' undercarriage, and small outrigger wheels retracting into wingtip fairings, but failed to attain production status.

Bosun: In 1946, the Tupolev design bureau received a requirement for a light tactical bomber with pressurized accommodation for the crew. Work was initiated under the design bureau designation Tu-72, but this was supplanted by the Tu-73. Whereas the Tu-72 was to have been powered by two Rolls-Royce Nene turbojets and possess a defensive armament comprising two fixed forward-firing 23-mm NR-23 cannon and a similar pair of weapons in the extreme tail, the Tu-73 had the power of the two Nenes supplemented by a Rolls-Royce Derwent turbojet mounted in the extreme tail, and the tail gun position supplanted by

(Above) The Tupolev Tu-81 was the first version of the Tu-14 (Bosun) AV-MF bomber of the early 'fifties, much of the structural design being similar to that of the swept-wing Tu-82 (bottom right). The Tu-77 (immediately below right) was a Tu-2 derivative

dorsal and ventral barbettes sighted from lateral blisters.

The Tu-73 made its initial flight on 29 October 1947, although, in the event, it was preceded into the air by another jet bomber from the same design bureau, the Tu-77 which flew on 27 July 1947. The latter was essentially an interim design evolved primarily to afford some experience with the operation of turbojet-powered bombers at the earliest opportunity, being an adaptation of the basic Tu-2 airframe to take two Derwent turbojets and a nosewheel undercarriage. Factory trials with the Tu-77 were completed by 10 September 1947, this four-seat bomber having a loaded weight of 32,408 lb (14 700 kg), a maximum speed of 540 mph (870 km/h), and a maximum range of 1,370 miles (2 240 km). In the meantime, factory trials with the three-engined Tu-73 continued until 14 June 1948, a second three-engined prototype, the Tu-78, having joined the test programme on 17 April 1948, this differing primarily in utilizing the initial

The Myasishchev M-50, dubbed Bounder by the ASCC, was one of the most spectacular Soviet experimental combat aircraft of the 'fifties. The example illustrated above has afterburners on the inboard engines, the outboard units being attached to wingtip pylons

Soviet derivatives of the Nene and Derwent, the RD-45 and RD-500. A reappraisal of the design resulted in the auxiliary turbojet being discarded and the tail armament being reinstated, this modified version being designated Tu-81 by the design bureau, completing State Acceptance Trials between September and December 1952, and entering production for the Soviet Navy as the Tu-14 early in the following year.

Named *Bosun* by NATO, the Tu-14 was powered by two 5,952 lb (2 700 kg) s.t. VK-1 turbojets and the principal production version, the Tu-14T (*Torpedonosets*) which received the design bureau designation Tu-89, carried a cannon armament of four 23-mm NR-23 weapons and a maximum bomb load of 6,614 lb (3 000 kg). With a maximum take-off weight of 55,888 lb (25 350 kg), maximum fuel and a 2,205-lb (1 000-kg) offensive load, the Tu-14T attained a maximum range of 1,870 miles (3 010 km) at 33,135 ft (10 100 m), this altitude being reached in 46 min. At normal loaded weight of 46,297 lb (21 000 kg), the Tu-14T attained maxi-

mum speeds of 497 mph (800 km/h) at sea level and 525 mph (845 km/h) at 16,400 ft (5 000 m). The Tu-14T remained in service until the early 'sixties, and a swept-wing version of the basic design, the Tu-82, was flown in 1949, this being powered by two 5,952 lb (2 700 kg) VK-1s and attaining a maximum speed of 540 mph (870 km/h) at sea level, rising to 580 mph (934 km/h) at 13,125 ft (4 000 m). No production of the Tu-82 was undertaken.

Bounder: One of the most spectacular Soviet combat aircraft of the 'fifties was the experimental long-range strategic bomber to which the Air Standards Co-ordinating Committee gave the reporting name *Bounder* when it appeared in its initial form in 1957. This immense bomber, evolved by the team headed by Vladimir M. Myasishchev and possessing the design bureau designation M-50, would seem to have been conceived when the ADD concluded that the turbo-prop-powered Tu-20's greater range was more useful than the M-4's superior speed, the M-50 representing an attempt to combine a low-drag airframe with non-afterburning 28,660 lb (13 000 kg) s.t. Soloviev D-15 engines to achieve a substantial range at high subsonic speed. It is possible that the Myasishchev team underestimated the severity of the transonic drag rise, but before the M-50 was abandoned several prototypes were flown, the last of which (designated, according to some Soviet sources, the M-52) introducing afterburners on the inboard turbojets and transferring the outboard engines to horizontal pylons extending from the wingtips. In this form, the M-50 was probably capable of a short-period dash speed of M=1·4. Its approximate overall dimensions included a span of 83 ft (25,3 m), an overall length of 185 ft (56,2 m), and a gross wing area of the order of 2,700 sq ft (250,8 m²). Maximum loaded weight was some 300,000 lb (136 080 kg).

Brawny: Despite the fact that, by the early 'fifties, it was becoming increasingly obvious that the strike fighter was assuming the role previously performed by the *Shturmovik*, the V-VS was loath to abandon an aircraft category with which it had achieved such success, and accordingly, in 1953, prototypes were completed of a turbojet-driven *Shturmovik*, the Il-40, which was duly named *Brawny* by the ASCC. Of somewhat novel appearance, the Il-40 was powered by two 5,942 lb (2 700 kg) s.t. Mikulin AM-5F turbojets which were mounted side-by-side in the centre fuselage and fed via individual ducts, twin circular intakes being provided in the extreme nose with effluxes emerging just aft and below the wing root trailing edges. The thick-section wing accommodated four 37-mm N-37 cannon, and a tail-mounted barbette carried two 23-mm NR-23 cannon for rear defence, this being directed by the second crew member seated over the wing trailing edge. The Il-40 was heavily armoured but, nevertheless, attained a maximum speed of 600 mph (964 km/h) at low altitude, its range being 620 miles (1 000 km). Development was abandoned in 1955 when the task for which the Il-40 had been designed was assumed by the MiG-15.

Brewer: Developed primarily as a tactical attack bomber to succeed the Il-28 with the *Frontovaya Aviatsiya*, the aircraft dubbed *Brewer* by the Air Standards Co-ordinating Committee is one of three current third-generation derivatives of the original Yak-25 (see *Flashlight*) all-weather interceptor, the others being *Firebar* and *Maestro*. Designated Yak-28 in V-VS service, *Brewer* differs from its predecessors in having

The Myasishchev M-50 (Bounder) was possibly abandoned as a result of an underestimation of the transonic drag rise

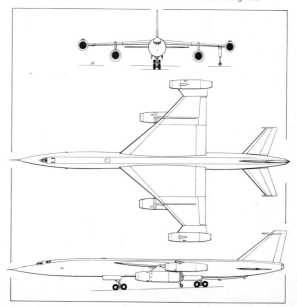

Assigned the reporting name Brawny, the Il-40 (above and below) represented an attempt to produce a turbojet-driven Shturmovik

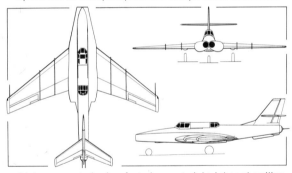

a higher-mounted wing featuring a straight inboard trailing edge and sharp leading-edge sweepback inboard of the engine nacelle. Possessing larger, more powerful engines, it also has increased tailplane sweep, enlarged vertical surfaces, and a widely-spaced 'bicycle' undercarriage in place of the 'zero-track' tricycle undercarriage of the Yak-25 and Yak-27. The Yak-28 (see page 242) possesses an internal

weapons bay in its strike version (*Brewer A*), but this feature is deleted from the tactical reconnaissance model (*Brewer-D*). The Yak-28 first appeared in 1959, and entered service with the V-VS during the early 'sixties, variants appearing in 1960 including the Yak-28I (*Brewer-C*) and Yak-28L (*Brewer-B*).

AIRSCREW-DRIVEN TRANSPORTS AND LIAISON AIRCRAFT

Cab: The reporting name *Cab* was allocated to both the Soviet-manufactured DC-3 and Lend-Lease C-47s. Prior to World War II, the Soviet government purchased through *Amtorg*, the Soviet Trading Corporation in the USA, a number of DC-3s which, from July 1937, operated in concert with ANT-35s over the *Aeroflot* Moscow–Riga–Stockholm service under the Soviet designation PS-84. The Soviet government also acquired a manufacturing licence for the DC-3, the task of supervising the adaptation of the transport for Soviet production being given to Boris Lisunov, the actual conversion being undertaken by Vladimir Myasishchev, I. P. Tolstykh and I. P. Mosolov. Accordingly, when the licence-built DC-3 entered service with both the V-VS and *Aeroflot* in 1940 it received the designation Li-2. The Li-2 differed from the DC-3 in several respects. Powered by the Shvetsov M-62IR or M-63R nine-cylinder radial frequently fitted with the shutter-type cold-weather cowling, the Li-2 had a starboard rear entry door, and most examples delivered to the V-VS featured a manually-operated turret with a single 7·62-mm ShKAS machine gun over the radio compartment. Production of the Li-2 was supplemented during 1941–44 by Lend-Lease deliveries of the C-47A and B to the Soviet Union, 709 being allocated of which two were lost in the USA prior to departure. Some Li-2s are still utilized by *Aeroflot* in the airline's Northern, Polar and Far East Directorates.

Camp: Evolved to meet both a V-VS requirement for a tactical transport with rear loading facilities and an *Aeroflot* demand for a commercial freight- and passenger-carrying aircraft to replace the Li-2 in the remoter areas of the Soviet Union, the An-8, named *Camp* by the ASCC, was powered by two 5,100 e.s.h.p. Kuznetsov NK-6TV-2 turboprops, and the first of five prototypes flew in the autumn of 1955, production of a series of 100 aircraft commencing during the following year. The An-8 featured a glazed observation nose, a single 23-mm NR-23 cannon in a tail position, two four-wheel main undercarriage bogies retracting into bulges standing proud from the slab-sided fuselage, and an integral loading ramp. Maximum loaded weight was 83,776 lb (38 000 kg), maximum and long-range cruising speeds were 373 mph (600 km/h) and 298 mph (480 km/h) respectively, and maximum range was 2,175 miles (3 500 km).

As the original 42—48-seat capacity specified by *Aeroflot* was changed to a demand for 75-seat capacity, the Antonov bureau revised the basic design by replacing the two NK-6TV-2 turboprops with four 4,000 e.s.h.p. NK-4 turboprops, the basic wing structure remaining relatively unchanged, and this being married to an enlarged and pressurized fuselage. The new model was flown in 1957 as the An-10 *Ukraina* (see *Cat*), and as this offered a significant improvement in both performance and capacity over its twin-engined predecessor, the An-10 was adapted to take a rear fuselage essentially similar to that of the An-8, this subsequently being manufactured as the An-12 (see *Cub*), production of the An-8 being discontinued after the completion of the original batch of 100 aircraft, the production model discarding the NK-6 turboprop in favour of the 4,000 e.s.h.p. Ivchenko AI-20V. The An-8s were, for the most part, delivered to the V-VS with which they have since served, performing a variety of tasks which include paratroop training and even the monitoring of radioactive fallout, an example engaged in the last-mentioned role being intercepted on 11 May 1966 some 70 miles (113 km) north-east of Ullung Island, off Korea's eastern coastline.

Cart: In 1945, *Aeroflot* formulated a requirement for a 50—

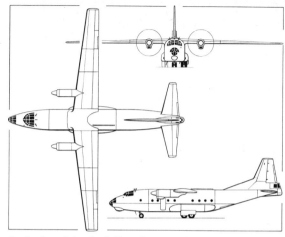

Production of the An-8 (Camp) was restricted to a batch of 100 aircraft, most of which were assigned to the V-VS

Single examples of two transport derivatives of the Soviet copy of the B-29 were flown, one being the Tu-70 (Cart) above, and the other being the Tu-75 illustrated by the general arrangement drawing (below), the upper sideview showing the Tu-70 for comparison

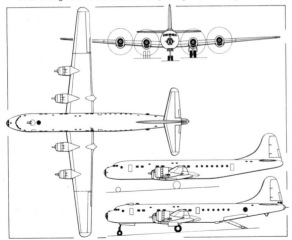

60-passenger long-range four-engined transport, and to meet this demand the Tupolev bureau adapted the wings, power plant, tail surfaces and undercarriage of the Tu-4 heavy bomber (see *Bull*) to marry with an entirely new fuselage accommodating a crew of seven and 48 passengers, this flying on 27 November 1946 as the Tu-70 which, eight years later, received the reporting name of *Cart*. Employing the same 2,200 hp ASh-73TK engines as those of the Tu-4, the Tu-70 possessed a maximum loaded weight of 105,820 lb (48 000 kg), a range of 3,045 miles (4 900 km), and attained a maximum speed of 353 mph (568 km/h) at 29,530 ft (9 000 m). It competed with the Il-18 (see *Clam*) for *Aeroflot* orders, but a reappraisal of the airline's immediate requirements led to the conclusion that forecasts of traffic volume over *Aeroflot's* longer routes had been over optimistic, and the Tu-70 was abandoned, only one prototype being completed. However, in 1950 a military derivative of the Tu-70 was flown as the Tu-75. With maximum loaded weight increased to 124,782 lb (56 600 kg), and a maximum payload of 22,046 lb (10 000 kg), the Tu-75 featured ventral freight doors fore and aft and was demonstrated over

Tushino in July 1951, but no production was undertaken for the V-VS.

Cat: The identification name *Cat* was applied by the ASCC to the An-10 *Ukraina* medium-haul commercial transport which was flown for the first time in March 1957. Pre-production examples were powered by Kuznetsov NK-4 turboprops, but production models standardized on the Ivchenko AI-20 with a similar 4,000 e.s.h.p. rating. The An-10 entered service with *Aeroflot* in July 1959, and possessed an 84-seat capacity, but in the same year the An-10A made its début, supplanting the earlier model on the assembly line and entering *Aeroflot* service in February 1960. The An-10A differed from its predecessor in having an additional

The directional stability problems suffered by the An-10A (Cat) are indicated by the combination of auxiliary endplate fins and single ventral fin seen below and the definitive twin splayed ventral fins seen above right

The Ilyushin Il-18 (Clam) was designed to meet an Aeroflot requirement abandoned as a result of reappraisal of the airline's immediate requirements. The designation was to be resurrected a decade later for a turboprop-driven transport (see Coot)

6 ft 6¾ in (2,0 m) section inserted in the fuselage and 100-seat capacity. The An-10V (to which the design bureau designation An-16 was initially applied) was a high-density version for 132 passengers flown in 1963. The An-10 was phased out of *Aeroflot* service during 1972–73 following a series of structural failures.

Clam: Built to meet the same *Aeroflot* requirement as the Tu-70 (see *Cart*), the Il-18 was first flown on 30 July 1947, eventually being named *Clam*. Powered by four 2,200 hp ASh-73TK engines, the Il-18 accommodated a crew of six and 60 passengers, empty and loaded weights being 62,809 and 93,696 lb (28 490 and 42 500 kg) respectively. Performance included maximum and maximum cruising speeds of 365 and 317 mph (587 and 510 km/h), and maximum range was 3,850 miles (6 195 km), but development was

abandoned for similar reasons to those that had dictated the discarding of the Tu-70, and only a single prototype was built. A decade later, the designation 'Il-18' was resurrected and applied to a new turboprop-driven transport (see *Coot*) which bore no relationship to the earlier design other than a common design origin.

Clank: An aerial survey aircraft based on the An-24RT and having a redesigned forward fuselage, designated An-30, has been assigned the reporting name *Clank* (see page 135).

Cleat: The largest commercial passenger transport aircraft until the début of the Boeing Model 747, the Tu-114 *Rossiya*, named *Cleat* by the Air Standards Co-ordinating Committee, employed the wing, tail assembly, undercarriage power plant and other components of the Tu-20 bomber (see *Bear*).

Completed in prototype form in the autumn of 1957, the Tu-114 was initially powered by 14,795 e.s.h.p. Kuznetsov NK-12M turboprops but was subsequently re-engined with NK-12MV turboprops rated as 15,000 e.s.h.p. The fuselage of the Tu-114 was of appreciably larger diameter than that of the Tu-20 and was some 21 ft (6,40 m) longer, overall length being 177 ft 6 in (54,10 m). Accommodation was provided for a maximum of 220 passengers. Some 30–35 Tu-114s were built for use by *Aeroflot* but had been largely phased out by the beginning of 1975. An AWACS derivative of the Tu-114 currently serves with the V-VS (see *Moss*). The designation Tu-114D (*Dalny* or 'Long Range') was applied to direct conversions of the Tu-20 bomber which were employed for a short period by *Aeroflot* over high-priority long-distance routes within the Soviet Union.

Clod: The identification name *Clod* was allocated to the small STOL feederliner and light utility transport developed by the Antonov bureau, and flown for the first time on 15 March 1958. Designated An-14 (see page 126) and known as the *Pchelka* (Bee), this aircraft underwent protracted development and did not attain quantity production until 1965. The three prototypes of the An-14 were initially powered by 260 hp AI-14R engines and featured untapered wings of 64 ft 11½ in (19,80 m) span. A development of the basic design, the An-28 powered by two 810 e.s.h.p. Isotov TVD-650 turboprops, has passenger accommodation increased from 6–7 to 15 (see page 127). The An-14 has been built for both civil and military roles.

The Tu-114 (Cleat), which was in process of being phased out of service early 1975 after several years restricted to internal services, had made 50,000 passenger-carrying flights with Aeroflot by mid-1974, totalling more than 155m miles (250m km)

The Il-12 (Coach) formed the backbone of the V-VS logistic support element and Aeroflot until supplanted by the Il-14 (Crate)

Coach: In 1943, Sergei Ilyushin's design team initiated work on a potential successor to the Li-2 (see *Cab*) in competition with the design bureau of V. G. Yermolayev which was evolving a transport derivative of the Yer-2 bomber. The Ilyushin proposal was selected for further development as the Il-12, a prototype being flown early in 1946, and the type entering service with the V-VS in 1947 and *Aeroflot* in 1948, the initial production version being supplanted at an early stage by the Il-12B (Б) with dorsal fin, improved exhaust system, and other refinements. The Il-12, named *Coach* under the ASCC system, continued in production until supplanted by the Il-14 (see *Crate*) in 1953, between 2,000 and 3,000 examples having allegedly been manufactured.

Cock: The largest turboprop-driven transport aircraft in the world, the An-22 *Antei* (Antaeus) is primarily a military transport, but three of the five prototypes were delivered to *Aeroflot* for evaluation and some 50 An-22s were included in the inventory of this operator in 1974. Active development of a commercial model accommodating 300–350 passengers and 66,140 lb (30 000 kg) of freight appears to have been abandoned. Flown for the first time on 27 February 1965, the An-22 (see page 128) can carry three tracked carriers for single *Frog* or twin *Ganef* surface-to-

surface missiles, self-propelled guns, etc., and, dubbed *Cock* by the ASCC, the first production aircraft were delivered to the V-VS during the summer of 1967.

Coke: The An-24 short- to medium-range commercial transport (see page 130) was flown for the first time in April 1960, two prototypes being followed by five pre-production examples completed in 1961. Allocated the reporting name *Coke*, the An-24 entered *Aeroflot* service in September 1963. The initial production An-24 was a 44-seater and, like its mixed freight-and-passenger variant, the An-24T (*Transportny*), was powered by 2,550 e.s.h.p. Al-24A turboprops. The similarly powered 50-seat An-24V (Б) followed, this in turn giving place to the refined An-24V *Seriiny II*, variants being the An-24TV (*Transportny*) quick-change version with a convertible freight hold, and the An-24RV (*Reaktivny*) with a Tumansky RU-19-300 auxiliary turbojet of 1,980 lb.s.t. in the starboard engine nacelle for use under hot-and-high conditions. The An-24P (П) is a firefighting version (the suffix letter indicating *Protivopozharny*, or 'Fire Protection') with special provision for the low-altitude parachuting of fire-fighters, and the An-30 (*Clank*) is an aerial survey variant (see page 135) with a raised flight deck and extensively glazed nose. A further development with both civil and military applications, the An-26 has an electrically-operated rear loading ramp and is stressed for a higher *g*-load factor (see *Curl*).

Colt: One of the very few post-war biplanes to be manufactured in really large numbers, the An-2, known as the *Colt* to NATO, has been in continuous production for more than 25 years, and numerous variants have been evolved. The An-2 (see page 121) was flown for the first time in 1947 as the SKh-1 (*Selsko-khozaistvenny*-1 or 'Rural Economy-1'), having been evolved to meet a requirement formulated by the Ministry of Agriculture, one prototype having a 730 hp ASh-21 engine and another having a 1,000 hp ASh-62IR. The production version, which appeared in 1949, standardized on the ASh-62IR, and early variants included the

An-2ZA (*Zondirovanie Atmosfery* or 'Air Sampling'), a special high-altitude meteorological variant with a turbo-supercharged ASh-62IR/TK engine and an observer's cockpit immediately forward of the tail assembly (this model having the design bureau designation An-4); the An-2V (*Vodyanoi* or 'Water Floatplane') with twin light metal floats (and the design bureau designation An-6), and the An-2NRK (*Nochnoi razvedchik-korrectirovshchik* or 'Night Reconnaissance and Air Observation Post Aircraft'), this being an experimental variant with a twin fin-and-rudder tail assembly and dorsal turret mounting a single 23-mm cannon. The An-2P (*Protivopozharny* or 'Fire Protection') is a water-bombing floatplane model, and the An-2M (*Modifikatsirovanny* or 'Modified'), introduced in 1964, is an agricultural model featuring a redesigned tail assembly and an ASh-62M engine in a redesigned cowling.   The manufacture of the An-2 has been undertaken in China since 1957 as the *Fong Chou*, and in Poland since 1960, production in the latter country alone approaching 6,000 by the beginning of 1974.

Coot: When, in the summer of 1957, flight trials began of a new commercial transport designed by Ilyushin's bureau, the designation Il-18, originally bestowed 10 years earlier on a piston-engined transport prototype (see *Clam*), was resurrected, the Air Standards Co-ordinating Committee applying the reporting name *Coot* to the type.   Two pre-production examples were produced, and the Il-18 *Moskva* (see page 141) entered service with *Aeroflot* in April 1959.   The 75-seat initial production version was followed by the 84-seat Il-18B (Б) and by the 89-seat Il-18V (В) in 1961.   In 1964, the Il-18I (И) appeared with 4,250 e.s.h.p. AI-20M turbo-props in place of the 4,000 e.s.h.p. AI-20K engines of the Il-18V, accommodation for 110–122 passengers made possible by the lengthening of the pressurized section of the fuselage by the deletion of the unpressurized tail cargo hold, and a 32 per cent increase in fuel capacity.   Redesignated Il-18D (Д), this model entered *Aeroflot* service in 1965, together with the Il-18Ye (Е) which was similar apart from

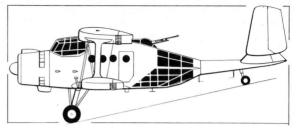

The An-2NRK (or An-2K) was an experimental night reconnaissance and air observation post version of the An-2 (Colt)

having the same fuel capacity as the Il-18V.   A maritime patrol derivative of the Il-18 is designated Il-38 (see *May*).

Cork: In 1947, the Yakovlev design bureau completed prototypes of a small feederliner powered by two 750 hp ASh-21 radials and carrying a crew of two and 10–12 passengers. Designated Yak-16 and assigned the reporting name *Cork*, the aircraft attained a maximum speed of 193 mph (310

The Yak-16 (Cork) was an early postwar attempt on the part of the Yakovlev bureau to produce a small feederliner

The Yak-12 (Creek—A) was initially built with the M-11 engine (as illustrated) but the vast majority received the AI-14R

km/h) and a maximum cruising speed of 180 mph (290 km/h), range being 620 miles (1 000 km). The Yak-16 did not prove successful and no production was undertaken.

Crate: Derived from the Il-12 (see *Coach*), a new transport, the Il-14, entered production for both the V-VS and *Aeroflot* in 1953, commencing service in the following year. Allocated the reporting name *Crate*, the Il-14 (see page 139) had ASh-82T engines in place of the ASh-82FN engines of the earlier aircraft, a twin-tube thrust augmentation exhaust

The Yak-10 (below) was the immediate predecessor of the Yak-12, with which it shared a close family resemblance, but its poor characteristics resulted in production being limited to 40

system, a revised wing and redesigned tail surfaces. To differentiate between military and civil models manufactured in parallel, the latter was designated Il-14P (*Passazhirskii* or 'Passenger'). In 1956, some structural revisions were made and the fuselage lengthened by 3ft 4 in (1,0 m), this model being designated Il-14M (*Modifikatsirovanny*) and providing accommodation for 24—28 passengers. Licence production of the Il-14P was undertaken in East Germany by the VEB Flugzeugwerke, 80 being built of which the first flew in April 1956. Approximately 80 Il-14Ps were also manufactured in Czechoslovakia as Avia-14s, production continuing with the Il-14M as the Avia-14-32 and, in freighter form, as the Avia-14T, a photographic survey model being designated Avia-14FG. Production of the Il-14 in the Soviet Union terminated in 1958, but development continued in Czechoslovakia where, in 1960, the 42-passenger Avia-14-42 was produced, this being a pressurised model with circular cabin windows. Approximately 3,500 Il-14s of all versions were built and some 300 of these remained in airline service at the beginning of 1975.

Creek: Immediately after the end of World War II, the Yakovlev bureau began design of a three—four-seater light utility monoplane which flew in 1946 as the Yak-10. Powered by an M-11 engine, the Yak-10 did not offer entirely satisfactory characteristics, suffering weight and control problems, and production was confined to 40 aircraft, work being meanwhile initiated on an extensively revised version of the basic design which was assigned the designation Yak-12 (this having been previously allocated to a two-seat trainer which had been abandoned—see *Crow*). The initial production series was powered by the 160 hp M-11FR-1 or M-11L engine, but in 1952 a new version, the Yak-12R (*Razvitoi* or 'Developed') appeared with a 240 hp AI-14R engine, development having been held up for several years for political reasons. This was succeeded by the Yak-12M (*Modifikatsirovanny*) in which an all-metal structure supplanted the mixed structure previously employed, and in 1956 licence manufacture of this model began in Poland. With the allocation of reporting names by the Air Standards Co-ordinating Committee in 1954, the Yak-12, -12R and -12M became the *Creek-A*, *-B* and *-C* respectively. In 1957 yet a further development appeared, the Yak-12A (*Aerodynamichesky*), this becoming the *Creek-D*. The Yak-12A represented a major aerodynamic redesign, new wings being introduced, the Vee-type bracing struts giving place to single struts, a new tailplane being fitted, and the cockpit glazing being extended. Licence manufacture of the Yak-12M and Yak-12A in Poland was undertaken during 1956–60.

Crib: In 1945, Yakovlev produced the Yak-8 light twin-engined feederliner, design of which, owing much to the Yak-6 of 1943, had been initiated in the previous year on behalf of *Aeroflot*. Powered by two 150 hp M-11 engines, the Yak-8 carried a crew of two and six–eight passengers, but *Aeroflot* demanded larger-capacity higher-performance aircraft, and relatively few transports of this type were built. Nevertheless, the ASCC christened it *Crib*.

Crow: Ten years prior to the formulation of the ASCC naming system a side-by-side two-seat light low-wing training monoplane was produced by the Yakovlev bureau. Powered by a 145 hp M-11E engine, and featuring a retractable undercarriage, this trainer was designated Yak-12 and was tested during the winter of 1945–46. The side-by-side seating arrangement did not find favour, and development was abandoned in favour of a parallel trainer design, the Yak-18, only one example of the Yak-12 being produced. Nevertheless, in the belief that the Yak-12 had been manufactured in numbers, the ASCC bestowed the name *Crow* on this type. Later, the designation Yak-12 was resurrected and applied to the successor of the Yak-10 high-wing cabin monoplane (see *Creek*).

Cub: Evolved from the An-10 (see *Cat*), the An-12 freighter first appeared in 1959 and has since been in continuous production. Serving in extremely large numbers with the

The Yak-8 (Crib) light feederliner was designed for Aeroflot in 1944, but this organization had changed its requirements by the time the prototype flew and only a few were built

V-VS, the An-12 (see page 124) differs from the An-10 primarily in having a redesigned rear fuselage embodying an integral loading ramp, and has the reporting name *Cub*.

Cuff: Designed specifically for use by *Aeroflot* as a local-service airliner, the Be-30 was flown for the first time on 3 March 1967, and was named *Cuff* by the ASCC. For initial flight trials, the first prototype was powered by 740 hp ASh-21 air-cooled radial engines, this subsequently being re-engined with Turboméca Astazou XII turboprops, but the

Although only one example of the low-wing Yak-12 (below) was built in 1945, it was allocated the reporting name Crow nine years later in the mistaken belief that it had been built in numbers

The Be-30 (Cuff) was intended to meet an Aeroflot requirement for a local-service airliner, the definitive series prototype flying on 18 July 1968. Weighing 7,937 lb (3 600 kg) empty and having a max take-off weight of 12,919 lb (5 860 kg), the Be-30 was to have joined Aeroflot in 1970, but was ultimately rejected

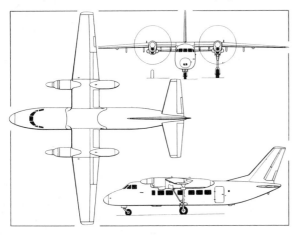

pre-production Be-30 was powered by Glushenkov TVD-10 turboprops of 970 e.s.h.p. The Be-30 had a standard seating arrangement for 14 passengers and offered maximum and maximum cruising speeds of 304 mph (490 km/h) and 286 mph (460 km/h) respectively, but although production was initiated, *Aeroflot* was dissatisfied with the capabilities of *Cuff*, production and further development being discontinued.

Curl: A derivative of the An-24RT (see *Coke*) with both civil and military applications, the An-26 (see pages 132—3) features a rear fuselage of 'beavertail' type but is otherwise structurally similar to the An-24V *Seriiny II*. The An-26 has been allocated the reporting name *Curl*.

JET TRANSPORTS

Camel: The Soviet Union's first jet transport, the Tu-104, which was given the reporting name *Camel*, is a derivative of the Tu-16 (see *Badger*) medium bomber, and employs basically similar wings, tail assembly and undercarriage, with de-rated civil versions of the bomber's engines. The Tu-104 prototype was flown for the first time on 17 June 1955, and the initial aircraft delivered to *Aeroflot* for crew training and route proving were designated Tu-104G (Г) for some obscure reason, this indicating *Grazhdansky* ('Civil'). The first production model was powered by 14,880 lb (6 750 kg) s.t. AM-3 turbojets and accommodated 50 passengers, this being succeeded by the Tu-104A of 70-seat capacity with AM-3M turbojets uprated to 19,180 lb (8 700 kg) s.t. The first Tu-104A was used in September 1957 to establish a number of international speed and load-carrying records as the Tu-104Ye (Е), and the Tu-104B (Б) was a 100-passenger version with a 3 ft $11\frac{1}{4}$ in (1,20 m) longer fuselage which appeared in September 1958. Re-engined with 21,385 lb (9 700 kg) s.t. AM-3M-500 engines, the capacity increased to 100 passengers, the Tu-104A became the Tu-104V (В), and with similar power plants the Tu-104B (Б) became the Tu-104D (Д).

The Tu-104B (Camel), above, was the initial 'stretched' version of the Soviet Union's first jet transport, most later being re-engined to become Tu-104Ds. The Tu-104 had largely been phased out of service by 1975, a small number remaining with Aeroflot

Candid: Flown in prototype form for the first time on 25 March 1971, the heavy commercial and military freighter assigned the reporting name *Candid* is generally similar in concept to the Lockheed C-141A StarLifter. Four Il-76s were participating in the flight test programme during 1973 when it was anticipated that certification for commercial operation would be received during the course of 1974. (See pages 151–2).

Careless: Announced in the spring of 1966 as a potential successor to the Tu-104, Il-18 and An-10 over medium-to-long stage lengths, the Tu-154 (see pages 235–6) was first flown on 4 October 1968, and was allocated the reporting name *Careless*. Current development is concentrated on the Tu-154A which has been re-engined with Soloviev D-30KU turbofans.

Charger: The world's first supersonic commercial transport

to fly, the Tupolev Tu-144, assigned the reporting name *Charger*, flew for the first time on 31 December 1968, and exceeded M=1·0 initially on 5 June 1969 and M=2·0 on 26 May 1970. The production prototypes, the first of which joined the development programme during September 1971 (see pages 232–4), differ from the original prototype so extensively that they constitute virtually a new aircraft, a compound delta replacing the ogee wing planform, the engines being relocated, the overall dimensions being increased and retractable noseplanes being introduced.

Classic: Subjected to continuous modification throughout protracted development, the Il-62 (see page 148) entered service on *Aeroflot* long-haul routes in 1967, and was named *Classic* by the ASCC. The first of two prototypes was flown in January 1963 with 16,538 lb.s.t. Lyulka turbojets pending availability of the 23,150 lb.s.t. Kuznetsov NK-8 turbofan which was installed in the three pre-production Il-62s produced during 1964–65. The initial production series had the 23,150 lb (10 500 kg) Kuznetsov NK-8-4 turbofan, but this was supplanted by the 25,353 lb. (11 500 kg) s.t. Soloviev D-30-KU turbofan with the Il-62M which appeared in 1971. Both the NK-8-4-powered Il-62 and D-30-KU powered Il-62M remained in production at the beginning of 1974 when some 70 were in airline service.

Codling: The first Yakovlev-designed commercial transport since the abortive Yak-16 of 1947 (see *Cork*), the Yak-40 was flown for the first time on 21 October 1966, and has been named *Codling*. The Yak-40 (see page 247) is intended primarily as a successor to the Li-2 (see *Cab*) in *Aeroflot* service, and is unusual for an aircraft in its size category in having three turbofans. Production was expected to exceed 600 by mid-1975, and a 40-passenger high-density version and variants with 3,858 lb (1 750 kg) AI-25T turbofans have been proposed.

Cooker: Evolved in parallel with the Tu-104B (see *Camel*), the Tu-110 was a 78–100 seater flown for the first time in the spring of 1957 with four 12,125 lb (5 500 kg) Lyulka AL-5 turbojets. Apart from its power plants, the Tu-110, named *Cooker*, was essentially similar to the Tu-104B, and was claimed to have a high speed cruise of 559 mph (900 km/h) at 32,810 ft (10 000 m). As the Tu-110 offered few advantages over the Tu-104B, *Aeroflot* elected to pursue development of the latter for reasons of standardization, and only one prototype of the four-engined transport was completed.

Cookpot: Essentially a scaled-down Tu-104 (see *Camel*) to meet an *Aeroflot* requirement for a short-to-medium range turbofan-driven successor to the piston-engined Il-14 (see *Crate*), the Tu-124 (see page 227), named *Cookpot* by the ASCC, was flown as a prototype in June 1960. Having the distinction of being the first turbofan-powered airliner to have attained commercial service, scheduled operation by *Aeroflot* having commenced on 2 October 1962, the Tu-124

The Tupolev Tu-110 (Cooker) flew some two years after the Tu-104 from which it differed primarily in having four Lyulka AL-5 engines in place of two larger Mikulin turbojets. The Tu-110 was rejected by Aeroflot and only one prototype was flown

has been produced in several versions, the basic models being the 44-passenger Tu-124 and the 56-passenger Tu-124V (**B**). Versions with a de-luxe forward cabin are the 36-seat Tu-124K and 22-seat Tu-124K2, the 'K' suffix signifying *Kabine* (cabin). Some 90 Tu-124s were serving with *Aeroflot* at the beginning of 1974.

Crusty: Derived directly from the Tu-124 and known initially as the Tu-124A, the Tu-134 was flown in prototype form in the second half of 1962, five pre-production examples being manufactured in 1963–64. Named *Crusty*, the Tu-134, which entered international service in September 1967 and was joined by the stretched Tu-134A in the Autumn of 1970, is illustrated and described on page 229.

AIRSCREW-DRIVEN FIGHTERS AND FIGHTER-BOMBERS

Fang: The last piston-engined fighter to be designed and manufactured in the Soviet Union, the La-11 was flown for the first time in 1947 under the design bureau designation La-140, and was intended primarily for the escort role. Like its predecessor, the La-9 (see *Fritz*), the La-11 was an all-metal stressed-skin single-seater with a laminar-flow wing and a 1,850 hp ASh-82FNV radial engine, and armament comprised a similar trio of asymmetrically-arranged 23-mm Nudelman-Suranov NS-23 cannon, but internal fuel capacity was increased from 181·5 to 242 Imp gal, (825 to 1 100 l), which, with the addition of wingtip tanks, provided a maximum range of 1,584 miles (2 550 km). Normal loaded weight was 8,810 lb (3 996 kg), a maximum speed of 419 mph (674 km/h) was attainable at 20,340 ft (6 200 m), and ceiling was 33,630 ft (10 250 m). The La-11 entered service with the V-VS in 1948, remaining in first-line use until the early 'fifties, and being supplied in small numbers to the Sino-Communist and North Korean air arms, receiving the reporting name *Fang* from the Air Standards Co-ordinating Committee.

The La-126PVRD (above) was a ramjet-boosted version of the La-7 (Fin) tested in 1946, and the La-9 (below) entered V-VS service in 1946 and was eventually assigned the reporting name Fritz

The La-9RD (above) was flown in 1947 with two RD-13 pulse jets boosting speed by 79 mph (127 km/h) but vibration was excessive

Fin: At the end of 1943, a progressive development of the successful La-5 fighter was flown under the design bureau designation La-120, entering service with the V-VS during the spring of 1944. Powered by a 1,775 hp ASh-82FN, the La-7 was delivered during the war years in two versions, these being the so-called 'Moskva La-7' and 'Yaroslavl La-7', the former, manufactured in Moscow, having only two

The Yak-9P (below) was the final production variant of the basic Yak-9 (Frank) of which 16,769 examples were built 1942–47

20-mm ShVAK cannon, and the latter, built at Yaroslavl, having three of these weapons. During October 1944–February 1945, two aircraft were fitted with an RD-1 liquid fuel rocket motor in the extreme tail and flown under the designation La-7R (*Raketny* or 'Rocket'). The RD-1 offered 660 lb (300 kg) thrust for three minutes, but although speeds in excess of 435 mph (700 km/h) were attained for brief periods, the corrosive effect of the nitric acid vapour escaping from the inadequately-sealed tank resulted in the disintegration of the plywood monocoque structure. A further rocket-boosted version, the La-120R with a ZhRD-1 (*Zhidkostny Raketny Dvigatel*, or 'Liquid-fuel Rocket Engine') motor also rated at 660 lb (300 kg) thrust and a metal rear fuselage was demonstrated over Tushino in August 1946, the extra power boosting speed at 9,840 ft (3 000 m) by 53 mph (85 km/h) to 461 mph (742 km/h).

Another attempt to boost the power of the La-7 was represented by the La-126PVRD* fitted with two small VRD-430 (*Vozdushnoreaktivny Dvigatel* or, literally, 'Air Breathing Engine') ramjets beneath the wings, these having been developed by I. I. Bondaryuk. Tested between June and September 1946, the ramjet-boosted La-126PVRD displayed a 62 mph (100 km/h) increase in maximum speed over the standard La-7, but the serious drag resulting from the ramjets during cruising flight led to the discontinuation of flight testing. Withdrawn from first-line V-VS service by 1948, the La-7 remained in service with the *Československé letectvo* as the S 97 until 1950, and was allocated the reporting name *Fin*. A total of 5,753 was built.

Frank: Built in larger numbers than any other Soviet fighter of World War II, the Yak-9 was a progressive development of the Yak-1 and -7 fighters, and, during the war years, appeared in a variety of models, including the Yak-9B (*Bombardirovshchik* or 'Bomber'), the Yak-9M (*Modifikatsirovanny* or 'Modified'), the Yak-9T (*Tyazhely* or 'Heavy', and

*The Design bureau designation 'La-126' indicated the sixth basic modification of the La-120.

referring to the installation of the heavy 37-mm Nudelman-Suranov NS-37 cannon between the cylinder banks), the Yak-9D (*Dalny* or 'Long Range'), and the Yak-9U (*Usilenny* or 'Strengthened'). The last-mentioned model, which began to reach the V-VS late in 1944, was the first variant to have an all-metal airframe and the 1,700 hp VK-107A engine, and post-war development of this resulted in the Yak-9P (*Perekhvatchik* or 'Interceptor') which entered V-VS service in 1946 and was eventually to be dubbed *Frank* by the Air Standards Co-ordinating Committee. The Yak-9P, which differed from the Yak-9U primarily in having later radio and navigational equipment, carried an armament of one engine-mounted 20-mm ShVAK cannon and two 12·7 mm Berezin UB machine guns, and attained a maximum speed of 414 mph (666 km/h) at 16,400 ft (5 000 m). Fighters of this type served operationally with the North Korean air arm during the opening stages of the Korean conflict, and equipped elements of the *Polskie Wojska Lotnicze* until the early 'fifties.

Fred : One of the US combat aircraft supplied under Lend-Lease to the Soviet Union in large numbers during World War II was the Bell P-63 Kingcobra, more than two-thirds of the total production of which went to the V-VS. The actual quantity of aircraft involved was 2,421 P-63As and P-63Cs of which 10 were lost in the USA, nine in Canada and two in Alaska prior to delivery over the Alaskan–Siberian Ferry Route. Although it would seem that the Kingcobra was withdrawn from V-VS service shortly after the termination of hostilities, it was nevertheless allocated the reporting name *Fred* in 1954.

Fritz : Too late to see operational service during World War II, having been flown for the first time in 1945 under the design bureau designation La-130, the La-9 entered V-VS service in 1946, and possessed little more than a family resemblance to its immediate predecessor, the La-7 (see *Fin*). Mixed construction had given place to all-metal, and a laminar-flow section wing was employed. Power was

The Mikoyan Ye-2A (above) was a swept-wing contemporary of the Ye-5 (MiG-21) and was assigned the reporting name Faceplate

provided by an ASh-82FNV radial of 1,850 hp, and whereas early aircraft had four 20-mm ShVAK cannon, later production aircraft had four 23-mm NR-23 cannon, although one of the portside weapons was frequently removed. The La-9 attained 429 mph (690 km/h) at 20,510 ft (6 250 m), and possessed a range of 1,078 miles (1 735 km), and variants included the La-9RD of 1947 with a pulse jet or pulsating athodyd beneath each wing, and the tandem two-seat La-9UTI (*Uchebno-Trenirovochny Istrebitel* or 'Instructional Training Fighter'). Some La-9s were supplied to the Sino-Communist air arm, and although largely withdrawn from the V-VS by the early 'fifties, the type was given the reporting appellation *Fritz*.

JET FIGHTERS AND FIGHTER-BOMBERS

Faceplate : In the early 'fifties, a specification was prepared which called for a small and simple fighter with modest internal fuel capacity, capable of attaining the maximum possible speed which could be combined with good manœuvrability, climb rate and ceiling. Simple radar ranging was to be combined with cannon armament, and the aircraft had to be capable of dealing with high-altitude bombers in clear

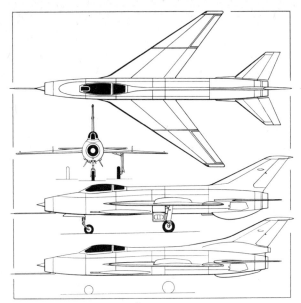

The general arrangement drawing above illustrates the Mikoyan Ye-2A, the lower sideview depicting the similar Ye-50

order to resolve finally the question of the potential superiority of the delta over more orthodox 55-deg swept surfaces for the new fighter, two aerodynamic prototypes were built by the Mikoyan OKB, these being identical in every respect apart from their wings, that with swept wings being designated Ye-2A and the delta-winged aircraft being the Ye-5. Flown in 1956, these aerodynamics test vehicles were demonstrated over Tushino on 24 June of that year, by which time the Ye-5 'tailed delta' arrangement had demonstrated superiority.

The delta-winged Ye-5 development aircraft was given the reporting name *Fishbed* by the Air Standards Co-ordinating Committee, and its swept-wing Ye-2A contemporary was named *Faceplate*. For some time it was believed in the West that the latter had been developed in favour of the former, and was the MiG-21, but, in fact, *Faceplate* had not progressed further than the aerodynamic test vehicle stage. The Ye-2A was powered by a single Tumansky R-11 two-spool turbojet rated at 11,244 lb (5 100 kg) with full reheat and was flown for the first time by V. A. Nefedov. Featuring an armament of three 30-mm NR-30 cannon, the Ye-2A had a loaded weight of 13,780 lb (6 250 kg) and allegedly attained 1,180 mph (1 900 km/h), or M=1·78, during its test programme, and could climb to 32,810 ft (10 000 m) in 1·3 min.

The Ye-2A was preceded by an aerodynamically generally similar mixed-power interceptor prototype, the Ye-50, first flown by V. P. Vassin in 1955. Possessing a similar fuselage, tail assembly and 55-deg swept wing, the Ye-50 was powered by a Tumansky RD-9Ye turbojet offering 8,378 lb (3 800 kg) with full reheat plus an ShRD-S-155 rocket motor in the rear fuselage. Weighing 18,740 lb (8 500 kg) loaded, the Ye-50 achieved 1,490 mph (2 460 km/h), or M=2·3, but range was only 280 miles (450 km).

Fagot: In March 1946, Iosef Stalin gave three design bureaux the task of developing swept-wing high-altitude day interceptors for service with the V-VS from the late 'forties. The specification called for a speed of Mach 0·9, a cannon arma-

weather conditions and operating from small frontline fields. As a result of extensive research at the TsAGI (*Tsentralny Aerogidrodinamichesky Institut*) and other aerodynamic development centres, it was concluded that the 'tailed delta' configuration, combining low wave drag and structural weight with good supersonic manœuvrability, was best suited to meet the requirement, although its poor subsonic lifting capacity limited any secondary ground attack role. In

ment, an endurance of at least one hour, high climb rate and manœuvrability above 33,000 ft (10 060 m), and the ability to operate under relatively primitive conditions. The fighter had to be optimized for the interception of bombers at very high altitudes under clear weather conditions, but had also to possess close support capability. The competing design bureaux were those of Lavochkin, Yakovlev, and Mikoyan and Gurevich, the last-mentioned of these winning the contest with its I-310 fighter which, also known as the Type 'S', powered by a Rolls-Royce Nene 2 and flown on 30 December 1947, was to enter production as the MiG-15 and, several years later, was to be named *Fagot*.

Neither the competitive La-168 nor Yak-30 attained flight test status until mid-1948, by which time the Mikoyan-Gurevich fighter had already attained production, this having been initiated in February following an accelerated test programme with the I-310 prototypes, first deliveries being made to the V-VS before the end of the year. Initial production MiG-15s were powered by the 4,850 lb (2 200 kg) s.t. RD-45 turbojet, but this was supplanted at an early stage by the 5,005 lb (2 270 kg) s.t. RD-45F (*Forsirovanny* or 'Boosted'). Equipment was extremely simple, the only electronics comprising an RSI-6M-1 high-frequency radio and navaid, and an RPKO-10M low-frequency homing receiver, and a gyro-type gun sight was accompanied by an armament of two 23-mm NS-23KM cannon with 80 r.p.g., and a single 37-mm N-37 cannon with 40 rounds. Hard points were built into the wings to take two 220-lb (100-kg) bombs, an alternative external load being two 54·4 Imp gal (247,5 l) drop tanks to augment the 321 Imp gal (1 460 l) internal fuel tankage, auxiliary tanks boosting range from 882 to 1,193 miles (1 420 to 1 920 km) at 236 mph (380 km/h) at 39,370 ft (12 000 m). The maximum attainable Mach number in horizontal flight was 0·911 at 36,090 ft (11 000 m) and at the clean take-off weight of 10,595 lb (4 806 kg), initial climb was 8,268 ft/min (42 m/sec).

Progressive development of the basic design resulted in the so-called SD which, with a VK-1 turbojet rated at 5,952 lb (2 700 kg) s.t., and a reduction of some 200 lb (90 kg) in empty weight as a result of a critical weight analysis of both airframe and systems, entered production as the MiG-15bis. This model also featured improved equipment which included an RSIU-3M VHF radio transceiver, an MRP-48P beacon receiver, an ARK-5 radio compass, an RV-2 or -10 radio altimeter, and an SRO IFF set. Licence

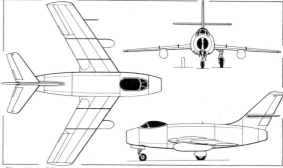

The Yak-30 (above and below) was designed to meet the same specification that produced the MiG-15

The MiG-15bis (Fagot) is seen above in service with the Polish air arm as the LIM-2 and (below left) in Czechoslovak service as the S 103. The MiG-15 was licence-built in both Poland and Czechoslovakia.   The prototype MiG-15bis was referred to as the SD

manufacture of the MiG-15 was undertaken in Czechoslovakia and Poland as the S 102 and LIM-1 respectively, the MiG-15bis being known as the S 103 and LIM-2, and variants of the basic design included the two-seat instructional MiG-15UTI (see *Midget*), the MiG-15Sbis specialized high-altitude interceptor with reduced armament, the MiG-15bisR (*Razvedchik* or 'Reconnaissance') with a vertical camera below the gun magazines, and MiG-15P (*Perekhvatchik* or 'Interceptor') with *Izumrud* (Emerald) AI radar. The last-mentioned version was first evolved in 1950 as a two-seater under the design bureau designation SP-5 (MiG-15UTI-P), but was subsequently manufactured in single-seat form.

Faithless: During the air display held on 9 July 1967 at Domodedovo, near Moscow, a single-seat single-engined STOL fighter-bomber of 'tailed delta' configuration made its début, and was named *Faithless* by the ASCC.   Obviously a product of the design bureau led by the late Artem Mikoyan in that it employed an essentially similar wing to that of the MiG-21 (see *Fishbed*), *Faithless* possessed a single propulsive turbojet in the 25,000 lb (11 340 kg) thrust category, and two vertically-disposed lift engines mounted aft of the cockpit. *Faithless* appeared to be in the 40,000 lb (18 145 kg) loaded weight category, and was presumed to be capable of speeds of the order of M=2·2, but development was apparently abandoned.

Fantail: The design bureau of Semyon A. Lavochkin was instrumental in producing the first Soviet swept-wing aircraft, the La-160, which flew for the first time in September 1947, and an essentially similar wing was adopted for the La-168 designed in competition with the Mikoyan-Gurevich team's I-310 and the Yak-30, this having sweepback angles of 37 deg 20 min at the leading edge and 35 deg at quarter chord, a constant thickness/chord ratio of 9·5 per cent, and an aspect ratio of approximately 6 (the competitive I-310's wing possessing similar sweepback but having a thickness/chord ratio of 11 per cent and an aspect ratio of 4·85). Whereas both the Mikoyan-Gurevich and Yakovlev bureaux selected the RD-45 derivative of the Rolls-Royce Nene to achieve the desired power-to-weight ratio, Lavochkin elected

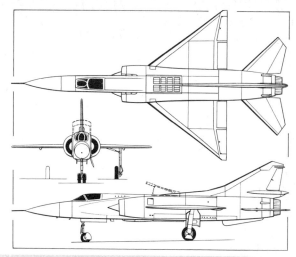

The Mikoyan-designed STOL fighter assigned the reporting name Faithless was publicly demonstrated in July 1967, and was presumably competitive with the STOL version of the Su-15 (Flagon)

55

The La-168 (above and below) was a product of the same programme as the MiG-15 and immediate predecessor of the La-15 (Fantail)

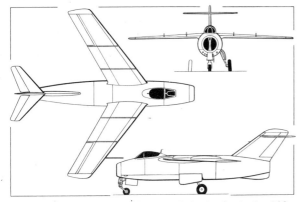

to use the lower-powered Derwent derivative for the La-168. However, the fact that the substantially more powerful I-310 proved to be barely heavier than the La-168 necessitated a reappraisal of the latter in order to achieve a more acceptable thrust-to-weight ratio, and at the beginning of 1948, work

was begun on two further prototypes, the La-174 and the La-176.

The La-168 was completed with a 3,527 lb (1 600 kg) s.t. NII-1 (*Nauchnoissledovatelsky institut V-VS*, or 'Scientific and Research Institute of the V-VS', the organization allocated the responsibility of adapting the Rolls-Royce Derwent for production in the Soviet Union) in the early summer of 1948, its most significant feature being its shoulder-mounted wing which offered a neater internal arrangement than the mid wing of the I-310, the structure of which ran straight through the intake ducts, but the narrow-track, fuselage-mounted undercarriage offered poor lateral stability on the ground. Carrying the specified armament of one 37-mm N-37 cannon and two 23-mm NS-23 cannon, the La-168 possessed a normal loaded weight of 9,727 lb (4 412 kg), providing a thrust-to-weight ratio of 0·36.

The La-168 was quickly joined by the La-174 (not to be confused with the La-174TK competitor for the Yak-23 for which see *Flora*), which, powered by the production version of the NII-1, the RD-500, bore a close similarity to its predecessor. In endeavouring to reduce drag, overall wing span had been reduced from 31 ft 2 in (9,50 m) to 28 ft 11½ in (8,82 m), the fuselage nose was shortened, the vertical tail surfaces were enlarged, and numerous detail changes were introduced which, with structural revisions and the replacement of the N-37 cannon by a third NS-23, reduced normal loaded weight by 1,239 lb (562 kg) to 8,488 lb (3 850 kg), thrust-to-eight ratio being raised to 0·41. The La-174 successfully completed State Acceptance Trials in August 1948, and was ordered into production for the V-VS as the La-15, which, in due course, received the ASCC reporting name of *Fantail*. Lacking the necessary altitude performance for the intercept role, the La-15, which joined the V-VS in 1949, was confined to the ground attack fighter elements with which it remained until the late 'fifties. The production La-15 carried either two or three 23-mm Nudelman-Rikhter NR-23 cannon, these having an 850 rpm rate of fire as compared with the 550 rpm offered by the earlier

Nudelman-Suranov NS-23. Performance included a maximum speed of 637 mph (1 025 km/h) at 16,400 ft (5 000 m), or approximately M=0·9, this altitude being attained in 3·2 min, and maximum range on internal fuel was 737 miles (1 185 km) at 32,810 ft (10 000 m). A tandem two-seat conversion training version was evolved under the design bureau designation La-180, this being delivered in small numbers as the La-15UTI.

Produced in parallel with the La-174, the La-176 was a more direct competitor for the Yak-30 and MiG-15, being powered by a similar RD-45F turbojet to that installed in the Yakovlev and Mikoyan-Gurevich fighters. Following closely the aerodynamic concept of the La-15 alias La-174, the La-176 was marginally scaled up overall, and its wings were swept 45 deg. at quarter-chord. By the time the La-176 flew the MiG-15 had already attained service status with the V-VS, but the Lavochkin fighter acquired a measure of fame on 26 December 1948 when it was believed that, while being flown by I. Ye. Fedorov, it had achieved M=1·0. It was eventually to be concluded that an ASI error had been involved, but the La-176 did exceed M=1·0 in a shallow dive during the following month while being flown by O. V. Sokolovsky.

Fargo: Possessing the distinction of being the first turbojet-driven fighter of indigenous Soviet design to fly, the I-300, designed by Mikoyan and Gurevich, flew on 24 April 1946, an hour before the first prototype of the Yak-15 (see under *Feather*) made its initial flight. Two design bureaux had been allocated the task of producing in the shortest possible time twin-jet fighters powered by the newly-acquired German turbojets and capable of attaining 560 mph (900 km/h). One of the two bureaux, that of Pavel Sukhoi, chose an orthodox configuration with wing-mounted turbojets, this emerging as the Su-9, but the Mikoyan-Gurevich bureau elected to mount the turbojets side-by-side in the centre fuselage, achieving lower profile drag by reducing the wetted area compared with that of the competitive Sukhoi fighter.

Artem Mikoyan and Mikhail Gurevich initiated work on their fighter in February 1945 under the design bureau designation I-300 (F), the construction of three prototypes proceeding in parallel with detail design.

Each powered by two BMW 003A turbojets of 1,760 lb (800 kg) s.t., the three prototypes were completed in a

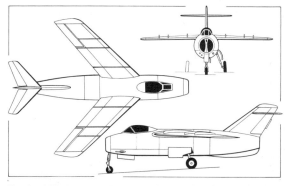

The La-176 (above and below) was the first Soviet aircraft to exceed M=1·0 in a dive, this taking place in January 1949

The tandem two-seat La-180 (above) was manufactured in small numbers as the La-15UTI

remarkably short time, the first, as previously mentioned, flying on 24 April 1946 with Alexei Grinchik at the controls. Initial trials took level speed up to 466 mph (750 km/h), a speed of 566 mph (910 km/h) at 16,400 ft (5 000 m) being

The La-15 (below), assigned the reporting name Fantail, served until the late 'fifties in the ground attack fighter role

recorded during the second phase of the test programme, this being equivalent to M=0·78. However, on 24 May 1946, Grinchik crashed in the first I-300, losing his life. Testing of the remaining prototypes was continued by Mark Gallai and Grigori Shianov. One of the two surviving I-300 prototypes was demonstrated over Tushino during the Aviation Day of the Soviet Union Display on 18 August 1946, and on the following day, Mikoyan was ordered to initiate a 'crash' programme for the manufacture of 15 aircraft which had to be ready to participate in the October Revolution Parade on 7 November 1946, two-and-a-half months later! In the event, the second aircraft was ready on 5 October and the 15th on 21 October, but fog prevented their participation in the Parade.

Service trials of the fighter took place late in 1946, by which time it had received the official designation MiG-9. The BMW 003A turbojet had entered production in the Soviet Union as the RD-20, and the twin power plants of this type installed in the MiG-9 had 351 Imp gal (1 595 l) of fuel available in four fuselage tanks and six flexible wing tanks. The fighter featured the first nosewheel under-carriage used by a production V-VS combat aircraft, and armament comprised two 23-mm NS-23 cannon with 80 r.p.g. and one 37-mm N-37 cannon with 40 rounds. At a normal loaded weight of 11,023 lb (5 000 kg), the MiG-9 could attain an altitude of 16,400 ft (5 000 m) in 4·3 min., maximum speed at that altitude being 566 mph (910 km/h). Developments of the basic fighter included the MiG-9F (*Forsirovanny* or 'Boosted') with 2,205 lb (1 000 kg) s.t. RD-21 turbojets, the MiG-9FR with a pressurized cockpit, and the tandem two-seat instructional MiG-9UTI. The pressurized MiG-9FR, which appeared in 1948 and was the final version of the basic design to be built, had a redesigned forward fuselage with the two 23-mm cannon transferred to the portside and the 37-mm weapon to starboard so that the latter would not intrude into the pressurized cockpit. Although by 1954 the MiG-9 had virtually disappeared from V-VS service, it was allocated the reporting name *Fargo*.

(Above and below right) The MiG-9 (Fargo) was one of the first jet fighters to enter service with the V-VS but served relatively briefly, being phased out of the first-line inventory during 1949–50 to give place to more advanced fighters

Farmer: In the late 'forties, a requirement was formulated for a genuine transonic fighter, and both the Lavochkin and Yakovlev bureaux endeavoured to fulfil the requirement with a fighter powered by a single Lyulka-designed AL-5 turbojet of 11,023 lb (5 000 kg), these being the La-190 and Yak-1000 respectively. The La-190 flew in February 1951 and featured 55 deg. wing sweep, a delta tailplane, and a zero-track tricycle undercarriage with small wingtip-mounted outrigger stabilizing wheels. At 20,408 lb (9 257 kg), the La-190 was seriously overweight. Its armament comprised two 37-mm N-37 cannon, and a speed of 750 mph (1 190 kg) was attained at 16,400 ft (5 000 m), equivalent to approximately M=1·03, this altitude being attained in 1·5 minutes, but handling characteristics proved unacceptable. The competitive Yak-1000 was even less fortunate. Featuring a thin, short-span wing of near-delta planform, and a similar undercarriage arrangement to that of the La-190, the Yak-1000 revealed such poor characteristics during preflight tests that permission to fly the prototype was withheld.

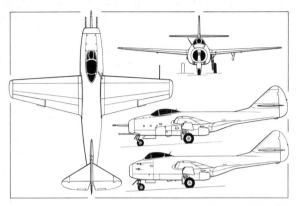

The plan, head-on and upper side views (above) depict the standard MiG-9 and the lower sideview illustrates the MiG-9FR

With the failure of the transonic La-190 and Yak-1000, a new requirement was drawn up in 1951 which called for a genuine supersonic fighter as a successor to the MiG-17 that was about to enter V-VS service, and the Mikoyan bureau initiated work on the twin-jet fighter, the I-350 alias Type SM, that was to attain V-VS service in 1955 as the MiG-19 and the first Soviet combat aircraft capable of attaining and maintaining speeds in excess of M=1·0. With its public début over Tushino in 1955, the MiG-19 was given the reporting name *Farmer*.

The MiG-19 (see page 166) was flown for the first time in 1953 powered by two small-diameter Mikulin AM-5 axial-flow turbojets mounted side-by-side in the rear fuselage. Comparatively few MiG-19s had been delivered before a slab-type tailplane was introduced, the designation being changed to MiG-19S, the suffix letter indicating *Stabilizator*.

Progressive development resulted in 1957, in the service début of the MiG-19SF (*Forsirovanny*) in which the AM-5s gave place to Tumansky-designed RD-9Bs. The MiG-19SF was dubbed *Farmer-C*, the *Farmer-B* appellation having been bestowed on the MiG-19PF (*Perekhvatchik* or 'Interceptor'),

The MiG-9FR (left) was the final development of the basic MiG-9 (Fargo) and, flown in 1948, featured a pressurized cockpit, an ejection seat and a redesigned fuselage nose in which the two 23-mm cannon were accommodated to port with the 37-mm weapon mounted to starboard so that it did not intrude into the pressurized cockpit

The Sukhoi Su-9, illustrated by the photograph (right) and the general arrangement drawing, was first flown on 18 August 1946 with two Jumo 004 turbojets as a competitor for the Mig-9 (Fargo). It attained 526 mph (847 km/h), M=0·67, at sea level and 559 mph (900 km/h), or M=0·78, at 16,400 ft (5 000 m) but was considered a 'warmed over Me 262'

this being a limited all-weather version of the MiG-19SF day interceptor. Before the MiG-19 was finally phased out of production in the Soviet Union in 1959, one further version appeared. This, the MiG-19PM (*Perekhvatchik Modifikatsirovanny*), differed from the MiG-19PF in having all cannon armament deleted and, in its place, launching shoes for four *Alkali* air-to-air missiles, the ASCC designation *Farmer-D* being applied to this model.

During its production life, the MiG-19 was the subject of a number of experimental programmes, one such, which bore the bureau designation SM-10, was a modified MiG-19S equipped for in-flight refuelling, trials with which were initiated in 1955. The SM-12PM tested late in 1957 had RS-26 turbojets of unspecified thrust, search and track radar in a conical intake centrebody and an enlarged dorsal spine. Armament comprised two *Alkali* AAMs and performance achieved during trials allegedly included a maximum speed of 1,069 mph (1 720 km/h), or M=1·6, a maximum ceiling of 57,090 ft (17 400 m) and the ability to climb to 32,810 ft (10 000 m) in 4 minutes. A modification of this experi-

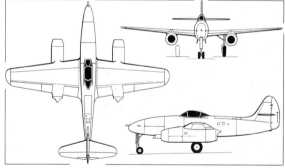

mental version, the SM-12PMU, had an externally mounted Dushkin RU-01S liquid rocket motor which enabled the aircraft to attain a maximum ceiling of 78,740 ft (24 000 m) during the course of 1958.

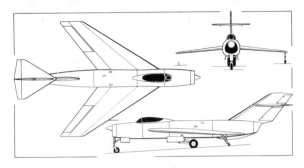

The La-190 (above) and the Yak-1000 (below) resulted from a specification for a genuine transonic fighter, this specification being replaced in 1951 by one which resulted in the MiG-19 (Farmer)

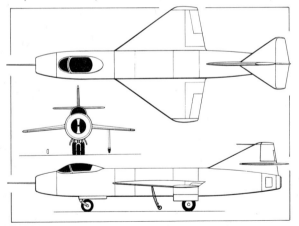

Earlier, during 1956, a pre-series MiG-19 with the bureau designation SM-30 was used for a series of catapult take-off trials, and a further experimental version, the SM-50, which was evaluated during 1959, had slightly more powerful RD-9BM turbojets each rated at 7,275 lb (3 300 kg) with reheat plus a U-19 rocket motor of 7,055 lb (3 200 kg) beneath the fuselage. Basically a modified MiG-19S airframe, the SM-50 attained a maximum speed of 1,118 mph (1 800 km/h) during trials and reached an altitude of 65,620 ft (20 000 m) in 8 minutes.

The MiG-19S was supplied to a number of air arms, the fighter being designated S 105 in service with the *Československé letectvo*, and production has also been undertaken *without* licence in China, Sino-Communist MiG-19S copies having been supplied to Pakistan, Albania and North Vietnam.

Feather: When the Mikoyan-Gurevich and Sukhoi bureaux were awarded the task early in 1945 of designing the first twin-jet fighters, the Lavochkin and Yakovlev bureaux were simultaneously instructed to develop single-jet fighters with equal haste, these also utilizing the newly-acquired German turbojets. I. F. Kolesov and his team had commenced the adaptation of the Jumo 004B for Soviet production as the RD-10, and both Lavochkin and Yakovlev were allocated this power plant for their respective fighters, but whereas the former designed an entirely new airframe, the La-150, the latter chose to adapt the airframe of the piston-engined Yak-3U (*Usilenny* or 'Strengthened') which flew as the Yak-15, this event taking place on 24 April 1946 at the same airfield where, an hour earlier, the I-300 had gained the distinction of becoming the first Soviet turbojet-powered fighter to have flown.

The Yak-3U had been the definitive production development of the basic Yak-3, and Yakovlev and his co-designer, Yevgenii Adler, merely introduced a new fuselage nose to house the 1,984 lb (900 kg) s.t. RD-10, arching the wing mainspar over the jetpipe to minimise the base area at the nozzle by lifting the jetpipe as high as possible, a stainless

The Yak-15 (right) was the first jet fighter to actually attain service status with the V-VS and was an adaptation of the piston-engined Yak-3U whereas its competitor, the La-150 (the first prototype of which is illustrated by the general arrangement drawing below right and on page 7), was an entirely original design

steel sheath being provided to protect the rear fuselage structure from the hot gases, and the tailwheel being replaced by a steel roller. Taxying trials with the first Yak-15 began in October 1945, but flight testing was delayed while the possibility of the jet efflux attaching to the fuselage at high incidences was explored in the full-scale TsAGI wind tunnel, together with the effect of throttle settings on trim owing to the thrust line being below the C.G.

Like Mikoyan, Yakovlev was instructed to produce 15 examples of the Yak-15 to participate in the abortive fly-past forming part of the October Revolution Parade of 7 November 1946. The Yak-15 completed State Acceptance Trials in May 1947, production of 280 being ordered as a single-seat fighter conversion trainer. Possessing a loaded weight of only 5,820 lb (2 640 kg), and carrying an armament of two 23-mm NS-23 cannon, the Yak-15 was structurally limited to M=0·68 which prevented the use of full power below 10,500 ft (3 200 m) owing to flutter, maximum speeds being 435 mph (700 km/h) at 8,200 ft (2 500 m), 476 mph (765 km/h) at 19,685 ft (6 000 m) and 459 mph

(740 km/h) at 29,530 ft (9 000 m).

Continued difficulties with the tailwheel led to the testing of the Yak-15U (*Usovershenstvovanny* or 'Improved') with

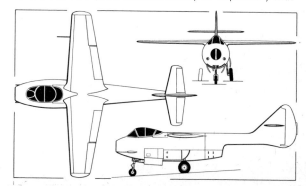

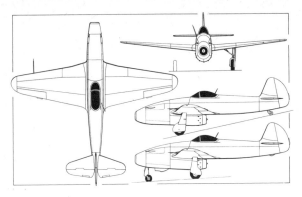

a nosewheel undercarriage, but as it was physically impossible to completely retract the nosewheel owing to the position of the engine, this was partly enclosed by a fixed fairing. The use of tricycle gear and the transfer of the main undercarriage members to the rear spar in consequence necessitated considerable redesign of the wing structure to take the landing loads, and the structure of the production Yak-15U was also stiffened to permit the introduction of wingtip tanks which would otherwise have decreased the placard speed.

From the outset the Yak-15 had been looked upon by Yakovlev as nothing more than an interim design pending availability of the Kolesov RD-10A turbojet of 2,205 lb

The Yak-15 (illustrated by the general arrangement drawing above) was, by minutes, the second Soviet jet fighter to fly, and was developed, via the Yak-15U (lower sideview) into the Yak-17 (below), the lower sideview illustrating the Yak-17UTI (see page 98)

(1 000 kg) s.t. which was to be installed in a partly re-designed airframe, this emerging late in 1946 as the Yak-17, eventually receiving the ASCC reporting name *Feather*. The increased rating of the RD-10A over the RD-10 was obtained by overspeeding the engine and accepting a bigger mass flow, and the necessary increase in intake area was achieved on the Yak-17 by cutting back the intake face. This change was accompanied by the provision of taller, more angular vertical tail surfaces.

The loaded weight of the Yak-17 at 7,055 lb (3 200 kg) was some 4 per cent lower than that of the competitive La-150's 7,359 lb (3 338 kg); maximum speed at 516 mph (830 km/h) at 9,840 ft (3 000 m) was marginally superior

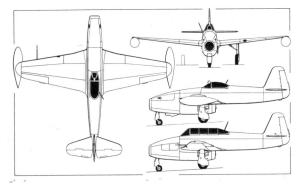

The Yak-17 (Feather), illustrated right, featured a stiffened wing to accept tip tanks, the repositioning of the main undercarriage members by comparison with the Yak-15 reducing internal wing fuel tankage. Lavochkin produced a series of competitive fighters, including the La-156 illustrated by the drawing (below right) and the photograph (opposite page)

and the range of 460 miles (740 km), obtained with the aid of wingtip tanks, was some 23 per cent better than that offered by the Lavochkin fighter. Furthermore, the airfield performance of the Yak-17 was immeasurably superior to that of the La-150 which, of similar pod-and-boom configuration, had a fuselage mounted narrow-track undercarriage. Whereas the Yak-17 had its engine and main undercarriage members mounted directly on the wing structure, the La-150 used heavy frames to carry these items, this feature contributing to a weight problem. The second prototype of the La-150, which was flown over Tushino on 3 August 1947, compensated for the excessive dihedral effects of the shoulder-mounted wing by introducing drooped wingtips, but trials were generally unsatisfactory. Three further La-150 prototypes had been built, these being fitted with the RD-10F (Forsirovanny) with short afterburner boosting available power to 2,425 lb (1 100 kg), but in April 1967, three months before the second prototype appeared over Tushino, La-150 development had been abandoned. Three further Lavochkin prototypes, the La-152, La-154 and La-

156, which were externally similar RD-10-powered aircraft coupling a narrower-section fuselage with an aft-positioned cockpit and mid-positioned wing, had also been built to compete with the Yak-17, and were tested during the early

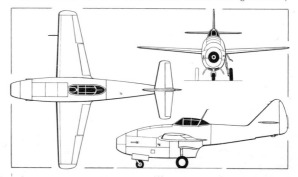

The La-250 (above and below) was evolved to meet the requirements of an essentially similar specification to that which resulted in the Tupolev Tu-28 (Fiddler) but proved unsuccessful and was abandoned during the course of 1958

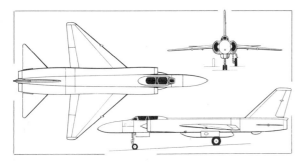

months of 1947 but quickly discarded, and the Yakovlev fighter, which had proved itself superior on most counts, entered quantity production for the V-VS and for supply in small numbers to several Soviet *bloc* countries, one or two

serving with the *Československé letectvo*, being dubbed S 100, and one being delivered to the *Polskie Wojska Lotnicze*. A total of 430 aircraft of this type was built, this figure including a proportion of two-seat trainers. For the tandem two-seat Yak-17UTI see *Magnet*.

Fencer: Relatively little was known of the aircraft to which the Air Standards Co-ordinating Committee has allocated the reporting name *Fencer* at the time of closing for press. However, it was believed to be a side-by-side two-seat variable-geometry aircraft reportedly designed by the Mikoyan bureau. The *Fencer* allegedly possesses a maximum take-off weight of the order of 66,140 lb (30 000 kg) and a 600-mile (965-km) tactical radius with a 6,000-lb (2 720-kg) ordnance load.

Fiddler: In the mid 'fifties, the Tupolev and Lavochkin design bureaux began work on two-seat long-range strike-reconnaissance and all-weather interceptor aircraft, producing the Tu-28 and La-250 respectively. The former (see page 222), which flew in prototype form in 1957, entered service with the V-VS during the early 'sixties, and is known as *Fiddler*, the fighter code name being applied despite the primary strike-reconnaissance role of the aircraft. Biased towards economical high-altitude operation, the Tu-28 has been seen with a large reconnaissance radar pack mounted ventrally, and for the intercept role carries such loads as four *Ash* air-to-air missiles. Current service models lack the ventral fins seen on early production examples, these possibly having proved unnecessary at the modest supersonic speeds of which the *Fiddler* is capable, and it may be assumed that the service designation of the interceptor variant is Tu-28P.

The La-250 '*Anaconda*', which was a very large tailed-delta powered by two 14,330 lb (6 500 kg) AL-7 turbojets (boosted to 19,840 lb/9 000 kg with afterburning), suffered an accident during early flight trials in June 1956 and another in November 1957, being abandoned in 1958.

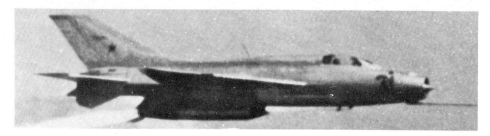

The Ye-66A (right) was a rocket-boosted pre-production MiG-21 (Fishbed) utilized to establish a zoom climb record in 1961, and embodying aerodynamic improvements later standardized by the MiG-21PF (Fishbed–D)

Firebar: An all-weather interceptor variant of the basic Yak-28 design (see *Brewer*), the Yak-28P (*Perekhvatchik*) features a dielectric nose cone, tandem seating for the two crew members with windscreen (and twin-wheel forward member of the 'bicycle' undercarriage) approximately 2 ft 6 in (76 cm) further forward than that of the parallel Yak-28 tactical strike aircraft (which later standardized on the lengthened fuselage) and the internal weapons bay deleted. The Yak-28P (see pages 245–6), which has been fitted with progressively more powerful versions of the Tumansky R-11 turbojet and upgraded avionics and missiles since its service introduction in 1963–64, has the reporting name *Firebar*, late production examples featuring a longer and more pointed nose cone.

The Fishbed–G (immediately above and below) was a low-speed lift engine test-bed conversion of the MiG-21PFM airframe

Fishbed: Designed initially for the pure air superiority role under clear weather conditions, the MiG-21 (see pages 170–5), known by the reporting name *Fishbed*, has been in continuous production for the past 16 years, having first entered service with the V-VS as a simple day fighter in 1959. The aerodynamic prototype of the MiG-21, the Ye-5 built for comparison purposes with the swept-wing Ye-2A (see *Faceplate*) which utilized an essentially similar fuselage, appeared over Tushino on 24 June 1956. The Ye-5 (*Fishbed-B*), which had flown for the first time earlier in 1956 with a pre-series R-11 turbojet rated at 11,244 lb with afterburning, featured a trio of airflow fences on the upper surface of each wing and twin splayed ventral fins. A small pre-production series of the MiG-21 (*Fishbed-A*) carried an armament of two semi-externally mounted 30-mm Nudelman-Rikhter NR-30 cannon with simple radar ranging in a small conical intake centrebody. Owing to the critical weight factor, the initial production model, the MiG-21F (*Forsirovanny*) which had an uprated Tumanski R-11 turbojet with an afterburning thrust of 12,676 lb (5 750 kg) and was referred to by NATO as the *Fishbed-C*, had the port NR-30 cannon removed. A pair of K-13 (*Atoll*) air-to-air missiles on underwing pylons was standardized, and as production of the MiG-21F progressed a vertical fin of broader chord was adopted and, later, a bullet fairing appeared at the base of the vertical tail surfaces to house the parabrake (previously stowed in a compartment alongside the ventral fin). Licence manufacture of the MiG-21F was undertaken in Czechoslovakia and a copy is being produced in China.

The initial clear-weather version of the MiG-21 was phased out of production in the late 'sixties', and the progressive development of limited all-weather and multi-role versions is described on pages 170–6.

Fishpot: Evolved in parallel with the Su-7 close-support and ground attack fighter (see *Fitter*), the Su-9 and Su-11 single-seat all-weather interceptors, initially both assigned the reporting name *Fishpot*, originally shared limited commonality of major components with the Su-7, the three aircraft having essentially similar fuselages and tail surfaces which, in the case of the Su-9 and Su-11, were married to a rather highly loaded 57 deg. delta-wing, the Su-7 having a wing swept 62 deg. on its leading edge. Two aerodynamic prototypes were displayed at Tushino in 1956, one having a housing for search-and-track radar over the air intake and wing root-mounted cannon (Su-9), and the other having a more orthodox circular air intake with a central diffuser cone accommodating the radar (Su-11). The latter was subsequently adopted for production, the Su-11 beginning to appear in V-VS service in 1959 with a Lyulka AL-7 engine. In 1961, a further development of the basic type appeared at Tushino, this (see pages 206–7) being dubbed *Fishpot-C* in the west. The later Su-11 differed from the initial production model primarily in having an enlarged air intake with an extended conical centrebody, an AL-7F-1 turbojet rated at 15,432 lb (7 000 kg) dry and 22,046 lb (10 000 kg) with full afterburning, and two *Anab* infra-red or semi-active radar homing missiles in place of the four *Alkali* missiles carried by the initial Su-11. During 1962, the Su-11 established FAI-homologated records for sustained altitude and a 500-km closed-circuit, the designation 'T-431' applied some years previously to an earlier Su-11 model employed to establish records being retained. For two-seat version see *Maiden*.

Fitter: Optimized for the ground attack role, the Sukhoi Su-7 has served with the V-VS for the past 16 years and has been widely exported. Progressively developed since it was seen in prototype form at Tushino in June 1956, the principal version, the Su-7BM (*Bombardirovshchik Modifikatsirovanny*), is known to NATO as the *Fitter-A*, is powered by a Lyulka AL-7F-1 turbojet and carries a cannon armament of two 30-mm NR-30s with 70 rpg. The Su-7BMK, 150 examples of which were supplied to the Indian Air Force, has provision for RATOG, and *Fitter-A* has ordnance loads distributed between four external pylons (two beneath the wings inboard of substantial airflow fences and two side-by-side beneath the fuselage) but some recent production examples feature two additional ordnance pylons immediately outboard of the main fences. A version of the Su-7BM, known as *Fitter-B*, featuring pivoting outer wing panels was demonstrated publicly in July 1967, and was initially thought to be purely a variable-geometry technology development aircraft. However, this model, designated Su-20, appeared in service with the FA in 1972 (see page 210). A tandem two-seat conversion training variant is designated Su-7U (see *Moujik*), this featuring a raised spinal fairing presumably housing fuel.

Flagon: A single-seat all-weather interceptor fighter apparently intended as a successor to the Su-11 (*Fishpot-C*), the Su-15 (see pages 208–9) is in large-scale service with the P-VO *Strany* (Air Force of the Anti-aircraft Defence of the Homeland) and some 700 aircraft of this type were reportedly included in the V-VS inventory at the beginning of 1974. Assigned the reporting name *Flagon-A* by the Air Standards Co-ordinating Committee, the Su-15 possesses an essentially similar wing to that of the Su-11 and is reportedly powered by two Lyulka AL-9 turbojets with afterburning thrusts of the order of 25,000 lb (11 340 kg). A STOL version with three direct lift engines mounted vertically in the centre fuselage (*Flagon-B*) was demonstrated at Domodedovo on 9 July 1967, but this variant is believed to have been a technology development aircraft rather than a potential operational model. A tandem two-seat version of the Su-15 has been reported.

Flashlight: The first genuine all-weather interceptor of Soviet design to attain service with the V-VS, the Yak-25* resulted from a specification issued in November 1951 calling for a twin-engined two-seat all-weather interceptor with relatively long search range radar employing a large dish scanner. Competing with the Yak-25 was the La-200 powered by two 5,952 lb (2 700 kg) s.t. Klimov VK-1 centrifugal turbojets installed in the fuselage, the forward engine drawing its air from intakes on each side of the radome and exhausting below the fuselage, a lower scoop intake feeding the aft engine which exhausted from the extreme tail. Armament comprised two 37-mm N-37 cannon with blast channels in the walls of the lower intake duct, and in order to attain the specified range of 2,175 miles (3 500 km), the La-200 had large underwing tanks which added 493 Imp gal (2240 l) to the 616 Imp gal (2 800 l) housed in the wings. A further development of the basic design, the La-200A,

*This designation had previously been applied to an unsuccessful single-seat fighter of 1947.

(Above) The STOL version of the Su-15 (Flagon–B) and (below) the Yak-25 (Flashlight–A) all-weather fighter, a general arrangement drawing of which appears on page 72

An example of the duplication of Sukhoi type numbers is illustrated by the use of the designation Su-15 for the current V-VS interceptor known in the West as Flagon (the STOL version being illustrated above), this having previously been assigned to the single-seat fighter (illustrated right and below) with two RD-45F engines which commenced its flight test programme in January 1949

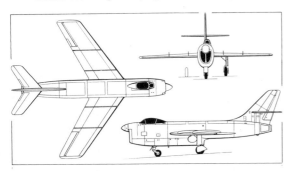

featured a circular nose air intake which fed both engines. By comparison, the Yak-25, despite its novel zero-track tricycle undercarriage with which the fighter virtually

(Above) The La-200A with nose air intake and (below) the La-200 with side and lower scoop intakes

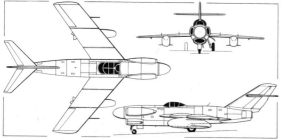

balanced on the twin-wheel aft member, was relatively conventional, with two 4,850 lb (2 200 kg) s.t. Mikulin AM-5 turbojets slung beneath its wings. The Yak-25 was flown for the first time in 1953, and after successfully completing State Acceptance Trials, entered production in the following year for the V-VS, and was named *Flashlight* by the ASCC.

Developed in parallel with the Yak-25 interceptor was the Yak-25R (*Razvedchik* or 'Reconnaissance') for the *Frontovaya Aviatsiya*, this having a redesigned forward fuselage in which the rear cockpit was deleted and a position provided for the second crew member in a sharply-pointed glazed nose, the designation *Flashlight-B* being allocated to this variant despite its radically different role, the basic interceptor model becoming retroactively *Flashlight-A*. Whereas the Yak-25 had an armament of two semi-externally mounted 37-mm N-37 cannon, the armament of the Yak-25R was restricted to one 23-mm weapon mounted in the starboard side of the forward fuselage. Performance of the Yak-25 was unspectacular but was improved from 1957 with the installation of the 5,730 lb (2 600 kg) Tumansky RD-9 engine, maximum speeds of 630 mph (1 015 km/h), or M=0·83, being attainable at sea level and 594 mph (956 km/h), or M=0·9 being reached at 36,000 ft (11 000 m).

Prior to the introduction of the RD-9 engine in the production Yak-25F airframe, the Yakovlev bureau had produced an aerodynamically refined version of the fighter, the Yak-27P, specifically intended for this power plant plus afterburner. The Yak-27P featured a sharply pointed nose radome to lessen drag and reduce rain erosion, a highly swept extension was introduced on the inboard wing leading edge to raise the critical Mach number, the wingtips were extended, and afterburners boosted the thrust of the RD-9 engines to 7,275 lb (3 300 kg) s.t. An aerodynamic prototype of the Yak-27P appeared over Tushino in 1956, and was dubbed *Flashlight-C*, but only limited series production was undertaken, possibly owing to the marginal performance increase offered over the RD-9-powered Yak-25 and its short time lead over more advanced all-weather interceptors. How-

Flipper: Considerable speculation was aroused in the West when, in June 1961, what at first sight appeared to be a large scaled-up MiG-21 (see *Fishbed*) was demonstrated over Tushino, and when, four months later, on 7 October 1961, a new 100-km closed-circuit record of 1,492 mph (2 400 km/h) was claimed for an aircraft referred to as the Ye-166, the two events were inevitably linked. However, the large Mikoyan-designed fighter seen at Tushino and promptly named *Flipper* by the ASCC had obviously been *twin*-engined, whereas the documentation eventually forwarded by the Soviet authorities to the FAI to corroborate the record claim stated that the Ye-166 had a *single* turbojet of 22,046 lb (10 000 kg). Some six years later, the puzzle was resolved by the appearance of the Ye-166 at Domodedovo, as it then became apparent that the record-breaking aircraft and the so-called *Flipper*, were, in fact, single- and twin-engined derivatives of the *same* basic design.

ever, the parallel tactical reconnaissance development, the Yak-27R (see page 241) or *Mangrove* with a similar forward fuselage to that of the Yak-25R, attained large-scale series production, and served in some numbers with the V-VS until the late 60's.

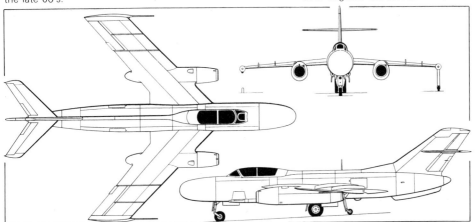

Now virtually phased out of the V-VS operational inventory, the Yak-25 (Flash-light—A), illustrated by the general arrangement drawing (left) and on page 69, was the first Soviet all-weather interceptor to achieve service. A progressive development, the Yak-27P, illustrated above left, embodied various aerodynamic refinements and after-burning engines but was built in relatively limited quantities

A specification was formulated in the late 'fifties for an interceptor of roughly twice the weight of the MiG-21, a requirement that was, in the event, to be fulfilled by the Sukhoi-designed Su-15. The Mikoyan OKB's contender in the interceptor contest would seem to have been produced in two versions; one with a single Lyulka AL-7F-1 turbojet with an afterburning thrust of 18,520 lb (8 400 kg), a 55-deg. swept wing and, for some inexplicable reason, the designation I-75F, and the other with two Tumansky R-11 turbojets mounted side-by-side in the rear fuselage and offering a total afterburning thrust of approximately 27,000 lb (12 250 kg). Yet a third model combined the Lyulka engine of the swept-wing aircraft with the tailed-delta configuration of the Tumansky-engined model. Apart from the respective rear fuselages, the last-mentioned aircraft was essentially similar to the twin-engined model, both, being highly-loaded tailed-deltas with clean gross weights of the order of 30,000–32,000 lb (13 610–14 515 kg), spanning some 30 ft (9,15 m), and having overall lengths of approximately 65 ft (19,80 m). The fuselage nose was slightly drooped, and an extremely large centre-body protruded from the circular air intake.

The single-engined delta featured a single centrally-positioned ventral fin, but the twin-engined model, the rear fuselage of which was of flattened oval section, sported twin splayed ventral fins. As the Ye-166, the former was progressively refined, the cockpit canopy being reduced in size to provide a smooth lead-in to an enormous dorsal fairing introduced to house some of the vast quantity of fuel needed for the record flights, gross weight rising to something of the order of 44,000 lb (19 960 kg). In its final Ye-166 form, this single-engined model is illustrated on page 19.

The swept-wing I-75F possessed, in fact, little commonality with either delta model owing to the repositioning of the

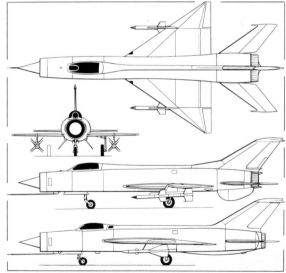

(Right) The photograph and general arrangement drawing (including upper sideview) illustrate the experimental fighter assigned the reporting name Flipper, the bottom sideview showing the I-75F

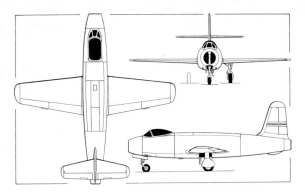

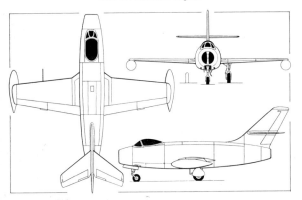

The Yak-19 (above) and the Yak-25 (below) were contempories of the Yak-23 (Flora), prototypes of all three aircraft flying in 1947 with the Derwent engine

cockpit and the other structural changes to the fuselage necessitated by the different wing carry-through structure. Like the deltas, the I-75F had a so-called *Uragan* (Hurricane) 5B search and track radar in a conical intake centrebody. Performance of the I-75F allegedly included a maximum speed of 1,430 mph (2 300 km/h), or M=2·16, and the ability to attain an altitude of 32,810 ft (10 000 m) in two minutes. Ceiling exceeded 65,600 ft (20 000 m) and clean gross weight was 25,090 lb (11 380 kg).

Comparable with the BAC Lightning, *Flipper* was evidently intended to carry two fully-active two-stage missiles, but there is evidence to suggest that these weapons proved too sophisticated for successful development, leaving only air-to-air missiles that required the target illumination of the immense X-band *Skip Spin* radar which *could* be accommodated by the Su-15. Thus, the programme was abandoned.

Flogger: The first combat aircraft embodying variable-geometry to attain service with the V-VS, the MiG-23 (see pages 177–8) was demonstrated in prototype form over Domodedovo on 9 July 1967, when it was assigned the reporting name *Flogger*. The initial service version of the MiG-23 (*Flogger-A*) was optimized for the intercept role, and late in 1972, the USAF Secretary stated his belief that *Flogger-A* possessed avionics comparable with those of the F-4J Phantom and had achieved limited V-VS service for the air superiority mission. During the course of 1973, a fighter-bomber version, the MiG-23B (*Flogger-B*), was demonstrated to an Indian Air Force mission to the Soviet Union. The MiG-23B (the 'B' suffix indicating *Bombardirovshchik*) retains the built-in cannon armament of the MiG-23 interceptor and differs primarily in avionics and in having two weapons pylons on the fixed wing glove and two beneath the fuselage. Gun armament comprises a GP-9 gun pack with a twin-barrelled GSh-23 23-mm cannon installed immediately aft of the nosewheel well. The MiG-23B was first deployed with the Group of Soviet Forces in Germany during 1973, a tandem two-seat operational version,

The Yak-23 (Flora), one of the prototypes of which is illustrated (right) was a simple and lightweight clear-weather interceptor, offering exceptional manoeuvrability and, for its time, an outstanding rate of climb. In the event, the Yak-23 was overtaken by the appreciably more advanced MiG-15 with the result that production and subsequent service were both strictly limited

the MiG-23U (*Flogger-C*), also being in service.

Flora: The acquisition of 30 Rolls-Royce Derwent and 25 Rolls-Royce Nene turbojets from the UK early in 1947 overcame the principal hurdle in the path of Soviet combat aircraft design development, the lack of powerful and adequately reliable engines. The lower-powered Derwent was favoured for what was envisaged as an interim generation of turbojet-driven fighters which, using simple, thoroughly orthodox air-frames would, nevertheless, offer a marked advance over the MiG-9 and Yak-17, and to the development of which the highest priority was attached. At the time the British engines were received, the Yakovlev OKB had reached an advanced stage of construction with prototypes of the Yak-19, a lightweight (4,850 lb/2 200 kg) conventional fighter with a 2,205 lb (1 000 kg) s.t. Kolesov RD-10A axial-flow turbojet fed via a simple circular intake in the extreme nose and exhausting in the tail. The one-piece two-spar wing

was mounted in the low-mid position, and had a thickness/chord ratio of 12 per cent. Armament comprised two 23-mm NS-23 cannon, a retractable tricycle undercarriage was fitted, and the pilot, who was provided with a simple ejector seat, was seated well forward beneath a single-piece sliding canopy.

With the receipt of the first Derwents, the second Yak-19 prototype was adapted hurriedly to take the British power plant in place of the RD-10A, the fatter centrifugal-flow engine having to be mounted further aft in the fuselage than the axial. This necessitated the provision of some ballast forward, the weight increase partly negating the advantages afforded by the substantial increase in power. Nevertheless, the Derwent-powered Yak-19, the second prototype of which was flown over Tushino on 3 August 1947, allegedly achieved 562 mph (904 km/h) in level flight at 16,405 ft (5 000 m). In the meantime, with the issue of the new V-VS requirement, the Yakovlev OKB had initiated the parallel

development of two Derwent-powered fighters, the Yak-23 and the Yak-25,* which retained the wing and undercarriage of the Yak-19, marrying these components to entirely new fuselages and tail surfaces. In view of the thrust losses

* The designation 'Yak-25' was to be resurrected some six years later for the twin-engined all-weather interceptor designed by the Yakovlev OKB and named Flashlight by the Air Standards Co-ordinating Committee.

associated with long intake and exhaust pipes such as were featured by the Yak-19, the Yak-23, which was eventually to be given the reporting name *Flora*, had its Derwent mounted in the forward fuselage and inclined downward at a slight angle from the longitudinal axis, the forward spar being arched over the jetpipe exhausting beneath the rear fuselage, and the pilot being seated well aft. The Yak-25 evolved in parallel followed more closely the aerodynamically cleaner lines of the Yak-19, but the diameter of the circular-section fuselage was marginally increased to ease installation of the Derwent turbojet, and all tail surfaces were swept.

Prototypes of both the Yak-23 and Yak-25 were flown in 1947, the former being the first to commence its test programme (in June), and while the latter proved marginally faster, attaining 590 mph (950 km/h), and offered the pilot a markedly superior view, the Yak-23 provided superior manoeuvrability, climb rate, acceleration and ceiling; factors which, coupled with better engine accessibility, led to its adoption for series production early in 1948 as a back-up programme for the La-15 and MiG-15 and an insurance against failure of the more advanced warplanes. Its principal competitor was the La-174TK (not to be confused with the La-174 prototype of the La-15 for which see *Fantail*) designed by Semyon Lavochkin's team. Of basically similar configuration to the earlier Lavochkin jet fighters (e.g., La-152, La-154, etc.), with a mid-mounted, unswept wing, an aft-mounted cockpit, and a narrow-track fuselage-mounted undercarriage, the La-174TK had a wing of only 5 per cent thickness/chord ratio (the 'TK' suffix indicating *Tonkoye Krylo* or 'Thin Wing'), and like that of the Yak-23, the Derwent engine was mounted in the forward fuselage at a slight downward angle and exhausted under the rear fuselage. However, the La-174TK did not complete flight testing until the early spring of 1948, by which time production of the Yak-23 had been initiated.

The Yak-23, which carried an armament of two 23-mm NS-23 (later NR-23) cannon with 90 rpg, entered service with the V-VS late in 1948, pre-production examples having the 3,527 lb (1 600 kg) NII-1 (the pre-production Soviet copy of the Derwent) and production models having the RD-500 (Derwent copy) of 3,505 lb (1 590 kg) s.t. The pilot was equipped with a rudimentary lightweight ejector seat without face blind, thigh guards, hood breaker, or even stabilizing drogue, and the fuselage fuel tanks had a total capacity of 202 Imp gal (920 l) which could be supplemented by two 41·7 Imp gal (190 l) wingtip tanks. The climb rate of the Yak-23 at 9,252 ft/min (47 m/sec) was second to none, maximum speed was 606 mph (975 km/h) at sea level and 590 mph (950 km/h) at 22,966 ft (7 000 m), and normal range at 335 mph at 32,810 ft was 575 miles, this being increased to 746 miles with tip tanks.

In 1949, 12 Yak-23s were delivered to each of the *Polskie Wojske Lotnicze* and the *Československé letectvo*, serving in the latter air arm as the S-101, and in the early 'fifties this type was supplied to the air arms of Albania, Bulgaria, Rumania and Hungary. A total of 310 Yak-23 fighters was built and one example of a tandem two-seat version, the Yak-23UTI, was evaluated.

Foxbat: Creator of a large number of FAI-recognized international records between 1965 and 1973 under the designa-

tion Ye-266 (see page 19), the MiG-25 is a titanium aeroplane designed for the dual intercept-reconnaissance role, has a shoulder-mounted cropped delta wing of comparatively low aspect ratio and is powered by two Tumansky

Only one example of the tandem two-seat Yak-23UTI (above) was built, but 310 examples of the single-seat Yak-23 (below and illustrated on page 75) were built for the V-VS and for export

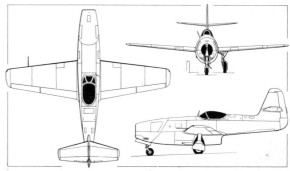

The La-174TK (above and below) was a competitor for the Yak-23 (Flora) and bore no relationship other than a common design origin to the La-174 prototype of the La-15 (Fantail)

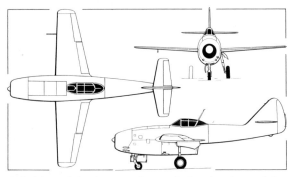

turbojets each having a maximum afterburning thrust of the order of 24,250 lb (11 000 kg). Possessing a short period dash speed of the order of M=3·2, or 2,100 mph (3 380 km/h), and a high-altitude maximum sustained speed of M=2·7, or 1,780 mph (2 865 km/h), the MiG-25 is believed to have a q (dynamic force) limitation restricting it to speeds of the order of 585–620 mph (945–1 000 km/h) at sea level. The high-altitude interceptor variant of the MiG-25, known to NATO as *Foxbat-A* and believed to have entered V-VS service in 1971–72, apparently has four wing stations for radar-homing air-to-air missiles and is equipped to receive signals from the ground-to-air digital transmission system known as *Markham* which enables tracking radars to feed data directly to the cockpit display. During 1971, the V-VS deployed to Cairo West airfield, Egypt, and Mers-el-Kebir, Algeria, units equipped with the reconnaissance version of the MiG-25, *Foxbat-B*, featuring a camera nose (see pages 179–80).

Freehand: Essentially a technology development aircraft presumably intended to further Soviet fixed-wing V/STOL design and operating techniques, the Yak-36 single-seat research aircraft was first publicly revealed in July 1967 at Domodedovo, where two examples were shown, one of these having a 16-round rocket pod beneath each wing as a representative ordnance load. Despite its obvious research role, the Yak-36 was assigned the reporting name *Freehand* by the Air Standards Co-ordinating Committee. The Yak-36 is powered by two turbojets mounted side-by-side in the base of the forward fuselage, each exhausting through a large-diameter louvred and gridded vectored-thrust nozzle, bleed air being supplied to 'puff-pipe' reaction control nozzles located at the end of a nose probe, at the tail and in wingtip fairings.

It is believed that about a dozen or so Yak-36s were built for trials purposes and one of these is reported to have undergone sea trials from a specially-fitted pad on the flight deck of the anti-submarine cruiser *Moskva*. The Yak-36 undoubtedly has some relationship with the fixed-wing V/STOL strike fighter and reconnaissance aircraft that has been developed for use by the AV-MF from the carrier *Kiev*, and reportedly combines a vectored-thrust arrangement with direct lift engines.

Fresco: In 1949, a refined development of the MiG-15 (see *Fagot*) was flown by I. T. Ivashchenko as the SI, this being

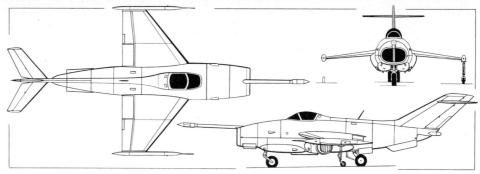

While believed to be primarily a technology development aircraft, the Yak-36 (Free-hand), illustrated by the general arrangement drawing right and the photograph below right, has reportedly served as a basis for a new V/STOL strike and reconnaissance fighter for shipboard use by the AV-MF

intended to meet a demand for a successor to the remarkable Mikoyan-Gurevich fighter which had begun to enter V-VS service some nine months earlier. Parallel developments of the basic MiG-15 were the SD (embodying a VK-1 engine and refinements resulting from a critical weight analysis of both structure and systems) and SP (embodying S-band *Izumrud* AI radar). Powered by a 5,952 lb (2 700 kg) s.t. VK-1 turbojet, the SI embodied the entire fuselage of the SD (alias MiG-15bis) forward of the rear frame of the engine plenum chamber unchanged. This was married to a new wing of thinner section and greater sweep angle (leading edge sweep ranging from 45 deg inboard to 42 deg outboard), overall span being reduced from 33 ft 0¾ in (10,08 m) to 31 ft 7⅛ in (9,63 m), and a third wing fence being provided to reduce the harmful effects of the new wing on low-speed stability. The rear fuselage was extended, increasing the fineness ratio, the air-brake geometry was revised, but the fixed-incidence tailplane was retained span and sweep angles being increased, and the vertical tail surfaces remained essentially unchanged. A competitor for the SI, the Yak-50, was produced by the Yakovlev OKB, and commenced its flight test programme early in 1950. Powered by a similar VK-1A turbojet, the Yak-50 was of essentially similar con-

figuration to that of the SI, with a mid-mounted wing swept 45 deg at quarter-chord, but the undercarriage was of zero-track tricycle type with wingtip stabilizing wheels, and generally similar to the undercarriage later adopted for the Yak-25 all-weather interceptor. Carrying an armament of one 37-mm N-37 and two 23-mm NR-23 cannon, the Yak-50

(Above) The LIM-6 is a modified version of the Polish-built MiG-17F employed by the Polskie Wojska Lotnicze for the ground attack role.   (Below left) The prototype of the MiG-17, the SI, that was first flown in January 1950

attained a maximum speed of 708 mph (1 140 km/h), but after protracted comparative trials, the SI was selected for series production as the MiG-17 in 1951, this later being given the reporting name *Fresco* (see pages 162–5).

The MiG-17 entered V-VS service in 1952, carrying an armament of one 37-mm N-37 and two 23-mm NR-23 cannon which was used with a simple lead pursuit optical gyro gunsight.   Some difficulties were evidently experienced with the narrow air-brakes mounted low on the rear fuselage of the initial production model, and therefore enlarged air brakes were introduced and these were repositioned on the fuselage, this modified version being dubbed *Fresco-C*, the initial model becoming *Fresco-A* and the appellation *Fresco-B* being given to the limited all-weather MiG-17P fitted with *Izumrud* (Emerald) AI radar and which later discarded the N-37 in favour of a third NR-23 cannon.   The decision to introduce the VK-1F engine with short afterburner boosting thrust to 7,452 lb (3 380 kg) may have been another factor influencing the repositioning of the air brakes, as it was obviously desirable to move the hydraulic actuators for the brakes from the vicinity of the afterburner itself.   The MiG-17F (*Forsirovanny*), or *Fresco-C*, featured a cut-back tail cone, exposing the end of the afterburner nozzle, and at a later stage the N-37 cannon was supplanted by a third 23-mm NR-23.   Licence production of the MiG-17F was undertaken in Poland as the LIM-5P, and in China as the F-4.

For the limited all-weather intercept role, a VK-1F-powered version equipped with the *Izumrud* AI radar, the MiG-17PF (*Perekhvatchik*), began to enter service in 1955, this having the conical scan dish mounted in a hemispherical radome on the intake splitter, the ranging unit being housed in an extended intake lip. The combat camera was moved from the top of the intake to the starboard side, and in order to provide room for the pilot's radar scope the windscreen was moved forward and the quarter lights modified. This variant, designated *Fresco-D*, was succeeded by the MiG-17PFU (*Fresco-E*) which had cannon armament supplanted by a quartet of small beam-riding *Alkali* air-to-air missiles, and a specialized ground attack version evolved in Poland in 1961 from the MiG-17F was designated LIM-5M. The latter featured a new plastic and fibreglass wing centre section extension of increased thickness, chord and leading-edge sweep to house twin-wheel main undercarriage members with low-pressure tyres and additional fuel tankage. Only a small number of LIM-5Ms were produced as a result of rebuilding LIM-5Ps, but a less extensive modification was adopted for large-scale service use. This, the LIM-6, intro-

duced a large braking chute housing projecting below the tail surfaces, RATOG and additional external ordnance pylons. The LIM-6 was still in first-line Polish service at the beginning of 1975, aircraft with modified ordnance racks to take a variety of air-to-surface missiles being designated LIM-6bis

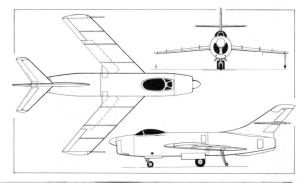

The Yak-50 (illustrated above right and immediately right) was evolved by the Yakovlev design collective in competition with the Mikoyan-Gurevich SI which was to be adopted as the MiG-17 (Fresco). An interesting feature of the Yak-50 was its zero-track tricycle undercarriage with wingtip stabilizing wheels

and modified for the tactical reconnaissance role as the LIM-6R. It is anticipated that these MiG-17 derivatives will be phased out of Polish service during the course of the year with the introduction of such types as the Su-20.

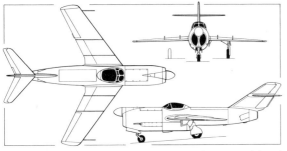

The Mikoyan I-320 (R-1) side-by-side two-seat interceptor (above) formed part of the same all-weather interceptor programme that resulted in the original Su-15 (see page 70)

HELICOPTERS

Hare: With the issue of a requirement for a three-seat communications helicopter late in 1947, the late Mikhail L. Mil, then Chief of the Scientific Research Laboratory for Helicopter Development attached to the TsAGI, established his own design bureau specifically to compete with the Yakovlev and Bratukhin bureaux in fulfilling the specification. Mil designed the GM-1, a conventional helicopter with single three-bladed main rotor and anti-torgue tail rotor powered by a seven-cylinder Ivchenko AI-26V engine of 575 hp, the first of three prototypes of which was completed and flown in September 1948. The competing Yakovlev design, the Yak-100, was a similarly-powered helicopter employing the same layout as the GM-1, the first prototype being completed in November 1948, and the Bratukhin contender, the B-11 of transverse rotor configuration with two AI-26GR engines, commenced flight trials before either of its competitors, the first prototype flying in June 1948. The B-11 suffered excessive vibration which led to the suspension of the test programme on 31 August 1948, and on 13 December shortly after testing had been resumed, the second prototype

The I-320 (R-1), left, underwent flight trials in 1950, having two turbojets mounted in tandem, one exhausting below the centre fuselage and the other in the tail. The first prototype had two 5,005 lb (2 270 kg) RD-45F engines, the second having two 5,952 lb (2 700 kg) VK-1s and armament comprised three 37-mm cannon

The general arrangement drawings depict (immediately right) the Bratukhin B-10 and (far right) the B-11, the latter also being illustrated by the photograph below right. Respectively three-seat observation and three-seat communications helicopters, the latter in competition with Mil's GM-1 (Hare), these helicopters were the final developments in Bratukhin's Omega series, with the open-framework rotor pylons being supplanted by fixed wings to offload the rotors in cruise. Development of the Bratukhin helicopters was abandoned in 1950

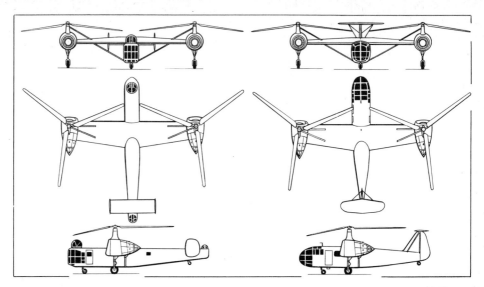

crashed. Modifications to the first prototype and further tests continued until May 1950 when further development of the B-11 was abandoned. Although more successful than Bratukhin's helicopter, the Yak-100 fared little better as it was not ready for State Acceptance Trials until the second half of 1950, by which time Mil's GM-1 had been selected for production.

The GM-1 completed State Acceptance Trials during the summer of 1949, and in September of that year was ordered into series production as the Mi-1 (see page 181), eventually receiving the ASCC reporting name *Hare*. The Mi-1 remained in production in the Soviet Union until the mid

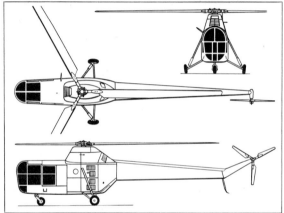

'sixties, and was manufactured under licence in Poland as the SM-1. Production variants included the Mi-1NKh (*Narodnoye-khozyaistvenny* or 'National Economy'), an all-weather multi-purpose model intended for forestry patrol and agricultural tasks, the Mi-1U (*Uchebny* or 'Instructional') fitted with dual controls, and the four-seat M-1A (*Aviataksi*).

Harke: Derived from the Mi-6 (see *Hoop*) for both military and commercial crane-type operations, the Mi-10 (see page 193) was first flown in prototype form in 1960 as the V-10 (*Vertolyot* or 'Helicopter'). Named *Harke* by the ASCC, the Mi-10 is virtually identical to the Mi-6 above the line of the cabin windows, but the depth of the fuselage is appreciably reduced and the tailboom is deepened to provide an unbroken lower line from nose to tail. A tall, long-stroke quadruped undercarriage straddles bulky items of freight, tracked vehicles, missiles, artillery, etc., and in 1965, a variant with a shorter undercarriage, the Mi-10K (*Korotokonogy* or 'Short-legged'), made its appearance, this having an additional cockpit gondola beneath the forward fuselage, the gondola featuring full flying controls and a rearward-facing seat.

Harp: To meet the requirements of a specification formulated in the late 'fifties and calling for a specialized anti-submarine warfare helicopter for shore-based and shipboard use by the *Morskaya Aviatsiya*, the late Nikolai Kamov's OKB developed the Ka-20 twin-turboshaft helicopter with three-bladed co-axial contra-rotating rotors. With two 900 s.h.p. Glushenkov turboshafts mounted side-by-side above the cabin, the Ka-20 was assigned the reporting name *Harp*, but when developed for production as the Ka-25 a new reporting name, *Hormone* (which see), was assigned despite strictly limited differences between prototype and production model.

Hat: The Ka-10M, which appeared in 1954 and received the

(Immediately above and below) The Yak-100 competitor for the GM-1

reporting name *Hat*, represented the final attempt on the part of Nikolai Kamov's OKB to produce a *Vozdushny mototsikl*, or 'Flying Motorcycle', a single-seat helicopter of minimum mechanical complexity for frontline observation and communications tasks. The first attempt to produce such a helicopter had been represented by the Ka-8 powered by an M-76 two-cylinder motorcycle engine modified to produce 44·8 h.p. Trials with the Ka-8, which began in 1947, were only partly successful owing to the unsuitability of the power plant, and only three prototypes were built, but with the availability of the 55 hp Ivchenko AI-4V four-cylinder engine, an improved design, the Ka-10, was produced, empty and loaded weights being raised from 403 and 606 lb (183 and 275 kg) to 516 and 827 lb (234 and 375 kg) respectively, rotor diameter being increased from 18 ft 4½ in (5,60 m) to 20 ft 1 in (6,10 m).

The first Ka-10 was flown in September 1949, and although underpowered like its predecessor, it attained a maximum speed of 56 mph (90 km/h), and possessed hovering and service ceilings of 1,640 and 6,500 ft (500 and 1 980 m). Four Ka-10 prototypes preceded eight pre-series Ka-10M (*Modifikatsirovanny*) helicopters which were produced in 1954, these differing in having modified rotor blade twist, a different rotor blade profile, twin vertical tail surfaces in place of the single surface of the Ka-10, and other changes. Although extensively tested, no further examples of the Ka-10M were built.

Hen: While engaged in the development of the Ka-10M (see *Hat*), the Kamov bureau began development of a two-seat helicopter of similar rotor configuration to meet a requirement formulated by the *Morskaya Aviatsiya*. Designated Ka-15, the new helicopter was flown in prototype form in 1952, and after successfully completing State Acceptance Trials, was ordered into production both for the Soviet Navy and, as the Ka-15M, for commercial operation. Powered by a 255 h.p. AI-14V engine, the naval Ka-15 could carry a depth charge on a rack attached to each side of the fuselage,

(Above) The Kamov Ka-10M which represented an attempt to evolve a simple 'flying motorcycle' and (below) the Ka-15 (Hen) built in limited numbers for civil and military roles

The Ka-18 (Hog) was a four-seater utilizing the same transmission, rotor pylon and rotors as the two-seat Ka-15M (Hen) and, like its predecessor, was built in limited quantities

the Ka-15M carrying stretcher panniers or agricultural chemical hopper or tanks in a similar position. The Ka-15M attained maximum and cruising speeds of 93 and 73 mph (150 and 117 km/h) respectively, had normal and maximum ranges of 180 and 290 miles (290 and 467 km), and weighed 2,500 lb (1 134 kg) in normal loaded condition. From late 1960, most Ka-15Ms were re-engined with the 275 h.p. AI-14VF engine. The Ka-15 was allocated the name *Hen*.

Hind: The first Soviet helicopter designed specifically for the gunship and assault transport roles, the Mil Mi-24, designed by the bureau 'named after M. I. Mil' and headed by M. N. Tishchenko, entered service in numbers during 1972–73 when it was assigned the reporting name *Hind*. The Mi-24 (see pages 198–9) employs the rotors, gearboxes, turbo-shafts, drive shafts and controls of the Mi-8 (*Hip*) transport helicopter, marrying these items to an entirely new fuselage and auxiliary wings carrying four pylons for anti-tank missiles or rocket pods.

Hip: Intended as a successor to the Mi-4 (see *Hound*), the

Mi-8 was flown for the first time in 1961 with a single 2,700 s.h.p. free turbine driving a similar four-bladed rotor to that of its predecessor, but the second and definitive prototype, flown on 17 September 1962, introduced a five-bladed main rotor driven by two 1,400 s.p.h. Izotov TV-2-117 turbines. Allocated the reporting name *Hip*, the Mi-8 (see page 190) entered production for the V-VS and for *Aeroflot* in 1963, both military and civil versions having clamshell-type rear loading doors. The basic military version has circular cabin windows and may be fitted with weapon carriers on out-riggers. Commercial models have square cabin windows, the standard version accommodating 28 passengers and the general utility version (Mi-8T) is equipped to carry internal or external freight. The Mi-8T has TV-2 engines uprated to 1,500 s.h.p., Doppler radar in the tailboom and an external cargo/rescue rig interconnected to a new automatic stabiliza-tion system to compensate for changes in CG. Total pro-duction of the Mi-8 exceeded 1,000 by mid-1973 when 300 had been exported and a float-equipped version was under development as the V-14.

Hog: Derived from the two-seat Ka-15M (see *Hen*), the four-seat Ka-18 utility helicopter, known to NATO by the reporting name *Hog*, employed the same transmission, rotor pylon and rotors as the earlier helicopter. Development of the Ka-18 was initiated in 1956, the helicopter flying in proto-type form in the following year, and from late 1960, series production Ka-18s had the original 255 h.p. AI-14V engine replaced by the 275 h.p. AI-14VF. The AI-14VF-engined Ka-18 had a maximum speed of 99 mph (160 km/h) and had a normal range of 186 miles (300 km) with three passen-gers and 20 minutes reserves cruising at 80 mph (130 km/h), empty and loaded weights being 2,274 lb (1 032 kg) and 3,311 lb (1 502 kg) respectively.

Homer: The subject of a protracted development, the first of two prototypes having flown in the autumn of 1968 with Soviet certification anticipated during the course of 1974, the Mi-12 (see pages 196–7) is currently the world's largest helicopter and has been assigned the reporting name *Homer*. The Mi-12 employs the dynamic components of the Mi-6 (see *Hook*), being, in effect, two Mi-6 power unit and rotor complexes mounted side-by-side at the tips of braced fixed wings and married to a fuselage and tail assembly of entirely new design. The Mi-12 established a number of FAI-homologated records in 1969, and two prototypes had completed their test programme by earlier 1974 when production was expected to be initiated.

Hoodlum: The Ka-26, which first appeared in 1965 with production deliveries commencing in the following year, is a light utility helicopter featuring a removable cabin which may be replaced by an open platform for bulky cargo loads or freight. Named *Hoodlum* by the ASCC, the Ka-26 (see page 157) is powered by two 325 h.p. Vedeneev M-14V-26 radial engines mounted externally, and features a similar rotor arrangement to earlier helicopters from the Kamov bureau.

Hook: First flown in 1957, and manufactured for both military and civil roles since 1959, the Mi-6 was, until the début of the Mi-12, the world's largest helicopter. In addition to serving with the V-VS, the military version of the Mi-6 has been supplied to Indonesia, Egypt and North Vietnam. The standard civil version accommodates 65 passengers, but a special 80-seater for *Aeroflot* is designated Mi-6P (*Passazhersky*). Auxiliary wings are fitted to off-load the main rotor in cruising flight, and these may be removed when the Mi-6 is operated in the crane role. Some 700 helicopters of this type had been delivered by mid-1973. The Mi-6 (see page 188) has the reporting name of *Hook*).

Hoop: Known in the Soviet Union as the *Vintokrilya* ('Screwwing'), the Ka-22 experimental transport convertiplane powered by two 5,622 e.h.p. Ivchenko TV-2 turboshafts was first demonstrated publicly over Tushino on 9 July 1961, and was allocated the reporting name *Hoop*. The Ka-22 carried its power plants at the tips of 67 ft (20,4 m) span fixed wings, the engines driving both conventional four-blade air-

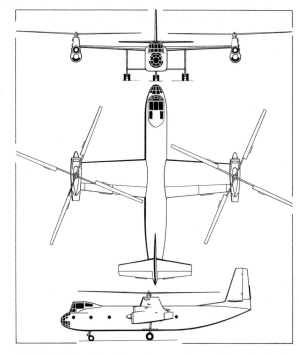

The Ka-22 Vintokrilya (Hoop) convertiplane of the early 'sixties established a number of FAI-recognized records

screws for forward flight, and four-blade side-by-side rotors for take-off, hovering and landing, a clutch on each engine enabling power to be progressively transferred to the tractor

airscrews after take-off. The Ka-22 established several FAI-recognized records in 1961, attaining an average speed of 227·4 mph (366 km/h) over a straight course, and lifting 36,343 lb (16 485 kg) to an altitude of 6,562 ft (2 000 m), but no further development was undertaken.

Hoplite: A derivative of the piston-engined Mi-1 (see *Hare*)

with increased capacity made possible by the installation of 400 s.h.p. Izotov GTD-350 turboshafts side-by-side above the cabin, the Mi-2 (see page 183) has been built in large numbers in Poland to where production and marketing were transferred after the completion of prototype development by the Mil bureau. Named *Hoplite* by the ASCC, the Mi-2 was initially flown in 1961 as the V-2 (*Vertolyet*) and entered series production in Poland in 1966 in accordance with an agreement signed in January 1964 under which the Polish WSK-Swidnik organization assumed responsibility for all further development. Production of the Mi-2 was continuing at the WSK-Swidnik in 1974.

Hormone: The production development of the Ka-20 (see *Harp*), the Ka-25, dubbed *Hormone* by the Air Standards Co-ordinating Committee, was first flown in pre-production form in 1967, and has since been developed in both commercial and military versions, an anti-submarine variant serving with the *Morskaya Aviatsiya* aboard the anti-submarine cruisers *Moskva* and *Leningrad*, and aboard *Kresta*-class missile cruisers. By comparison with the Ka-20, the Ka-25 (see page 154) *Hormone-A* ASW helicopters embodies some minor revision of the fuselage contours, and the civil Ka-25K features an hydraulic winch and an aft-facing glazed gondola beneath the nose for the winch operator.

Horse: Designed primarily as a military assault transport helicopter, the Yak-24 was flown for the first time on 3 July 1952, four prototypes being produced and these utilizing similar rotor heads, rotor blades and transmission systems to those of the Mi-4 (see *Hound*). Serious vibration and other defects delayed production until 1955, a limited number of helicopters of this type subsequently being produced for the V-VS, and the reporting name *Horse* being allocated by the ASCC. The initial model accommodated 20 troops, 18 casualty stretchers, or three M-20 *Pobyeda* staff cars, and this was supplanted in 1958 by the Yak-24U (*Usilenny* or 'Strengthened') which, first flown in December 1957, embodied autopilot, auto-stabilization, structural revisions, larger rotor blades, a 15·7-in (40-cm) increase in cargo cabin width, and endplate vertical tail surfaces. Powered by two 1,700 hp ASh-82V radials, the Yak-24U attained a maximum speed of 108 mph (174 km/h), and by comparison with the initial production version of the helicopter, the empty and loaded weights were increased from 23,384 and 31,460 lb (10 607 and 14 270 kg) to 24,251 and 34,899 lb (11 000 and 15 830 kg). A commercial version, the 30-passenger Yak-24A (*Aeroflotsky*), was evaluated by *Aeroflot* but was rejected, as was also the Yak-24K (*Kupe*), a lavishly-appointed nine-passenger model with substantially enlarged windows and airstair door, while the Yak-24P (*Passazhersky*), a 39-passenger version with two 1,500 s.h.p. Izotov turbines mounted above the cabin, failed to progress further than the advanced project stage. Production of the Yak-24 in all versions totalled only 40 machines.

Hound: Mikhail Mil's bureau began work on the Mi-4 (see page 185) in October 1951, and the first prototype was flown only 10 months later, in August 1952, rapidly passing its State Acceptance Trials and entering production before the end of the year. Dubbed *Hound* by the ASCC, the basic military version of the Mi-4 carried a crew of three and up to

14 troops, 3,525 lb (1 600 kg) of freight, a GAZ-69 Jeep-type vehicle, or a 76-mm anti-tank gun and crew. The Mi-4A was an improved version capable of taking slung loads, and an ASW version featured a search radar housing beneath the nose, dipping sonar and external racks for sonabuoys. Commercial exploitation of the design began in 1954 with the development of the Mi-4P (*Passazhersky*), a 10-passenger helicopter for *Aeroflot*, this being followed

The Yak-24U (Horse) introduced an autopilot and auto-stabilization but enjoyed only limited success and production of the Yak-24 in all versions totalled only 40 machines

by the Mi-4SKh (*Selskokhozaistvenny* or 'Rural Economy'), an agricultural version carrying 2,200 lb (1 000 kg) of chemical dust or 352 Imp gal (1 600 l) of chemical spray.

From 1960, all Mi-4s had metal rotor blades, and when production terminated in the mid 'sixties, several thousand helicopters of this type had been manufactured, licence production having also been undertaken in China.

MISCELLANEOUS AIRSCREW-DRIVEN TYPES AND TRANSPORT GLIDERS

Madge: With the end of World War II, all Soviet development of seaplanes was concentrated in the design bureau of Georgi M. Beriev which was reinstated at Taganrog, priority being given to a modern maritime patrol and reconnaissance flying boat with the design bureau designation LL-143, the prefix letters simply standing for *Letaiyushchaya Lodka*, or 'Flying Boat'. The LL-143 was a large gull-wing monoplane powered by two 2,000 h.p. ASh-72 radial engines, carrying a duty crew of eight plus a relief crew with a similar complement, and a defensive armament comprising a 23-mm

The first Soviet maritime patrol flying boat of post-World War II design to attain production, the Be-6 (Madge), above left and below, has now been supplanted by the Be-12 (Mail), but some examples are believed to serve still in fishery patrol roles, etc

NS-23 cannon in the bow, a pair of similar weapons in the tail and a remotely-controlled dorsal barbette. The LL-143 completed State Acceptance Trials in 1947, and was ordered into production as the Be-6, this flying boat eventually receiving the reporting name of *Madge*.

The Be-6 was flown for the first time in 1949 and by comparison with the LL-143 prototype, embodies some re-design of the forward hull, provision was made aft of the hull step for a retractable radome housing a search scanner, the ASh-72s were supplanted by 2,300 hp turbo-supercharged ASh-73TK engines, and, at a later stage, the single-cannon turret mounted in the extreme tail was removed to permit the installation of a magnetic anomaly detection stinger. By the late 'fifties, the Be-6 was the most widely-used flying boat of the *Morskaya Aviatsiya*, and remained so throughout the 'sixties, although it began to give place to the Be-12 (see *Mail*) from 1965. The Be-6 no longer remains in service for maritime reconnaissance and patrol but still performs second-line tasks and transport duties, and a number of flying boats of this type are operated by the Sino-Communist air arm. Weighing 41,500 lb (18 825 kg) empty and 51,600 lb (23 400 kg) loaded, the Be-6 has a maximum speed of 258 mph (415 km/h) at 7,875 ft (2 400 m) and cruises at 235 mph (377 km/h) at sea level range being 3,000 miles (4 900 km).

Mail: Intended as a successor to the piston-engined Be-6 (see *Madge*), the turboprop-powered Be-12 (see page 137) was first displayed over Tushino in 1961, and is believed to have flown for the first time in the previous year. Named *Mail* by the Air Standards Co-ordinating Committee, the Be-12 follows closely the basic configuration of the Be-6, and, during 1964, established six FAI-recognized records in the Class C.3 Group II for turboprop-powered amphibians, these including an altitude of 39,977 ft (12 185 m) without payload, 37,290 ft (11 366 m) with payloads of 2,205 and 4,409 lb (1 000 and 2 000 kg), 30,682 ft (9 352 m) with 22,046 lb (10 000 kg), and a maximum payload of 22,266 lb

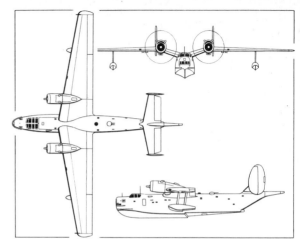

The Beriev Be-6 (Madge) maritime patrol flying boat in definitive form with MAD stinger replacing the original tail gun turret

(10 100 kg) lifted to an altitude of 6,560 ft (2 000 m). On 24 April 1968, the Be-12 established a 500-km closed-circuit record over 343·17 mph (553,28 km/h), following this on 9 October with a 1,000-km circuit record of 338·46 mph (544,69 km/h). Three speed-with-payload records were established during 1970, and in October 1972, the Be-12 raised the closed-circuit distance record to 1,259·25 miles (2 026·56 km) and a 2 000-km closed-circuit speed record of 345·97 mph (556,79 km/h). The Be-12 is currently the largest amphibian flying boat in service.

Mare: During the late 'forties, the Soviet Union was still evincing interest in large gliders for the assault transport role,

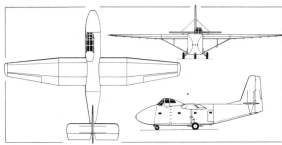

and among such gliders developed for use by the Aviation of the Airborne Troops were the Ilyushin Il-32, the Tsybin Ts-25 (see *Mist*), and the Yak-14 which received the ASCC appellation of *Mare*. The Il-32 and Yak-14 were both designed to meet a specification calling for a glider capable of carrying a 3·5 metric ton payload, and both possessed box-like fuselages with nose loading facilities, but whereas the Ilyushin contender for orders was of all-metal construction, its Yakovlev competitor was of wood. Both the Il-32

and Yak-14 were tested in 1948, but trials with the former were generally unsatisfactory, and the latter was ordered into production, several being towed over Tushino by Il-12 transports (see *Coach*) in 1949.

A shoulder-wing braced monoplane capable of accommodating 35 troops, wheeled or tracked vehicles, or freight, the Yak-14 had empty and maximum loaded weights of 6,825 and 14,881 lb (2 823 and 6 750 kg) respectively, and was normally towed by either the Il-12 or Il-14 at speeds up to 186 mph (310 km/h). Examples of the Yak-14 were delivered to the *Československé letectvo*, by which it was designated NK 14, and this assault glider remained in V-VS service until the mid 'fifties and its replacement by helicopters, a total of 413 being built.

Mark: At an early stage in the development of the I-26 fighter (which was to enter production as the Yak-1), Aleksandr Yakovlev initiated work on a tandem two-seat instructional version, the UTI-26, this flying in 1940 and entering production as the Yak-7. Progressive improvements embodied by the trainer airframe were standardized by a new single-seat model designated Yak-7A, and with further refinement and the cutting down of the rear fuselage decking for an all-round vision canopy resulting in the Yak-7B (**Б**), the two-seat model became the Yak-7V (**В**), and although it is extremely doubtful that any aircraft of this type remained in V-VS service by 1954 when the ASCC naming system was introduced, it was nevertheless allocated the name *Mark*.

Max: In continuous production in progressively developed versions for more than 25 years, the Yak-18 tandem two-seat primary trainer was flown for the first time in 1946, owing much to the experimental UT-2MV (see *Mink*) of 1943. The initial production model of the Yak-18 with a 160 hp M-11FR engine was introduced in 1947 as a successor to the UT-2, the first production variant being the Yak-18U which appeared in 1955, the 'U' suffix merely indicating *Usovershenstvovanny* or 'Improved', and modifications including a lengthened fuselage and a semi-retractable tricycle undercarriage.   In 1957, the Yak-18A entered service, the 'A' suffix indicating *Aerodynamichesky* and relating to the aerodynamic refinement of the basic design which included marginal increases in wing span and overall length, some enlarging of the cockpit canopy, and the replacement of the M-11 with its helmeted cowling by a 260 hp AI-14R in a cleaner, smooth cowling.   The Yak-18A (see page 237) was developed in parallel with a fully aerobatic single-seat model, the Yak-18P (*Pilotazhny* or 'Aerobatic'), intended for competition flying, this version entering production in 1961, a further single-seat variant evolved specifically for the 1966 Aerobatic Championships being the Yak-18PM (*Pilotazhny modifikatsirovanny*) with a 300 hp AI-14RF engine, reduced wing dihedral and various other changes.   The most recent derivative of the basic design is the Yak-18T (*Transportny*), a four-seater developed by Sergei Yakovlev and having a new fuselage centre section and new wing centre section.   First flown in 1967, the Yak-18T is currently most extensively used in the basic training role by the Aeroflot flying school at Sasovo.

May: The standard Soviet shore-based long-range maritime patrol aircraft, the Ilyushin Il-38 has been evolved from the

Built to the same requirement as the Yak-14 (Mare), the Ilyushin Il-32 assault glider (above) was tested during 1948

Il-18 transport (see *Coot*) in a similar fashion to the development of the US Navy's Lockheed P-3 Orion from the Electra transport.   Assigned the reporting name *May*, the Il-38 is believed to have flown as a prototype during 1967–68, entering service with the AV-MF early in 1970.   (See page 146).

Mink: In 1934, Aleksandr Yakovlev founded a line of two-seat primary training monoplanes with the AIR-9 (later redesignated Ya-9) which, in the following year, entered large-scale production in slightly modified form as the AIR-10 (later redesignated Ya-10), the designation being UT-2 in V-VS service.   Built in massive numbers (a total of 7,243 being delivered) with both the 125 h.p. M-11D and 110 h.p.

The Tsybin Ts-25 (Mist) transport glider built in small numbers

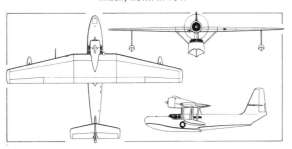

(Above and below) The Beriev Be-8 (Mole) light utility amphibian initially flown in 1947

M-11G until supplanted in production in 1946 by the Yak-18, the UT-2 was supplied to most Soviet *bloc* countries, remaining in service in some numbers until the early 'fifties, but having been largely phased out by the time it became the recipient of the reporting name *Mink*.

Mist: Prior to the issue of a specification for a 3·5 metric ton payload glider which produced the Il-32 and Yak-14 (see *Mare*), a requirement had been formulated for a smaller transport glider capable of carrying a 2·2 metric ton payload, and to meet this earlier specification., V. P. Tsybin produced the Ts-25. This glider was intended to fulfil both military and civil roles, and was evaluated by the Scientific Research Institute for Civil Aviation during 1947-48 to establish the feasibility of the use of gliders for carrying both freight and passengers over internal routes. With accommodation for 25 passengers, the Ts-25 was used experimentally on routes between Moscow, Novosibirsk, Gorki and Kuibishev. However, results were inconclusive, and the Ts-25 was built in small numbers for the Aviation of the Airborne Troops. One example was delivered to Czechoslovakia where it was evaluated as the NK-25, and the Ts-25 was given the reporting name *Mist* by the ASCC.

Mole: Despite the fact that the appellation *Mole* possesses but one syllable, it was, for many years, widely believed to have been allocated to a twin-jet flying boat allegedly designated Be-8. The system called, of course, for two-syllable names for turbojet-driven aircraft, and although the name *Mole* had been bestowed on the Be-8 it had *not* been misapplied; the Be-8 *was* piston-engined, and the jet-driven flying boat to which this designation was unofficially ascribed in the West was, in fact, the Beriev-designed experimental R-1 (*Reaktivny-1* or 'Reaction-1').

The Be-8 was a light all-metal utility amphibian which, flown in 1947, was powered by a single 700 h.p. ASh-21 radial engine, and was intended for ambulance, liaison, training and photographic tasks. Accommodating two crew members and six passengers, the Be-8 proved to possess a singularly unspectacular performance, which included a cruising speed of 137 mph (220 km/h) and relatively few examples were built, one of these being employed for hydrofoil trials. The Beriev R-1, to which the designation 'Be-8' had been erroneously attributed, was an experimental bomber flying boat powered by two 6,040 lb (2 740 kg) s.t. VK-1 turbojets and flown for the first time on 30 May 1952. With a crew of three, a defensive armament of two fixed forward-firing 23-mm NR-23 cannon and two similar weapons in a remotely-controlled tail barbette, and a 2,205-lb (1 000-kg) bomb load, the R-1 had an all-up weight of 37,480 lb (17 000 kg), and attained speeds of 472 mph (760 km) at sea level and 497 mph (800 km/h) at 22,965 ft (7 000 m). Only one prototype was built but this provided valuable information on the problems of turbojet-driven flying boats in general and the effects of porpoising at high planing speeds in particular.

Moose: In 1946, the Yakovlev OKB produced the prototype of a new training monoplane powered by a 730 h.p. ASh-21 radial engine. By international definition the new trainer came within the basic category but in the Soviet Union it was considered to be a *fighter*-trainer and consequently it received the apparently illogical official designation (in view of the fact that odd numbers were reserved for fighters) of Yak-11, and the type was eventually named *Moose* by the ASCC. The Yak-11 basic trainer began to enter V-VS service in 1948, and, in 1953, was placed in production under licence in Czechoslovakia. Embodying some design refinements, the first Czechoslovak-built Yak-11 flew on

29 October 1953 as the Le-10. This designation was subsequently changed to C 11, and when production terminated

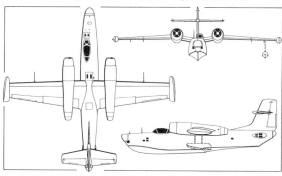

(Above right and below) The Beriev R-1 flown in May 1952 was the first Soviet jet flying boat and predecessor of the Beriev Be-10

The Beriev-designed MBR-2 dated from 1931, and was still engaged on fishery patrol tasks in the Black Sea and elsewhere when assigned the reporting name Mote by the ASCC

in 1956 a total of 707 had been built, Czech production machines being exported to the air arms of Bulgaria, Austria, Hungary, Poland, the UAR, and the Soviet Union. All manufacture of the Yak-11 was transferred to Czechoslovakia, and when, in 1954, the Yakovlev OKB projected a variant with a retractable tricycle undercarriage, the prototype was built in Czechoslovakia as the C 11U, but only one example of this variant was produced. Production of the Yak-11 totalled 3,859 machines.

Mop: One of the most important maritime patrol flying boats employed during World War II by the *Morskaya Aviatsiya* was the GST, a licence-built derivative of the Consolidated Model 28 built at Taganrog. Three examples of the Model 28 together with a manufacturing licence were purchased by *Amtorg* in 1938, and 18 Consolidated technicians accompanied the aircraft to the Soviet Union to assist in establishing production. The designation 'GST' stood for *Gidrosamolyot Transportny*, or 'Seaplane Transport', and was, in fact, intended to camouflage the primary role of maritime patrol for which the flying boat was required. The transport model was actually designated MP-7 (*Morskoy Passa-*

zhersky), and apart from lacking provision for defensive and offensive armament, it differed from the GST in having 870 hp M-62IR engines in place of the 950 hp M-87s. Soviet production of the GST was supplemented by the Lend-Lease supply of 137 PBN-1 and 48 PBY-6A amphibious versions of the basic design, and both these and the GST continued in service with the *Morskaya Aviatsiya* until finally supplanted by the Be-6 (see *Madge*) in the mid 'fifties, subsequently being relegated to fishery patrol and transport tasks, and the GST was accordingly allocated the reporting name *Mop*.

Moss: An airborne warning and control system (AWACS) derivative of the Tu-114 (see *Cleat*), the Soviet designation of which was uncertain at the time of closing for press, has been assigned the reporting name *Moss* by the Air Standards Co-ordinating Committee. This aircraft became known to Western intelligence agencies in the mid 'sixties, and first appeared in service with the V-VS in 1970. Apparently retaining the wings, tail surfaces, power plant and undercarriage of the Tu-114, *Moss* (see pages 224–5) is primarily intended to locate low-flying intruders and vector interceptors towards them.

Mote: One of the most elderly of Soviet aircraft to be the recipient of a reporting name from the ASCC was the Beriev-designed MBR-2 (*Morskoy Blizhny Razvedchik* or 'Marine Short-Range Reconnaissance') flying boat which, designed in 1931, was for many years the backbone of the coastal patrol elements of the *Morskaya Aviatsiya*. The MBR-2 entered production at Taganog in 1934, the initial model being powered by a single 680 hp M-17B engine pylon-mounted and driving a pusher airscrew, a commercial derivative being the MP-1 (*Morskoy Passazhersky*). A major rework of the design in 1935 was accompanied by the introduction of the 830 h.p. AM-34N engine, and this improved MBR-2 was the most widely utilized model of the flying boat during World War II, and, in 1954, was to receive the reporting name *Mote*. The AM-34N-powered MBR-2 could be fitted with a fixed wheel undercarriage or skis, and carried a defensive armament of a single 7·62-mm ShKAS machine gun in an open bow turret and a similar weapon in a manually-operated dorsal turret.   Maximum speed was 151 mph (243 km/h), and empty and loaded weights were 7,024 and 9,359 lb (3 186 and 4 245 kg) respectively, attainable ranges being 596 miles (960 km) with 148 Imp gal (670 l) and 932 miles (1 500 km) with 195 Imp gal (886 l) at 121 mph (195 km/h).   Commercial derivatives were the MP-1bis and MP-1T (*Transportny*), the latter having a strengthened cabin deck and a freight-loading hatch.   A total of 1,300 MBR-2s had been completed when production terminated in 1942, and the type was operated extensively on fishery patrol duties in the Black Sea in the late 'forties and early 'fifties.

Mug: A Soviet flying boat of World War II vintage that always possessed an element of mystery was the Che-2 which, designed by Ivor V. Chetverikov and eventually dubbed *Mug* by the ASCC, was for many years ascribed to the design bureau of Georgi M. Beriev and believed to be the Be-4.   The prototype of the Che-2 had flown in the summer of 1937 at Sevastopol as the MDR-6 (*Morskoy Dalny Razvedchik* or 'Marine Long-Range Reconnaissance'), a three-seat all-metal flying boat featuring bow and dorsal gun turrets and powered by two 730 hp M-25E radial engines. In 1938, the M-25E engines were supplanted by 960 hp M-63s, and as the MDR-6A, the flying boat was placed in production at Taganrog, deliveries commencing in 1939 and continuing until 1941 when 50 aircraft of this type had been completed for the *Morskaya Aviatsiya* and the designation had been changed to Che-2.   The Che-2 attained a maximum speed of 224 mph (360 km/h) at 16,400 ft (5 000 m), cruising at 137 mph (220 km/h) at sea level, and defensive armament comprised a 7·62-mm ShKAS machine gun in the bow turret and a 12·7-mm UB machine gun in the dorsal turret.

Although no further production of the Che-2 took place

after the delivery of 50 examples to the *Morskaya Aviatsiya*, development and refinement of the basic design continued until 1946 under the design bureau designation MDR-6B, experimental models being the MDR-6B-1 with 1,050 hp liquid-cooled M-105 engines, the MDR-6B-2 in which a major effort was made to reduce aerodynamic and hydrodynamic drag, the MDR-6B-4 embodying further aerodynamic refinement and M-105PF engines, and, finally, the MDR-6B-5 with a new, deeper hull, 1,700 h.p. VK-107 engines, a crew of four, a 20-mm Berezin B-20 cannon in a bow turret, and two similar weapons in an electrically-operated dorsal turret.

Mule: Designed to meet a 1926 V-VS demand for a simple, reliable elementary training biplane powered by the five-

The Chetverikov Che-2 was built in small numbers during 1939–41 as the MDR-6A (above) and refined developments of the design included the MDR-6B-4 (below)

(Above) The Polikarpov Po-2 (Mule) production of which was reinstated in Poland in 1948, and (below) the tandem two-seat version of the Yak-17, the Yak-17UTI (Magnet)

cylinder M-11 air-cooled engine, the Polikarpov Po-2 became the 'maid-of-all-work' of Soviet aviation, 13,500 being manufactured up to mid-1941, a further 6,500 being produced by 1944 when the type was finally phased out in the Soviet Union, only to be resumed in Poland in 1948, being manufactured under licence as the CSS-13 for agricultural tasks, and as the CSS-S-13 for the ambulance role.   Origin-

ally designated U-2, the Po-2 was popularly known as the *Kukuruznik* ('Corn Cutter'), and served in a variety of versions, these including the Po-2AP (*Aviatsionny Pilitel*) single-seat agricultural model; the Po-2GN (*Golos neba* or, literally, 'Voice of the Sky') with loud speaker and amplifier for psychological warfare; the Po-2NAK (*Nochnoartillerisky Korrectovovshchik* or 'Night Artillery Correction Aircraft'); the Po-2VS (LNB) night intruder (*Voiskovy Seriiny—Legky nochnoi bombardirovshchik*, or 'Military Series—Light Night Bomber'); the Po-2P (*Poplavkovy* or 'Floats'); the Po-2S (*Sanitarny* or 'Ambulance') three-seater, the S-1 having open cockpits, the S-2 having an enclosed cockpit for the medical attendant and a faired aft fuselage for a stretcher, and the S-4 with a cylindrical stretcher container above each lower wing; the Po-2ShS (*Shtabny svyaznoi* or 'Staff Liaison'), and the Po-2SP (*Spetsialnovo Primenenya* or 'Special Tasks') for topographical survey, aerial photography, air taxi and other roles.

This elderly biplane was named *Mule* by the ASCC, and is still flying in some numbers, more than 40 years after first entering service, most aircraft having the 125 hp M-11D radial engine.

JET TRAINERS AND MISCELLANEOUS TYPES

Maestro: An advanced operational conversion training version of the Yak-28 (see *Firebar*) serves with the V-VS as the Yak-28U and has been named *Maestro* by the Air Standards Co-ordinating Committee.   The Yak-28U has the shorter fuselage of the early production Yak-28 tactical strike fighter. The internal weapons bay is retained but the glazed nose is deleted and a separate cockpit windscreen and canopy is provided for the pupil pilot.

Magnet: The first tandem two-seat jet conversion trainer to be manufactured for the V-VS, the Yak-17UTI (*Uchebno-Trenirovochny Istrebityel* or 'Instructional Training Fighter') completed its flight test programme in April 1948 and entered

service towards the end of the year. Apart from the insertion of a second cockpit with dual controls in the space occupied by the radio equipment in the single-seater, the reduction of the armament to a single 12·7-mm UB machine gun in the starboard side of the nose, and the deletion of the fixed nosewheel fairing, the Yak-17UTI, named *Magnet*, was virtually identical to the standard Yak-17 fighter (see *Feather*).

Magnum: In the late 'fifties, the V-VS established a specification for a basic jet trainer to the modern formula; a simple and robust aircraft capable of catering for elementary through to advanced curricula, and suitable for standardization by all Warsaw Pact air arms. Design of the trainer was envisaged as an Eastern *Bloc* contest, the specification being issued to the Czechoslovak and Polish industries as well as to the Soviet aircraft industry. The Soviet contender in the contest was provided by the Yakovlev OKB whose Yak-104 project was selected for development from design studies tendered by several bureaux, and, as the Yak-30,* flew in 1960.

The Yak-30, allocated the reporting name *Magnum* by the ASCC, was an extremely clean, all-metal stressed-skin low-wing tandem two-seater, with an aft-sliding one-piece cockpit canopy and a small RU-9 single-shaft turbojet developed by S. K. Tumansky and rated at 1,984 lb (900 kg). The Yak-30 possessed a normal loaded weight of 4,960 lb (2 250 kg), and its performance included a maximum speed of 410 mph (660 km/h), an initial climb rate of 3,543 ft/min (18 m/sec), and a range of 600 miles (965 km), and a single-seat version which was identical apart from the deletion of the aft cockpit was developed in parallel as the Yak-32 (see *Mantis*). The Yak-30 underwent competitive evaluation with the Czechoslovak L 29 (see *Maya*) and the Polish TS-11, the contest winner being declared the L 29 which was promptly adopted for the V-VS. Thus, no production of the Yak-30 was undertaken, six prototypes being completed,

*The designation 'Yak-30' had previously been applied to the unsuccessful Yakovlev competitor for the MiG-15.

The Yak-32 (Mantis), above, was a single-seat version of the tandem-two seat Yak-30 (Magnum), only prototypes being built

but shortly after the choice of the L 29, one of the Yak-30 prototypes was employed on 22 September 1961 to establish a class speed record of 476·78 mph (767,31 km/h) over a 15–25-km course, the Tumansky-designed turbojet being referred to as the TRD-29 rated at 1,875 lb (850 kg) s.t., and all-up weight being quoted as 4,762 lb (2 160 kg), but three days later, when another Yak-30 prototype was used to establish a class altitude record of 52,913 ft (16 128 m), the TRD-29 was stated to have a thrust of 2,315 lb (1 050 kg).

Maiden: A tandem two-seat conversion training version of the Su-11 (see *Fishpot-C*) single-seat all-weather interceptor has been assigned the reporting name *Maiden*. The cockpit arrangement is similar to that of the Su-7U (see *Moujik*), the *Spin Scan* search-and-track radar appears to be installed and it is presumed that *Maiden* retains full operational capability.

Mallow: Owing much to experience gained with the experimental R-1, the Beriev Be-10 maritime patrol and reconnaissance flying boat was powered by two Lyulka AL-7PB turbojets of 14,330 lb (6 500 kg) thrust and established an

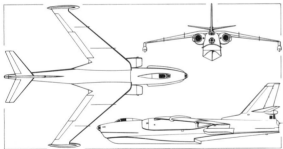

impressive series of international records in 1961, including a speed record for seaplanes of 566·69 mph (912 km/h) over a 15–25 km course, a 1 000-km closed-circuit record of 544·56 mph (875,86 km/h) with a payload of 11,023 lb (5 000 kg), and a seaplane altitude record of 49,088 ft (14 962 m). Production of the Be-10, which was assigned the reporting name *Mallow*, was apparently confined to a

pre-series, presumably for operational evaluation, but no quantity production followed. The Be-10 had empty and gross weights of the order of 53,000 lb (24 040 kg) and 90,000 lb (40 823 kg) respectively, operational radius probably being of the order of 1,300 miles (2 100 km) with a nominal weapons load of 4,400 lb (2 000 kg).

Mandrake: Flown in 1956 as a single-seat high-altitude strategic reconnaissance aircraft utilizing basically similar fuselage, tail surfaces and undercarriage to those of the Yak-25 (see *Flashlight-A*) which were married to a new long-span unswept wing, the type assigned the reporting name *Mandrake* is believed to have the official Soviet designation of Yak-26. Clandestine high-altitude reconnaissance flights over China, India and Pakistan were reportedly performed by *Mandrake* as recently as 1971–72 (see page 240).

Mangrove: A progressive development of the Yak-25R tactical reconnaissance aircraft (*Flashlight-B*) which was a variant of the Yak-25 (*Flashlight-A*) all-weather interceptor, the Yak-27R is an equivalent parallel development of the Yak-27P interceptor, and was built in substantial numbers for V-VS use in the Tac-R role. Assigned the reporting name *Mangrove*, the Yak-27R (see pages 241–2) includes sensors in the radio and infra-red regions in its internal equipment and can carry underwing sensor pods.

Mantis: Developed in parallel with the Yak-30 tandem two-seat trainer (see *Mangum*), the Yak-32 differs from the two-seater solely in having the aft cockpit deleted, and performances of the two aircraft were essentially similar. On 22 February 1961, a Yak-32 prototype established a new Class C-1d record by climbing to an altitude of 48,860 ft (14 283 m), the thrust rating of its Tumansky-designed RU-19 turbojet being quoted as 1,764 lb (800 kg), and its all-up weight as 4,710 lb (2 137 kg). Only two prototypes of the Yak-32 were built, and these were named *Mantis*. The Yak-32 attained a maximum speed of 435 mph (700 km/h) and had an endurance of 2·75 hours.

Mascot: A training variant of the Il-28 light tactical bomber (see *Beagle*), the Il-28U, allocated the reporting name *Mascot*, has the ventral radome and nose glazing deleted, and a second cockpit installed ahead and below the standard cockpit.

Maya: With the selection of the L 29 *Delfin* jet basic trainer by the V-VS, the Czechoslovak-manufactured aircraft was allocated the name *Maya* by the Air Standards Co-ordinating Committee.

Midget: Most Soviet fighters are eventually modified to produce two-seat operational or advanced trainers, and the MiG-15 (see *Fagot*) was no exception, the tandem two-seat MiG-15UTI appearing as a prototype in 1949. As with most such Soviet conversions, the aircraft's overall length was held constant. The rear seat was raised so that the instructor could see directly forward over the pupil's head in gunnery training, the windscreen being enlarged to suit. Licence production of the MiG-15UTI was undertaken in Czechoslovakia as the CS 102 and in Poland as the SBLim-1. From the beginning of 1967, all SBLim-1 trainers remaining

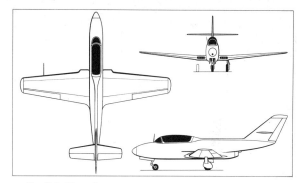

The Yak-30 tandem two-seat version of the Yak-32 (Mantis)

with the *Polskie Wojska Lotnicze* were fitted with the power plant, rear fuselage and tail surfaces of obsolescent LIM-2 (licence-built MiG-15bis) fighters as SBLim-2 trainers. The MiG-15UTI is named *Midget* by the ASCC.

Mongol: The two-seat operational training version of the MiG-21 single-seat fighter (see *Fishbed*) has been progressively developed since first introduced into service by the V-VS, changes largely paralleling those applied to contemporary single-seat models. The initial model of the MiG-21U (assigned the reporting name *Mongol*) was a straightforward adaptation of the MiG-21F with a second seat inserted behind the normal cockpit. (See page 176).

Moujik: A tandem two-seat advanced conversion training version of the Su-7 (see *Fitter*) is designated Su-7U and has been assigned the reporting name *Moujik*. A second cockpit is inserted aft of the standard cockpit, the instructor's seat being positioned higher than that of the pupil, each seat being enclosed by a separate aft-hinging canopy, and a spine has been introduced between aft cockpit and vertical fin.

THE AIR FORCES OF THE SOVIET UNION

The Air Forces of the USSR, or *Voenno-vozdushniye Sily* (V-VS), comprise together what is numerically the largest of the world's air arms. While precision concerning numbers of aircraft is not possible on present knowledge, the consensus of opinion of western intelligence agencies suggests that the current active inventory of the V-VS comprises marginally in excess of 10,000 combat aircraft.

Commanded by Chief Marshal of Aviation Pavel Stepanovich Kutahov, the V-VS consists of the following principal components: the Air Force of the Anti-aircraft Defence of the Homeland, or *Protivo-vozdushnaya Oborona (Strany)* which is usually abbreviated as P-VO *Strany* and has been a separate command of the Armed Forces of the USSR since 1948; the Long-range Aviation, or *Aviatsiya Dal'nevo Deistviya* (ADD); the Frontal Aviation, or *Frontovaya Aviatsiya* (FA); the Transport Aviation, or *Voenno-transportnaya Aviatsiya* (V-TA), and the Naval Air Force, or *Aviatsiya Voenno-morskovo Flota* (AV-MF).

The P-VO *Strany* is responsible for the aerial defence of the main centres of industry and population, and comprises anti-aircraft artillery, surface-to-air missiles, ground-based and airborne control and early warning radar, and a substantial interceptor force with supporting transport, communications and liaison units. The P-VO *Strany* Headquarters in Moscow exercises overall control of the Warsaw Treaty Organization air defence and warning system, and deploys its forces in two P-VO Districts, the *Moskovsky Okrug P-VO* (Moscow) and the *Bakinsky Okrug P-VO* (Baku). Elsewhere in the Soviet Union air defence is the responsibility of the P-VO units assigned to the various Military Districts which tie in with the P-VO *Strany* but which come under the direct control of the local Military District Air Command Headquarters.

The interceptor fighter component of the P-VO *Strany*, the *Istrebitel'naya Aviatsiya P-VO Strany* or IAP-VO *Strany*, employs the Divisiya (Division) as its largest unit for organizational purposes, this comprising three and sometimes more regiments (*polki*) each usually possessing three squadrons (*eskadrilii*) of 12 aircraft. One squadron in each regiment normally possesses a secondary operational and combat proficiency training commitment but each squadron usually includes in its inventory 2–3 dual role (i.e., equipped to fulfil both training and operational functions) aircraft, units operating single-seat aircraft normally possessing a ratio of 1 : 4/5 two-seaters (e.g., Su-11 single-seat interceptor squadrons including some tandem two-seat Su-11Us). All three squadrons in each regiment operate the same aircraft type.

The IAP-VO *Strany* traditionally enjoys priority in re-equipment with new types of interceptor fighter as introduced, and at the beginning of 1975, at least half of the more than 600 interceptors deployed in the two P-VO Districts were of the Sukhoi Su-15 (*Flagon*) type, a small proportion comprising the specialised high-altitude interceptor version of the MiG-25 (*Foxbat-A*) and the remainder being made up by the Sukhoi Su-11 (*Fishpot-C*) and the Yak-28P (*Firebar*). Transport support is provided by the Antonov An-12 (*Cub*) and the Ilyushin Il-14 (*Crate*) which are assigned at divisional level, although the latter is giving place to the An-26 (*Curl*), and communications and liaison tasks are performed by An-2s, An-14s and various helicopters.

The IAP-VO formations—as distinct from the main IAP-VO *Strany*—assigned to each Military District and to the groups of Soviet forces deployed outside the borders of the USSR are subordinate to the local Air Command Headquarters and, in effect, form an integral part of the respective District or Forces Group aviation components. The principal Military Districts are Moscow, Leningrad, Baltic, Kiev, Volga, Trans-Caucasian, North Caucasian, Carpathian, Ural, Odessa, Byelo-Russia, Central Asia, Turkistan, Trans-Baikal, Siberian and Far East. The Forces Groups comprise the Northern Group of Forces with Headquarters at Legnica, Poland, the Southern Group of Forces with Headquarters at Tokol, Hungary, the Central Group of Forces with Headquarters at Milovice, Czechoslovakia, and the Group of Soviet Forces in Germany with Headquarters at Wünsdorf. In addition, there are a number of Frontier Troop Districts (eg, Eastern Frontier District) to which IAP-VO formations are assigned.

Each District includes IAP-VO regiments according to its importance, this factor also usually governing priority in re-equipment, but during the early 'seventies, the progressive reduction in the proportion of obsolescent aircraft being operated by the IAP-VO was being accompanied by some numerical decline in the home defence interceptor force which, excluding the IAP-VO *Strany*, is believed to currently comprise some 55—60 regiments with a total of 2,000—2,200 interceptor fighters. By the beginning of 1975, it was calculated that some 45 per cent of the IAP-VO was equipped with the Yak-28P, the Su-15 and the Tu-28P (*Fiddler*). A further 25 per cent of the operational inventory was made up of the Su-11 and the remaining 30 per cent consisted of versions of the MiG-21 (*Fishbed*) and various obsolescing types (eg, MiG-17, MiG-19) which are likely to have been phased out within the next two years. The ageing Tu-28, employed primarily to mount standing patrols over areas not screened by SAMs around the Soviet periphery, was being phased out from late 1974 when an interceptor version of the Tu-22 was being introduced.

For the detection of low-flying intruders, the IAP-VO employs a derivative of the obsolete Tu-114 commercial transport (see pages 40—41), this AWACS (airborne warning and control system) aircraft, which has been assigned the reporting name *Moss* (see pages 224—5), working in conjunction with interceptors and presumably fulfilling a secondary function on behalf of the FA in assisting strike

The Yak-28P (top right) and the Su-11 (right) are now being progressively replaced in the regiments of the P-VO Strany

103

(Above and below) The Tu-22 supersonic reconnaissance-bomber currently spearheads the ADD. The downward-ejection seats of two crew members can be seen lowered (above) and the Bee Hind radar and 23-mm cannon tail barbette may be clearly seen (below)

aircraft to elude enemy interceptors. A more advanced AWACS aircraft with a look-down capability over land as well as water is expected to be phased into service during the closing years of the present decade, together with interceptors possessing a look-down/shoot-down radar/ missile system.

The strategic component of the V-VS, the ADD, has progressively diminished in importance with the growth of the the Strategic Rocket Forces, or *Raketny Voiska Strategicheskovo Naznacheniya*, and now possesses fewer than 200 ageing Tu-20 (*Bear*) and M-4 (*Bison*) heavy bombers (as compared with a peak strength of 700–800 in the late 'fifties and early 'sixties, and approximately half the heavy bombers remaining in the ADD have been adapted as carriers for stand-off missiles, while some 40–50 M-4s now fulfil the tanker role. As withdrawn from the ADD, the majority of the Tu-20s and a proportion of the M-4s have been adapted for use by the AV-MF in the long-range maritime and 'ferret' roles with optical and non-optical sensors, and for anti-shipping missile control (*Bear-D*).

The ADD has maintained a rather larger force of medium bombers currently spearheaded by upwards of 300 Tu-22s (*Blinder*) with a steadily declining but numerically similar force of obsolescent Tu-16s (*Badger*), but capability is currently being upgraded by the introduction of a variable-geometry bomber, assigned the reporting name *Backfire*, which was being phased in by the ADD during the course of 1974, and which is believed to possess an intercontinental role. The ADD still possesses a strategic reconnaissance commitment, emphasis during the late 'sixties and early 'seventies being on the surveillance of those areas of China bordering on the USSR. The largest component of the ADD is the *divisiya* which normally comprises three regiments each with three 10-aircraft squadrons with attached refuelling tanker elements.

The principal tactical element of the V-VS, the FA, is also the largest operational component, possessing 4,500–5,000 combat aircraft, these excluding almost 2,000 tactical aircraft used in training roles. The FA has undergone steady reorganization during the late 'fifties and throughout the 'sixties, and the large Frontal Aviation Army (*Frontovaya Aviatsionnaya Armiya*) with its component aviation corps (*aviatsionny korpus*) no longer exists, the largest formation being the *divisiya*, elements attached to a Forces Group or Military District being referred to by the designation of the Group or District (eg, Aviation of the Northern Group of Forces, or *Aviatsiya Severnoi Gruppi Voisk*). Each *divisiya* is normally equipped with aircraft performing one role (eg, close support, tactical strike, tactical reconnaissance, etc) but not necessarily with one aircraft type, transport and support components being assigned at *divisiya* level, and communications and liaison elements at regimental level. During the course of 1974, FA elements were enjoying an infusion of new equipment, such as the MiG-23B (*Flogger*) variable-geometry tactical strike aircraft and Mi-24 (*Hind*) gunship and assault transport helicopter, both of which appeared in service with the Group of Soviet Forces in Germany; the Su-20 (*Fitter-B*) variable-geometry close-support fighter, and a new two-seat variable-geometry strike fighter comparable with the General Dynamics F-111 of the

The Sukhoi Su-7 ground attack fighter (above right and immediately right) is currently numerically the most important combat aircraft in the FA inventory, but operational use by the Arab and Indian air forces in recent years has revealed various shortcomings, such as an overly modest range and ordnance limitations

105

The Yak-28I
(Brewer—C), left, is
the most widely-used
tactical strike and
reconnaissance air-
craft, and the MiG-21,
illustrated at the foot
of the page in its
MiG-21PFM form, is
numerically by far the
most important com-
bat aircraft employed
by the major com-
ponents of the V-VS

USAF and assigned the reporting name *Fencer*.

Apart from these newer types, the principal aircraft operated by the FA comprise the Yak-27R (*Mangrove*) tactical reconnaissance aircraft, various tactical strike, tactical reconnaissance and electronic countermeasures versions of the Yak-28 (*Brewer*) and dual-role (intercept and fighter-bomber) versions of the MiG-21 (*Fishbed*), but obsolescent types still serving with the FA in some numbers include the MiG-17F, the MiG-19S and the Il-28, these now being largely relegated to the close support role in Military or Frontier Districts of minor importance. The FA formations are assigned in much the same way as IAP-VO formations, according to the importance of the Group of Forces or Military District, deployments changing with variations in

The An-12 (above and below right) provides the backbone of the V-TA and is seen below disgorging an ASU-85 85-mm assault gun

world tensions. For example, by late 1974, some 18–20 Divisions or 2,000–2,200 aircraft, mostly of the FA, were on permanent assignment to the Military Districts bordering on Chinese territory, between Tadzhikistan (Central Asian M.D.) and the Pacific, but any increase in Sino-USSR tension could result in this V-VS force being increased by 50 per cent within seven days.

Individual FA units are, on occasions, deployed outside the Soviet Union and the Warsaw Treaty Organization countries and, during the early 'seventies, both fighter (MiG-21MF) and reconnaissance (MiG-25) units were deployed to Egypt, and the FA is believed to have a commitment for intelligence gathering over countries on the Soviet periphery (e.g., over-flights of Iranian territory by MiG-25s).

The primary transport component of the V-VS, the V-TA, has increased its airlift capability enormously over the past decade with the increase in emphasis on vertical envelopment

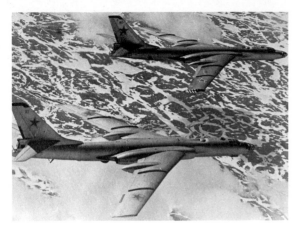

tactics, and now reportedly possesses in excess of 600 An-12 (*Cub*) general-purpose tactical transports and upwards of 70 An-22 (*Cock*) long-range heavy transports, as well as several hundred Il-14 (*Crate*) and An-24/26 (*Coke/Curl*) aircraft. The V-TA also possesses an inventory of 1,200–1,400 helicopters, including about 500 Mi-6 (*Hook*) and Mi-10 (*Harke*) heavy helicopters, the remainder being mostly Mi-4 (*Hound*) and Mi-8 (*Hip*) types. A semi-autonomous force, the largest component of which is the *divisiya* with a statutory strength of three regiments each with three or four squadrons of 10 fixed-wing aircraft or 12–16 helicopters, the V-TA possesses its own training organization and has a primary commitment to the airborne forces which include seven 7,000-man airborne divisions of which half, together with their support elements, can be airlifted simultaneously over short-to-medium ranges. For governmental transport missions, small numbers of Il-18s, Il-62s, An-24s, Yak-40s and other types are used, but these aircraft are not included in the V-TA inventory and are maintained by Aeroflot.

The AV-MF has assumed steadily increasing importance in recent years and is expected to undergo a major expansion of seagoing capability during the second half of the present decade with the introduction of the Soviet Navy's first genuine aircraft carriers, the *Kuril* class. Intended primarily

(Above) Tu-16s of the AV-MF attached to the Northern Fleet. The furthermost aircraft is equipped to perform the role of tanker, a refuelling hose being extended from the starboard wingtip

(Left) The Moskva anti-submarine cruiser has a complement of approximately 20 Ka-25 helicopters, and armament includes two banks of five torpedo tubes, 12-barrel MBU anti-submarine rocket launchers, SA-N-3 Goblet SAMs, 57-mm AA guns and twin launchers for ASW missiles

The Beriev Be-12 (Mail) maritime reconnaissance amphibian is extensively employed by the AV-MF, that illustrated (right) belonging to the Red Banner Pacific Fleet. The Be-12 has served the AV-MF for more than a decade, has a weapon bay in the hull and an external stores pylon under each wing for homing torpedoes or depth bombs

for the direct support of the four Soviet Fleets—Baltic, Northern, Black Sea and Pacific—the AV-MF is still primarily shore-based, the only AV-MF units deployed aboard naval vessels at the present time being the Ka-25 (*Hormone*) ASW helicopters operating from platforms aboard *Kresta* and *Kara* class cruisers and from the *Moskva*-class half-deck 'anti-submarine cruisers'.

Organized along identical lines to the other Air Forces of the V-VS and, despite its naval affiliation, employing military ranks, the AV-MF forms a substantial shore-based force but, since the mid 'fifties, has possessed no interceptor fighter element, the air defence of all ports and naval installations being the responsibility of the IA-PVO. The primary roles of the shore-based AV-MF elements are now long-range maritime surveillance and ELINT (electronic intelligence) for which the Tu-16 (in its *Badger–D*, *–E* and *–F* versions), the Tu-20 (in its *Bear–C*, *–D*, *–E* and *–F* versions), the M-4 (in its *Bison–B* and *–C* versions) and the Ilyushin Il-38 (*May*) are employed, medium-range ASW reconnaissance being performed by the Be-12 (*Mail*) amphibious flying boat. The anti-shipping strike task is fulfilled by some 275 examples of

the Tu-16 (in its AS-5 *Kelt*-equipped *Badger–G* version), supplemented over the past three years by some 50 Tu-22 (*Blinder*) bombers possibly limited to free-fall weapons or short-range missiles as distinct from the long-range anti-ship missiles of the Tu-16. For shorter ranges, the Il-28T (*Beagle*) has now apparently been largely supplanted by the Yak-28 (*Brewer*).

For the short-range ASW task, the Ka-25 is now used almost exclusively, the ASW version of the piston-engined Mi-4 having apparently been phased out of the operational role, and for the support of the *Morskaya Pekhota*—literally naval infantry, more akin to the British Marines than to the present-day USMC—the Mi-8 helicopter is used and this is likely to be supplemented by the Mi-24.

The first of the two *Moskva*-class anti-submarine cruisers began sea trials in the autumn of 1967, and was soon joined by her sister ship. These two vessels, the *Moskva* and the *Leningrad*, each operate up to 20 Ka-25 helicopters and have a full load displacement of 18,000 tons (18 291 tonnes). The first of the *Kuril*-class aircraft carriers, the *Kiev*, is known to have commenced working up during the Autumn of

(Above) The L 29 (Maya) and (below) the Su-7U (Moujik) trainers

1974, having been launched from the Nikolayev Nosenko yard on the Black Sea in December 1972, and is expected to be joined by a sister ship, the *Minsk*, during 1977–78. The *Kuril*-class vessels have a full load displacement of some 36,000 tons (36 580 tonnes) and have angled flight decks but have no aircraft catapults or arresting cables, indicating that fixed-wing aircraft operations are limited to V/STOL. In all probability, these vessels will embark some 30 Ka-25 helicopters and 15–20 fixed-wing V/STOL strike and re-connaissance fighters reportedly utilizing a combination of vectored thrust and direct lift and perhaps derived from the Yak-36 (see pages 78–79).

The total inventory of the AV-MF at the present time is believed to number about 1,200 aircraft of all types of which something over half may be considered as first-line fixed-wing aircraft and rotorcraft. The force includes limited communications, liaison and transport capability, but for any major logistic support the V-TA is utilized. Flying and technical training schools are shared with the other Air Forces of the V-VS, personnel completing their training at specialist schools operated by the AV-MF.

The V-VS training organization embraces numerous technical and specialist schools for the instruction of both V-VS personnel and pupils from the numerous countries receiving Soviet military equipment, and instructors from the organization are seconded on a rotational basis to Algeria, Cuba, Egypt, Iraq, North Vietnam, the Somali Republic, South Yemen, Syria and the Yemen Arab Republic. Pupil pilots normally receive both primary and basic instruction (on the Yak-18 and Yak-11) with the schools of the para-military DOSAAF (Volunteer Society for Co-operation with the Army, Aviation and the Fleet) organization prior to induction by the V-VS, this permitting specialization at a relatively early stage in the training programme. An all-through jet training syllabus has been employed by the V-VS since 1965, basic instruction being provided on the L 29 Delfin (*Maya*), some 2,000 examples of this type having been supplied to the V-VS from Czechoslovakia which is also supplying its successor, the L 39 Albatross, deliveries of which to the USSR commenced during 1974. Future combat aircraft pilots usually progress to the MiG-15UTI (*Midget*), type conversion following in the case of fighter pilots via the MiG-21U (*Mongol*), MiG-23U (*Flogger*), Su-7U (*Moujik*), Su-11U (*Maiden*), or Yak-28U (*Maestro*), advanced and operational flying training being conducted at regimental level. Experiments have been conducted in dispensing with the MiG-15UTI in the training sequence and some type conversion has been conducted direct from the L 29 and without benefit of the dual-control versions of combat aircraft previously listed.

Flying and technical training schools are distributed throughout the USSR, and the training organization includes three academies, the *Voenno-vozdushnaya Inzhenernaya Akademiya im. Prof. N. Ye. Zhukovsky* which has components in both Moscow and at Shchelkovo, north-west of Moscow, the *Voenno-vozdushnaya Akademiya im. Yu. A. Gagarin* at Monino, near Shchelkovo, a command, staff and tactical academy, and the VIRTA (*Voennaya Inzhenivnaya Radio-tekhnicheokaya Akademiya*), the radio and electronic engineering academy named after Marshal of the Soviet Union L. A. Govorov, at Kharkov. One of the most important flying schools is the *Kachinskoye Vyshee Voennoye Aviatsionnoye Uchilishsche im. A. F. Myasnikov* near Volgograd, believed to be the largest military flying school in the world, and there are Pilots' Higher Schools at Boriso-

(Above right) Kamov Ka-25 (Hormone) ASW helicopters of the AV-MF and (immediately right) an artist's impression of the new Soviet aircraft carrier Kiev which was known to have commenced trials in late 1974. The Kiev has no catapults or arresting cables and will have a mix of helicopters and fixed-wing V/STOL aircraft

glebsk and Barnaul, and a combined Pilots' and Navigators' Higher School at Stavropol. Other V-VS advanced flying training schools including those at Tambov, Orenburg, Balashov (near Saratov), Syzran, Chernigov, Kharkov and Yeisk (near the Sea of Azov). There are advanced navigational schools at Chelyabinsk and Voroshilovograd, and there are aeronautical technical schools at Tambov, Riga, Vasilkov (near Kiev), Archinsk, Irkutsk and two at Kharkov. The higher schools have a four-year course and the others have three-year courses. Students pass out with the rank of lieutenant. From the higher schools the qualification is

Pilot (Navigator), Engineer (Diploma), etc.

The P-VO training organization includes an advanced flying training school at Armavir, a technical aviation school at Daugavpils, radio-technical schools at Vilnyus and Krasnoyarsk, a command-electronics school at Pushkin, near Leningrad, and anti-aircraft rocket schools at Engels, Opochka (near Pskov), Gorky, Yaroslavl, Ordzhonikidze and Zhitomir. Technical schools are situated at Voronezh, Kaliningrad and Perm.

Outside the structure of the V-VS are the air components of additional forces usually referred to in the West misleadingly (and inaccurately) as 'para-military'. These are the KGB (Committee of State Security) which, embodying the Border Guard, possesses an estimated 125,000–175,000 troops, and the MVD (Ministry of Internal Affairs) which is believed to have a strength of 175,000–200,000. Both organizations possess substantial numbers of helicopters (Mi-4s and Mi-8s) and small utility aircraft (An-2s and An-14s) which, in addition to liaison and logistic support roles, perform (in the case of KGB aircraft) border patrol tasks (for which armament is carried) and the support of KGB and MVD armoured components.

(Above left) An Su-7BMK ground attack fighter landing with braking chute deployed and RATOG still attached, and (immediately left) a MiG-21PFMA interceptor taking-off. Both Su-7 and MiG-21 originally entered service with the V-VS in 1959, and have since been continuously manufactured in progressively improved versions

AEROFLOT

Aeroflot, the Soviet airline, is a vast undertaking and cannot be compared with any western airline. It is really almost the whole of Soviet 'civil' aviation and its name is a contraction from *Grazhdanskaya Vozduzhnaya Flot*—the Civil Air Fleet.

The best-known activities of Aeroflot are the operation of major domestic air services, services between the USSR and Europe, and its intercontinental operations—all worked by fleets of jet and turboprop aircraft. But these, although important, are only a small part of Aeroflot's overall activities which include operation of an enormous number of regional and local services within the USSR, including scheduled helicopter services; large-scale aerial agriculture; ambulance work; forest fire patrol and fire-fighting; fishery and ice patrols; powerline inspection; survey work of great variety, and heavy lifting in connection with construction work. These are just some of the most important aspects of Aeroflot's very varied duties.

In order to undertake this wide range of aerial activity it is necessary to have a very large fleet of aircraft in many categories. Some types are in service in very large numbers, certainly in hundreds, and in the case of such a type as the An-2, Aeroflot may operate fleets numbered in thousands. Very few details have ever been released concerning the size of the various Aeroflot fleets although the total number of Ilyushin Il-18s alone has been stated to be in excess of 600. Single-engined An-2 biplanes and, perhaps, some of the helicopters are employed in even larger numbers.

Aeroflot has, at least since 1934, been organized as a number of territorial directorates with, at some periods, a number of aviation groups in addition, and these directorates would appear to be largely autonomous. At present there are 31 directorates, being: Arkhangelsk, Armenia, Azerbaydzhan, Byelorussia, Central Regions and Arctic, Eastern Siberia, Estonia, Far East, Georgia, Kazakhstan, Kirghizia, Komi, Krasnoyarsk, Latvia, Lithuania, Magadan, Moldavia, Moscow Transport, North, North Caucasia, Polar Aviation, Tadzhikistan, TsUMVS (International), Turkmenistan, Tyumen, Ukraine, Ural, Uzbekistan, Volga, Western Siberia and Yakutia. Each directorate has its own administration, fleet, maintenance organization and sphere of responsibility. Some appear to have their own aircraft liveries.

The main services, known as all-Union, cross the boundaries of the individual directorates and this type of operation is undertaken by most of the directorates. In addition, each directorate is responsible for operating regional and local services within its territory and for the other tasks in which Aeroflot is engaged. The International Directorate is responsible for most, but not all, international services.

In 1972, Aeroflot carried about 82 million passengers and

An Aeroflot An-22 at Salekhard, on the Arctic Circle, being loaded with heavy equipment for the Medvezhie gas field on the northern Tyumenskaya, with An-24s in the foreground

(Left) Aeroflot's latest long-haul equipment: Tu-144 (foreground), Il-76 and Il-62M

Year	Passengers (Millions)	Unduplicated Route Network (mls)	(km)
1923	0·0002	260	(420)
1928	0·0007	9,780	(9 300)
1932	0·03	19,785	(31 900)
1937	0·2	57,975	(93 300)
1940	0·4	89,415	(143 900)
1950	1·5	183,555	(295 400)
1955	2·5	199,770	(321 500)
1958	8·2	216,985	(349 200)
1959	12·2	220,835	(355 400)
1960	16·0	223,750	(360 100)
1962	27·0	247,780	(398 800)
1963	32·0	248,550	(400 000)
1964	36·8	267,190	(430 000)
1965	42·1	270,260	(435 000)
1966	47·2	290,550	(467 600)
1967	55·1	310,690	(500 000)
1968	62·0	341,750	(550 000)
1969	68·0	372,820	(600 000)
1970	71·4	372,820	(600 000)
1971	78·0	403,890	(650 000)
1972	82·0	480,325	(773 000)

two million tonnes of cargo and mail over a network of about 480,000 miles (773,000 km), but it appears that only about one million of the passenger total was on international services. It is estimated that more than 3,500 cities, towns and settlements in the USSR are served by regular Aeroflot operations but no complete overall timetable or map is published and, indeed, it would be almost an impossible task to produce one. International and all-Union timetables are published—although they do not appear to show all flights—and there are regional timetables. Aeroflot international routes have grown considerably in recent years and now extend from Tokyo and Jakarta in the east to Montreal, New York, Havana, Lima and Santiago (Chile) in the west. There are numerous routes to Africa, with Brazzaville and Dar-es-Salaam being the southernmost terminals.

The development of Aeroflot has to a very great extent been dependent on the availability of equipment and this aircraft-allied expansion and improvement is described later. Although Soviet air transport is now organized on such an enormous scale, it lagged far behind Europe, the Americas and Australia in pre-war days. The Chief Air Fleet Administration was founded in May 1918, and in 1921 there were some experimental passenger and mail flights with a converted Sikorsky *Il'ya Muromets* bomber, but no regular Soviet domestic air services were operated until early in 1923. However, the joint Soviet–German airline, Deruluft, began international services over the Königsberg–Kowno–Smolensk–Moscow route on 1 May 1922, using a fleet of Fokker F III single-engined monoplanes. In March 1923, Dobrolet was founded and a regular service was opened between Moscow and Nizhniy Novgorod (now Gor'kiy), and a gradual development of routes took place. The fleet included one de Havilland 34, a Vickers Vimy Commercial, some air force machines (mostly D.H.9As), and, later, Junkers F 13s and the Soviet AK-1 were introduced. One Soviet source states that F 13s opened the Nizhniy Novgorod service.

Two other Soviet airline organizations were founded in 1923, Ukrvozdukhput, which operated in the Ukraine with Dornier Komets and, later, Kalinin K-4s; and Zakavia, which, for a short time worked services from Tbilisi to Baku and Yerevan. Zakavia was taken over by the Ukrainian airline in 1925, and in 1930 it was itself merged with Dobrolet to form Dobroflot. Further reorganization, in 1932, brought Aeroflot into being. In 1933 Glavsevmorput (Administration of Northern Sea Routes) was formed and this organization began operation with flying boats and did much to pioneer northern operations.

It is a surprising fact that up until the war much of Soviet air transport was undertaken by single-engined Kalinin and STAL' monoplanes, and various models of the R-5 and U-2 biplanes. About 70 twin- and three-engined ANT-9s were used, there were about 40 Lockheed Orion-like KhAI-1s, and a small number of twin-engined PS-89s (ZIG-1s). The

The Il-18D (foreground) and An-12 (background) together form a substantial proportion of the Aeroflot fleet. Between 500 and 600 of the various models of the Il-18 operate over Aeroflot's domestic and international routes and at least 200 examples of the An-12 serve scheduled and non-scheduled domestic and international cargo operations. The two aircraft are seen here at the new Dnepropetrovsk Airport

low-wing all-metal twin-engined PS-35 (ANT-35) was exhibited at the 1936 Paris *Salon*, and this type was partly responsible for operation of the Moscow–Riga–Stockholm service which began on 1 July 1937. But this work was shared by some imported Douglas DC-3s, and the Soviet Union secured a licence to build the type—known as the PS-84 and, from September 1942, as the Lisunov Li-2. Numbers of C-47s were supplied to the Soviet Union under Lease-Lend and many of these were allocated to Aeroflot. The Li-2 became Aeroflot's main type of aircraft, many still being used on local services and for cargo certainly until the summer of 1972. The single-engined types continued to serve in large numbers and there were during the war numerous transport conversions of military types, including the SB-2 and SB-2bis.

Having played its part in the war, Aeroflot emerged as a fairly primitive organization still with a fleet of Li-2s and numerous types of single-engined aircraft. The aircraft were to remain camouflaged for several years; crews were shabbily dressed and airports were of very poor standard. There is considerable evidence that most of the flying was VFR—frequently at very low altitude in order to maintain visual contact. These facts are not presented as criticism, but rather to set a baseline in order to show the enormous progress made by Soviet civil aviation in subsequent years. Further to emphasize the conditions at that time, it should be mentioned that in 1945 Aeroflot carried a total of only 530,000 passengers and 74,000 tonnes of freight and mail. By 1950 passenger traffic had trebled—to 1·5 million—and cargo had more than doubled. The route network in 1950 measured just over 183,000 miles (295 000 km).

In presenting a picture of Aeroflot, it must be related to the terrain and conditions in the USSR. The country is vast—more than eight million square miles (20 720 000 km²)—and there is wide variation in topography and climate—from the heat of mountainous Central Asia to the ice and snow of the northern tundra. The population exceeds 200 million, with concentrations in large cities and industrial regions but extremely sparse in many areas. Surface transportation is, in general, poor and inadequate; air transport offers enormous advantages and it is official policy that, over all but the shortest routes, aviation shall provide the prime means of transport.

After the war, it was Aeroflot's task to maintain and improve essential domestic communications and only very limited international operations were undertaken—mostly to neighbouring Communist countries and to Finland. It was only after consolidation of domestic routes and the availability of reasonably competitive aircraft that Aeroflot began to emerge as an international airline to take its place on world air routes.

In 1955, Aeroflot carried two-and-a-half million passengers and 258,000 tonnes of cargo and mail over a network of more than 199,000 miles (320 000 km), and this development had to a large extent been made possible by the production of two Soviet twin-engined aircraft, the Il-12—introduced in August 1947—and a developed version, the Il-14, which went into service in November 1954. These Ilyushins were built in immense numbers and replaced Li-2s on the main routes. Il-12s actually operated services right across the country and covered the distance between Moscow and Vladivostok in 33 hours with nine intermediate stops.

A major modernization plan for Aeroflot was embarked upon in 1953, and the first result of this was the production of the twin-jet Tupolev Tu-104, initially with 50 seats. The type went into service, over the Moscow–Omsk–Irkutsk route, on 15 September 1956, and, including the 70-passenger Tu-104A and 100-passenger Tu-104B, about 250 of these high-performance aircraft entered Aeroflot service, and many were, until recently, still in use on both domestic and international routes. It was the Tu-104 which first enabled Aeroflot to develop international services on a competitive basis—international destinations including (in chronological sequence) Prague, Delhi, Tirana, Cairo, Pyongyang, Copenhagen, London, Vienna, Rangoon, Ja-

A recent type to join the Aeroflot fleet, the Tu-154 (immediately and below right) began regular domestic services in February 1972 and flew its first international services during the following August. The Tu-154 is progressively replacing the Il-18 on medium length domestic and international routes

karta, Berlin, Stockholm and Zürich.

Useful as the Tu-104 was to prove, Aeroflot urgently required some workhorse aircraft for heavy traffic routes, and two of these were introduced in 1959—the low-wing four-turboprop Ilyushin Il-18 between Moscow and Alma Ata and Moscow and Adler/Sochi on 20 April, and the similarly powered high-wing Antonov An-10 between Moscow and Simferopol on 22 July that year.

The Il-18, originally with 80 seats, went into large-scale production, was produced in a number of versions with seating for up to 122, and became the backbone of the Aeroflot fleet—somewhere around 600–650 being used on domestic and international routes.

The An-10 was a more specialized aircraft capable of operating from rough airfields and it never operated any international scheduled services. The first production aircraft had 85 seats, but the developed and slightly longer An-10A, which entered service early in 1960, had standard accommodation for 100 passengers. An-10s and 10As are known to have been operated by seven Aeroflot directorates and the Moldavia Directorate equipped its An-10As with 118 seats. A civil and military cargo version of the An-10

was the An-12 and both types were built on the same production lines. The An-10s were all withdrawn in 1972 following a major fatal accident that May, but the An-12 continues in widescale Aeroflot service on scheduled and non-scheduled domestic and international cargo operations. The effect of large-scale introduction of turbine-powered aircraft on Aeroflot's operations is well shown by the fact that passenger traffic increased from $2\frac{1}{2}$ million in 1955 to 16 million in 1960. In the same period cargo and mail volume again more than doubled.

Although Aeroflot's greatest need had been fleets of medium-haul aircraft with about 85–100 seats, there was a requirement for a long-range high-capacity aeroplane for the operation of long domestic and international stages. To meet this requirement the 120–220-passenger Tupolev Tu-114 was developed from the Tu-20 strategic bomber. The Tu-114 was an unusual aeroplane; it was the largest and heaviest commercial transport until the introduction of the Boeing 747; it had a wing featuring 35 deg sweep but was powered by four 12,000 s.h.p. (later 15,000 s.h.p.) turbo-props and, with a maximum speed of 540 mph (870 km/h), was the fastest propeller-driven transport aeroplane. It is believed that only about 30 Tu-114s were produced, and the type entered service in April 1961 on the Moscow–Khabarovsk route. Subsequently it was used on services to Havana, Delhi, West Africa and Tokyo, and it was used to inaugurate Aeroflot's first North Atlantic services—to Montreal. On trans-Siberia routes it operated joint Aeroflot/Japan Air Lines and Aeroflot/KLM services. Most Tu-114s appear to have been withdrawn by 1973, except for a few on domestic routes.

Having acquired large fleets of turbine-powered aircraft for its major routes, Aeroflot needed to modernize its short-haul equipment and two types were produced for these operations. They were the twin-turbofan Tu-124 and the twin-turboprop Antonov An-24. The Tu-124 was essentially a 44–56-passenger scaled-down derivative of the Tu-104 and, entering service on 2 October 1962, was, by more than two-and-a-half years, ahead of any other short-haul turbofan-powered transport. It had numerous short-comings, however, and only about 100 are thought to have been built. It was followed, in 1967, by the larger capacity rear-engined Tu-134 which is in service in quite considerable numbers on shorter domestic and international routes. The An-24 is in the Fokker F.27 category—a high-wing mono-

plane capable of operating from modest airfields. It began regular passenger service on 31 October 1962, and is now in service in hundreds and operated by almost every Aeroflot directorate.

Even after the commissioning of this massive fleet of

The An-2M (above and below) is widely used by Aeroflot for agricultural tasks, an immense fleet of aircraft of this type being included in this operator's inventory (see pages 121—123)

The Tu-144 (described on pages 232–234 and illustrated above and below left) is expected to commence internal services during 1975

turbine-powered aircraft, Aeroflot still had some outstanding requirements. One was for a long-range high-capacity jet aircraft; another was at the other end of the scale, a modern small-capacity jet for rough field operation on local services.

The Ilyushin Il-62 was designed to meet the long-haul requirement, this resembling the British VC10 with its four rear-mounted turbofans. Having accommodation for 168–186 passengers, it was introduced in 1967 on some domestic routes. The Il-62 began working on the Moscow—Montreal route in September of that year, subsequently taking over most of the Tu-114 operations and, in July 1968, opened Aeroflot's services to New York. About 50 Il-62s are thought to have been in Aeroflot service by mid-1973, the latest version, the Il-62M-200, offering seating for up to 198 passengers. The Soviet local service jet is the Yak-40 with three rear-mounted turbofans and seating for up to 32 passengers. It can take-off with a ground run of about 765 yards (700 m), entered service in September 1968, brought modern airline standards to a large number of remote communities, and is in service in large numbers—probably not less than 350.

With its first turbine types introduced in the period 1956–1959, Aeroflot had to face, in the mid 'sixties, the problem of obtaining a replacement for the Tu-104, An-10 and Il-18,

The substantial helicopter component of Aeroflot includes numerous Mi-8s (above) and Mi-2s (below) for a variety of tasks

As Aeroflot implemented its massive re-equipment programmes and had the ability to provide improved service, so the airline worked hard to bring itself into line with the air transport operations of the West. Aircraft interiors rapidly changed from being replicas of Victorian railway carriages to become in a short space of time almost indistinguishable from Western standards. Crews were smartly dressed; ground transport improved; publicity and all other aspects of airline operation underwent an enormous transformation. Airports were rebuilt and new ones constructed; navigation and lighting systems were improved, and when high standards had been achieved, considerable effort was put into encouraging tourist traffic (although many routes are still barred to foreigners), and the Soviet Union became a member of ICAO (International Civil Aviation Organization).

In addition to its fixed-wing fleet, Aeroflot has large numbers of helicopters—certainly far more than any other non-military operator. Piston-engined Mi-4s were the first to provide scheduled passenger services but these are being replaced by twin-turbine Mi-8s. The very big Mi-6 and Mi-10 cargo and crane types play an important role but have never gone into scheduled service. In the development stage is the world's largest helicopter, the Mi-12. It has lifted a load of more than 40 tons and is likely to be used in conjunction with the Il-76 high-wing jet freighter which first appeared in 1971. Intended as another quantum leap ahead for Soviet aviation is the Tupolev Tu-144 supersonic transport. Initially Aeroflot is to operate a fleet of 30 over long-haul domestic and international routes, starting late 1975. Although the Tu-144 could shorten journey times over the longer Soviet routes, one of Aeroflot's greatest future needs will be high-capacity aircraft for operation on dense traffic routes and one of the aircraft being designed for this role is the 350-passenger Il-86. Having flown some 87·5 million passengers in 1974, which was an increase of 3·5 million over 1973, Aeroflot's traffic targets for 1975 have been set at 117 million passengers and just under 2 500 000 tonnes of mail and freight.

and one which could cater for the enormous traffic generated by these types. Thus, the Tu-154 was produced to meet these needs. It is a rear-engined trijet in the Boeing 727-200 category. It went into service in November 1971, with a standard layout for 152 passengers and is likely to become one of the most important aircraft in the Aeroflot fleet—it has been reported that the airline is to acquire no fewer than 600.

DIRECTORY OF CURRENT SOVIET AIRCRAFT

On the following pages are described and illustrated in alphabetical order of design bureau and numerical sequence of assigned type number current Soviet civil and military aircraft, together with commercial aircraft at present under development (i.e., Il-86 and Yak-42) and of which provisional details had been revealed at the time of closing for press. Some types of civil (e.g., Tu-104, Yak-12, Po-2) and military (e.g., MiG-15bis, Yak-25) aircraft now obsolete but still flying in small numbers in the Soviet Union and elsewhere have been omitted from this directory but are to be found under ASCC reporting names.

ANTONOV AN-2 (COLT)

Greeted as an anachronism at the time of its debut in possessing a biplane configuration, the An-2, which flew as a prototype on 31 August 1947 and the first product of the design bureau established in the previous year by Oleg K. Antonov, has nevertheless been one of the most successful of Soviet aircraft manufactured since World War II. It is today the most widely used aircraft of Soviet origin, having been exported to some 40 countries, and, with the possible exception of the MiG-15 series, has been built in larger numbers than any postwar Soviet aircraft if foreign licence manufacture is included in the total.

Designed solely for agricultural tasks to meet a requirement formulated by the Ministry of Agriculture, the An-2 rapidly proved to have much wider application than had been originally envisaged, serving in an enormous variety of roles, including crop dusting and spraying, forestry patrol and water bombing, light passenger and freight transportation, parachute training, glider towing, aerial survey, air ambulance and casevac, tactical logistic support, and navigational and radio training. An extremely robust biplane with an all-metal semi-monocoque fuselage and fabric-covered metal wings and tailplane, the An-2 couples a low wing loading with full-span slotted flaps and ailerons, and automatic slats on the leading edges of the upper mainplanes, these features combining to afford excellent short take-off and landing performance, and rendering the aircraft ideally suited for bush-flying.

The manufacture of the An-2 has been undertaken in

Paratroop-training An-2s of the Polskie Wojska Lotnicze (above) and the para-military DOSAAF organization (below)

The An-2ZA high-altitude meteorological aircraft with a supercharged ASh-62IR/TK engine and aft-positioned observer's cockpit

built. Licence production in Poland was approaching 6,000 aircraft by late 1974 but was expected to phase out during the course of 1975, and several thousand additional aircraft of this type are known to have been manufactured in China.

The basic model originally manufactured in the Soviet Union offers dual controls for two crew members seated side-by-side on the flight deck and has provision for a third seat for a flight engineer. Up to 10 passengers or as many as 14 paratroops can be accommodated on lightweight folding seats, alternative loads including six casualty stretchers and a medical attendant or 2,756 lb (1 250 kg) of freight, and the standard commercial passenger versions have either seven individual seats with a central aisle or four two-seat sofas. The agricultural variant with long-stroke undercarriage is fitted with pumping and spraying equipment under the fuselage and wings, and the main cabin accommodates a hopper with a capacity of 2,645 lb (1 200 kg) of dry or 308 Imp gal (1 400 l) of liquid pesticides or fertilizers. Several variants of this initial model were produced in the Soviet Union (see page 42).

(see page 42)

The Mielec-built versions of the An-2 are essentially similar to the basic Soviet model but have been assigned a series of suffix letters as follows: An-2T is the basic general-purpose transport accommodating up to 12 passengers or

China since 1957 as the *Fong Chou*, the first locally-built example having been completed in December of that year, and since 1960, the An-2 has been in continuous production at the WSK-Mielec in Poland to which all production of this type was progressively transferred from the Soviet Union where more than 5,000 examples of the An-2 had been

Substantial numbers of An-2s are operated by the V-VS in the light utility transport and logistic support roles, and particularly for the supply of the remoter border defence posts, as well as parachute training and for the instruction of radio operators and navigators

The general arrangement drawing (right) illustrate the An-2M, the bottom sideview depicting for comparison the standard An-2

3,307 lb (1 500 kg) of freight; An-2TP offering a higher standard of passenger comfort; An-2P intended solely for passenger transportation and accommodating 12 passengers in an improved cabin; An-2TD paratroop transport and training version; An-2S ambulance variant with accommodation for six stretcher patients and a medical attendant, and the An-2R agricultural version with similar capability to the equivalent model built in the Soviet Union.

In 1964, production of the An-2, which had been in process of phasing out, was reinstated in the Soviet Union with a revised agricultural version, the An-2M (*Modifikatsirovanny*), featuring redesigned, enlarged and more angular vertical tail surfaces, a revised engine mounting, and other modifications, metal bonding and welding being incorporated in the airframe production. A more efficient chemical dispensing system was employed, hopper capacity being raised to 431 Imp gal (1 960 l), and the An-2M could be operated by a one-man crew whereas earlier versions had specified a two-man crew. The agricultural equipment could be quickly removed to permit the accommodation of passengers on tip-up wall seating. Deliveries of the An-2M to Aeroflot began early in 1965.

The following specification relates to the An-2M:

Power Plant: *One 1,000 h.p. Shvetsov ASh-62M nine-cylinder radial air-cooled engine.* ***Performance:*** *Max speed, 157 mph (253 km/h) at 5,750 ft (1 750 m); econ cruise, 124 mph (200 km/h); operating speed, 93—100 mph (150—160 km/h); initial climb (clean) 550 ft/min (2,8 m/sec), (with spray gear), 395 ft/min (2 m/sec); service ceiling, 14,270 ft (4 350 m); range, 562 mls (905 km).* ***Weights:*** *Max take-off, 12,125 lb (5 500 kg).* ***Dimensions:*** *Span, 59 ft 8½ in (18,18 m); length, 42 ft 6 in (12,95 m); height, 13 ft 9¼ in (4,20 m); wing area, 765·3 sq ft (71,10 m²).*

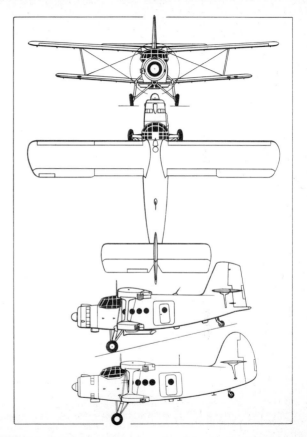

ANTONOV AN-12 (CUB)

Although evolved from the commercial An-10A (see page 39) primarily for the military role, entering service with the

V-TA in 1959, the An-12 is operated extensively as a commercial freighter by Aeroflot, Polish Air Lines, Air-Guinee, Iraqi Airways, Bulair and Cubana. Developed to meet a V-TA requirement for a general-purpose tactical transport carrying paratroops or miscellaneous Army loads, including wheeled or tracked vehicles, or surface-to-air and surface-to-surface missiles with support equipment, the An-12 is currently the most widely used V-VS transport aircraft and has also been supplied to the air forces of Egypt, India, Iraq, Indonesia, Algeria, Poland and Yugoslavia.

Differing from the An-10A primarily in having a redesigned rear fuselage embodying an integral loading ramp which may be lowered in flight for air-drop operations, a defensive tail gun position and revised tail surfaces, the An-12 has a heavy-duty freight floor designed for loadings of up to 307 lb/sq ft (1 500 kg/m²) and has a maximum payload of the order of 44,090 lb (20 000 kg). Possessing a flight crew of five, with pilot and co-pilot side-by-side on the flight deck, the engineer and radio operator behind the co-pilot and pilot respectively, and the navigator in the glazed nose compartment over the I-band *Toad Stool* navigational radar, the

(Above left) An-12 tactical transports of the V-TA, in excess of 600 aircraft of this type being available to the V-VS for logistic support, more than 200 additional An-12s being included in the inventory of Aeroflot. (Immediately left) A commercial An-12V differing from the majority of aircraft of this type in having no tail turret

An-12 has two 23-mm NR-23 cannon with *Gamma-A* radar warning in the tail turret which is occupied by a sixth crew member. Up to 100 paratroops may be carried and these may be despatched within one minute with the ramp doors hinged upward inside the cabin, and vehicles that may be carried include the PT-76 chassis-mounted ZSU-23-4 SP anti-aircraft system with its *Gun Dish* tracking radar, the PT-76 light amphibious tank, the ASU-57 or ASU-85 self-propelled assault guns, the BRDM-1 reconnaissance car, and BTR-60 or BTR-152 armoured personnel carriers. The personnel manning these vehicles are housed in a compartment aft of the flight deck which may accommodate up to 14 men.

Early examples of the commercial model, the An-12V, retained the tail turret glazing, but later aircraft have a fairing replacing the complete turret. One of the An-12Vs operated by Aeroflot was tested with broad skis with shallow curved-vee planing surfaces and equipped with heating and braking devices. This form of undercarriage was intended to enable the An-12V to operate from unprepared snow-covered surfaces. More than 900 An-12s are believed to have been built of which approximately one-third were intended for commercial operation.

The following specification relates to the late production An-12V:

Power Plant: *Four 4,000 e.h.p. Ivchenko AI-20K turbo-props.* **Performance:** *Max speed, 444 mph (715 km/h); max cruise, 373 mph (600 km/h); normal cruise, 342 mph (550 km/h) at 25,000 ft (7 500 m); initial climb rate, 1,970 ft/min (10,0 m/sec); service ceiling, 33,500 ft (10 200 m); range (with 22,050-lb/10 000-kg payload and one hour reserves), 2,110 mls (3 400 km).* **Weights:** *Empty, 61,730 lb (28 000 kg); normal loaded, 119,050 lb (54 000 kg); max take-off, 134,480 lb (61 000 kg).* **Dimensions:** *Span, 124 ft 8 in (38,00 m); length, 121 ft 4½ in (37,00 m); height, 32 ft 3 in (9,83 m); wing area, 1,286 sq ft (119,5 m²).*

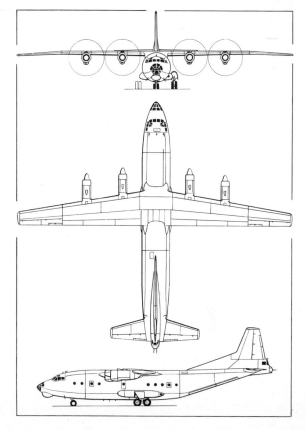

ANTONOV AN-14 (CLOD)

Developed to meet an Aeroflot requirement for a small utility transport offering a higher performance and standard of comfort than the general-purpose An-2 but possessing comparable short take-off and landing characteristics, the An-14 *Pchelka* (Little Bee) was flown for the first time on 15 March 1958 but suffered extremely protracted development with the result that series manufacture did not begin until 1965, and the definitive production model bore little more than a configuration similarity to the prototypes, a new

(Left and below) The An-14, of which several hundred examples were built, serves primarily with Aeroflot, but some (e.g., that seen below) are utilized by the V-VS for liaison tasks

126

long-span wing with tapered trailing edges outboard of the engine nacelles superseding the original shorter untapered wing, the fuselage contours undergoing some refinement and passenger capacity being increased, and uprated engines being introduced.

A braced high-wing monoplane with an all-metal semi-monocoque pod-and-boom fuselage and two-spar wing carrying full-span leading-edge slats and double-slotted trailing-edge flaps, the An-14 is intended for one-man crew operation. There is provision for a passenger beside the pilot and the main cabin normally accommodates six passengers in individual forward-facing seats with a central aisle, but a seven-seat cabin arrangement has also been offered. Passengers enter the cabin through clamshell rear doors which form the underside of the aft section of the fuselage pod, and emphasis is placed on simplicity of servicing in the field.

Several hundred examples of the An-14 were built, primarily for use by Aeroflot, versions including a five-seat executive transport, a light freighter, geological survey and photographic models, and an ambulance capable of accommodating six casualty stretchers and a medical attendant. A small number were delivered to the V-VS for the general-purpose role and a few have been exported for military duties, recipients including the air forces of the German Democratic Republic and Guinea.

Power Plant: Two 300 h.p. Ivchenko AI-14RF nine-cylinder radial air-cooled engines. Performance: Max speed, 138 mph (222 km/h) at 3,280 ft (1 000 m); normal cruise, 112 mph (180 km/h); initial climb, 1,000 ft/min (5,08 m/sec); service ceiling, 17,060 ft (5 200 m); range (max payload), 404 mls (650 km), (with 1,212-lb/550-kg payload), 444 mls (715 km), (with max fuel), 497 mls (800 km). Weights: Empty, 4,409 lb (2 000 kg); max take-off, 7,935 lb (3 600 kg). Dimensions: Span, 72 ft 2 in (21,99 m); length, 37 ft 6 in (11,44 m); height, 15 ft 2½ in (4,63 m); wing area, 427·5 sq ft (39,72 m²).

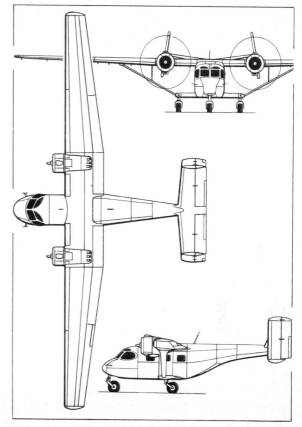

In October 1974, the An-22 covered a 3,107-mile (5 000-km) circuit with a 29·5-ton load at an average of 371 mph (597 km/h) and with a 34·44-ton load at 367 mph (590 km/h)

ANTONOV AN-22 (COCK)

The world's largest aircraft at the time of its appearance but subsequently surpassed in size by the Lockheed C-5A Galaxy, the An-22 *Antei* (Antheus) heavy military and commercial freighter established 14 payload-to-altitude records on 26 October 1967, attaining an altitude of 25,748 ft (7 848 m) with a payload of 220,462 lb (100 000 kg) and lifting a maximum payload of 221,443 lb (100 444,6 kg) to 6,560 ft (2 000 m). Further records for speed-with-payload were set on 19 February 1972 when an An-22 averaged 368·67 mph (593,32 km/h) over a 1,242·7-mile (2 000-km) closed circuit with a 110,231-lb (50 000-kg) payload, and, two days later, averaged 378·07 mph (608,45 km/h) over a 621-mile (1 000-km) closed circuit with the same payload.

The first of five prototypes of the An-22 was flown on 27 February 1965, two of these prototypes being used by Aeroflot on experimental freight services in 1967, and a

(Left) The third of five An-22 prototypes, this being one of the two utilized by Aeroflot on experimental freight services during 1967. (Above left) Current examples of the An-22 have two nose-mounted radars, one in a thimble-type fairing and one in a large undernose radome. Upwards of 70 An-22s were believed to be serving with the V-VS V-TA by the beginning of 1975 and others with Aeroflot

commercial production version was subsequently placed in service by the airline primarily to undertake special supply operations in the more remote and underdeveloped regions of the Soviet Union and elsewhere.   However, the An-22 was developed primarily as a long-range military transport for use by the V-VS V-TA, the examples of this heavy aircraft utilized by Aeroflot providing, in fact, a reserve for the military service to which three of the prototypes had been delivered. These participated in a display of mobility and vertical envelopment techniques at Domodedovo on 9 July 1967, unloading tracked carriers with twin SA-4 *Ganef* SAMs or single *Frog* battlefield support missiles, armoured personnel carriers and self-propelled assault guns.

Production deliveries of the An-22 (to the V-TA) began in the spring of 1967, and aircraft supplied to the V-VS and to Aeroflot since have been virtually identical.   The An-22 carries a crew of five—six and there is a compartment for 28–29 passengers immediately aft of the flight deck and separated from the main hold by a bulkhead.   There are rails in the roof of the hold for four travelling gantries, these continuing rearward on the underside of the large door, which, forming the underside of the rear fuselage, is raised upward inside the fuselage to facilitate the loading of large vehicles over the ramp.   Two winches, used in conjunction with the gantries, each have a 5,500-lb (2 500-kg) capacity. The An-22 is capable of taking-off in fully loaded condition within 1,420 yards (1 300 m) and landing within 875 yards (800 m).   Approximately 100 transports of this type were believed to have been delivered to the V-TA and Aeroflot by late 1974.

Power Plant: *Four 15,000 s.h.p. Kuznetsov NK-12 MA turboprops.*   **Performance:** *Max speed, 460 mph (740 km/h); max cruise, 422 mph (679 km/h); range (with max payload — 176,350 lb/80 000 kg), 3,107 mls (5 000 km), (with max fuel and 99,200-lb/45 000-kg payload), 6,800 mls (10 950 km); cruising altitude, 26,250–32,800 ft (8 000–10 000 m).*   **Weights:** *Empty equipped, 251,327 lb*

(114 000 kg); max take-off, 551,156 lb (250 000 kg).
Dimensions: *Span, 211 ft 3$\frac{1}{2}$ in (64,40 m); length, 189 ft 8 in (57,80 m); height, 41 ft 1 in (12,53 m); wing area, 3,713·6 sq ft (345 m²).*

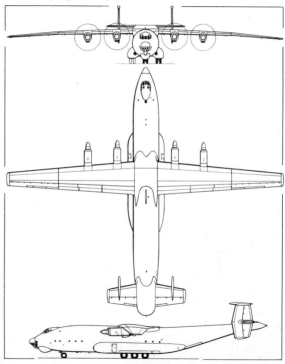

ANTONOV AN-24 (COKE)

Now the most widely used Soviet commercial transport, having been in continuous production for some 13 years with almost 1,000 having been delivered by late 1974 in a variety of versions, the An-24 short-range transport is numerically the most important airliner in the Aeroflot inventory in which it has succeeded the piston-engined Ilyushin Il-14. It also serves with Air Guinée, Air Mali, Balkan Bulgarian, Cubana, the Civil Aviation Administration

of China, Iraqi Airways, Interflug, Egyptair, Mongolian Airlines, Pan African Air Services, Polish Air Lines and Tarom, and small numbers have been delivered for military service with the V-VS and with the air forces of Czechoslovakia, Egypt, the German Democratic Republic, Hungary, North Korea, North Vietnam, Poland and Somalia.

Flown for the first time in April 1960, the An-24 was intended originally to accommodate 32–40 passengers but during the course of prototype construction a change in the Aeroflot requirement resulted in the aircraft being developed as a 44-seater. A second prototype and five pre-production aircraft, including two for static and fatigue testing, were employed for manufacturer's and State trials, and Aeroflot inaugurated services with the An-24 over the routes between Moscow, Voronezh and Saratov in September 1963. The initial production 44-seater was supplanted at an early stage by the 50-seat An-24V which gave place in turn, in 1968, to the An-24V Seriiny II embodying various refinements including an extended centre section chord with enlarged flaps, increasing gross wing area to 807·1 sq ft (74,98 m²) from

The initial production version of the An-24V (illustrated above left and immediately left) was the first version of of the An-24 to be built in really large numbers. The Seriiny II, introduced in 1968, featured an extended wing centre section chord and enlarged flaps, provision for the optional installation of AI-24T engines and other refinements

779·9 sq ft (72,46 m²), and AI-24 *Seriiny II* turboprops, which, having water injection and a similar rating to the initial AI-24 engines, could be replaced by 2,820 e.h.p. AI-24T turboprops to meet specific hot-and-high operating requirements. The *Seriiny II* aircraft has a normal flight crew of three and standard accommodation for 50 passengers in one-class four-abreast seating, but various optional mixed passenger/ freight and convertible cargo/passenger arrangements are offered.

Specialized freighters generally similar to the An-24V *Seriiny II* are the An-24T and An-24RT, the latter having a Tumansky RU-19-300 auxiliary turbojet of 1,984 lb (900 kg) thrust in the starboard engine nacelle for use under hot-and- high conditions, this permitting take-off with full payload from airfields at altitudes of up to 9,840 ft (3 000 m) above sea level and in temperatures up to ISA+30°C. Both models have provision for five crew members and the normal passenger door at the rear of the cabin deleted and replaced by a ventral freight door which hinges upward and aft for cargo loading. A 3,300-lb (1 500-kg) capacity electric winch hoists cargo through the ventral door and there is an electrically- or manually-operated 9,920-lb (4 500-kg) capacity conveyor in the cabin floor. The freight door may be opened in flight for air dropping, and provision is made for accommodating casualty stretchers in the air ambulance role. The An-24RV is similar to the *Seriiny II* passenger transport apart from having a similar auxiliary turbojet to that installed in the An-24RT.

A further specialized version is the An-24P (*Protivopozharny* or, simply, *Pozharny*) intended for fighting forest fires. First tested in October 1971, the An-24P carries parachutists and fire-fighting equipment which may be dropped in the vicinity of a fire.

The general arrangement drawing (right) depicts the standard An-24V, the lower sideview illustrating for comparison the An-24T specialized freighter with an upward-hinging freight door (dotted) and splayed ventral fins

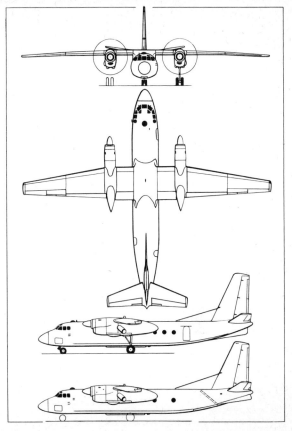

131

(Above) The An-24RT with auxiliary turbojet in the starboard engine nacelle and (below) an An-24V of the Somali Air Force

The following specification relates to the current An-24V *Seriiny II*:

Power Plant: *Two 2,550 e.h.p. Ivchenko AI-24 Seriiny II turboprops.* **Performance:** *Max cruise, 310 mph (498 km/h); best-range cruise, 280 mph (450 km/h) at 19,700 ft (6 000 m); initial climb, 1,515 ft/min (7,7 m/sec); service ceiling, 27,560 ft (8 400 m); range (max payload and reserves), 341 mls (550 km), (max fuel and 45 min reserves), 1,490 mls (2 400 km).* **Weights:** *Empty, 29,320 lb (13 300 kg); max take-off, 46,300 lb (21 000 kg).* **Dimensions:** *Span, 95 ft 9½ in (29,20 m); length, 77 ft 2½ in (23,53 m); height, 27 ft 3½ in (8,32 m); wing area, 807·1 sq ft (74,98 m²).*

ANTONOV AN-26 (CURL)

Derived from the An-24RT and intended for both military and civil applications, the An-26 was evolved during the late 'sixties with production deliveries commencing in 1969. Its principal new feature is a redesigned rear fuselage of 'beaver-tail' configuration incorporating a two-position door which may be lowered to form a conventional ramp for the loading of vehicles, or may be swung down and forward beneath the fuselage to permit straight-in loading of freight from ground vehicles at truck-bed height. The An-26 standardizes on the uprated AI-24T turboprop offered as an option on the An-24V *Seriiny II* and the basic structures of the two aircraft are similar, although that of the An-26 has been re-stressed to cater for higher weights.

The An-26 has a basic flight crew of five and can accommodate a variety of motor vehicles, including the GAZ-69 and UAZ-469, and similar electrically-powered mobile winch and electrically- or manually-powered conveyor to those of the An-24T and RT are provided. Tip-up seats along each wall accommodate up to 40 paratroops and standard operational equipment includes parachute static line attachments and retraction devices. Conversion for the troop transport role or as an ambulance with accommodation for 24 stretcher patients and a medical attendant may be undertaken in the field in 20–30 minutes.

The An-26 possesses rough-field capability, is being utilized as a tactical transport by the V-VS and has been supplied to a number of air forces as a successor to the Ilyushin Il-14, including the *Polskie Wojska Lotnicze.*

Power Plant: *Two 2,820 e.h.p. Ivchenko AI-24T turbo-props and one 1,984 lb (900 kg) Tumansky RU-19-300 auxiliary turbojet.* **Performance:** *Max speed, 335 mph (540 km/h) at 19,685 ft (6 000 m); long-range cruise, 273 mph (440 km/h) at 22,965 ft (7 000 m); initial climb, 1,575 ft/min (8,0 m/sec); service ceiling, 24,935 ft (7 600 m); range (with 9,920-lb/4 500-kg payload), 559 mls (900 km), (with 4,687-lb/2 126-kg payload), 1,398 mls*

(2 250 km). **Weights:** *Empty equipped, 37,258 lb (16 914 kg); normal loaded, 50,706 lb (23 000 kg) max take-off, 52,911 lb (24 000 kg).* **Dimensions:** *Span, 95 ft 9½ in (29,20 m); length, 78 ft 1 in (23,80 m); height, 28 ft 1½ in (8,57 m); wing area, 807·1 sq ft (74,98 m²).*

The An-26 employs an essentially similar airframe to that of the An-24RT apart from the rear fuselage which is of 'beavertail' configuration (see below), the two-position door being lowered to form a conventional ramp for the loading of vehicles

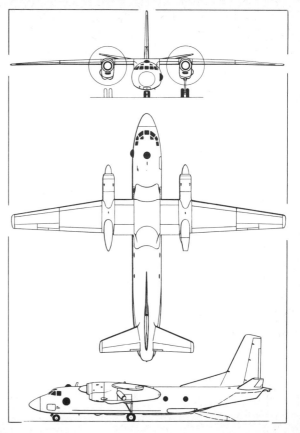

ANTONOV AN-28

Essentially a scaled-up, turboprop-powered derivative of the An-14 *Pchelka* light general-purpose aircraft (see page 126), the An-28 was flown in prototype form for the first time in September 1969, but has emulated its piston-engined predecessor in suffering a protracted gestation, State trials not being completed until the summer of 1972 and the definitive model not appearing until early 1974 when it was publicly displayed at Sheremetyevo International Airport, Moscow.

Initially referred to as the An-14M (*Modifikatsirovanny*), the An-28 retains little more than a similarity of basic configuration by comparison with the An-14 and possesses twice the capacity. During the course of development, progressive changes have been made to the wing and its high-lift devices, to the tail assembly and to the stub wings carrying the main units of the non-retractable levered-suspension undercarriage. Originally, all three members of the undercarriage were retractable, the main members retracting into fairings at the base of the fuselage and the nose-wheel retracting aft into the fuselage nose, but it was concluded that the marginal performance improvement provided by retractable gear was outweighed by the added weight and complication in which it resulted, and all prototypes subsequent to the first aeroplane have featured fixed gear.

Features shared by the An-28 with the An-14 include the hinged wing trailing edges comprising double-slotted flaps with the slats of the flaps extending to the wingtips and built into the single-slotted ailerons, and wide-tread low-pressure balloon tyres which permit operation at normal loaded weight from unimproved strips of 600–650 yards (550–600 m) length. The passenger version's cabin is arranged with 15 seats three-abreast (two to starboard and one to port), the seats folding back against the walls when the aircraft is operated in the freighter or mixed passenger/cargo roles. Access to the main cabin is provided by clamshell-type doors under the upswept rear fuselage.

The TVD-850 turboprops permit full-payload (2,865 lb/

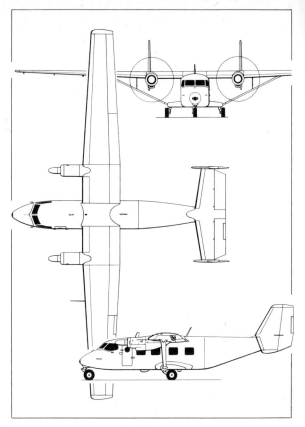

The An-28 is essentially a scaled-up derivative of the An-14

1 300 kg) operation under hot-and-high conditions, and it is anticipated that the An-28 will be operated over Aeroflot's shortest routes and particularly those which, currently operated by An-2 biplanes, have hitherto been relatively inaccessible to other types of fixed-wing aircraft. The An-28 has been proposed for parachute training, geological survey, fire fighting, rescue operations and agricultural tasks (with a 1,760-lb/800-kg capacity hopper in the fuselage), but its primary task is third-level passenger services from short, semi-prepared strips. Standard equipment includes a 550-lb (250-kg) capacity cargo-handling winch. At the time of closing for press it was anticipated that deliveries to Aeroflot would commence late 1974.

Power Plant: *Two 810 s.h.p. Isotov TVD-850 turboprops.*
Performance: *Max speed, 205 mph (330 km/h); max continuous cruise, 189 mph (305 km/h); service ceiling, 19,685 ft (6 000 m); range (with max payload), 560 mls (900 km), (with max fuel), 715 mls (1 150 km).* **Weights:** *Empty equipped, 7,716 lb (3 500 kg); normal take-off, 12,346 lb (5 600 kg).* **Dimensions:** *Span, 72 ft 2⅛ in (22,00 m); length, 42 ft 6⅞ in (12,98 m); height, 15 ft 1 in (4,60 m).*

ANTONOV AN-30 (CLANK)

A specialized aerial survey derivative of the An-24RT (see page 130), the An-30 initiated its test programme during the summer of 1973, and was expected to enter service with Aeroflot during the course of 1975 for mapping tasks in the remoter areas of the Soviet Union and as a successor to such types as the Avia 14FG (see page 141). It is also to be offered to foreign governments on a wet lease basis. The An-30 is structurally identical to the An-24RT apart from the forward fuselage which has been entirely redesigned. The nose is extensively glazed to provide the navigator with a wide field of vision and the size of the navigator's compartment has been increased by raising the flight deck, simultaneously improving the pilots' view.

For its primary task of aerial photography for map-making, the An-30 is provided with four large survey cameras which are mounted in the cabin and are operated by remote control by the crew photographer. Equipment includes a computer into which is fed a pre-programmed flight path, the computer subsequently controlling aircraft speed, altitude and direction throughout the mission. There are five camera hatches, as well as hatches permitting the use of laser, thermographic, gravimetric, magnetic and geophysical sensors. With the standard camera fit, a photographic swath ranging in width from 5·6 miles (9,0 km) to 9 miles (14,4 km) is possible from

an altitude of 19,685 ft (6 000 m). A crew of seven is normally carried and sufficient oxygen is provided to permit a high-altitude mission of eight hours endurance. The camera equipment may be replaced by other equipment suitable for microwave radiometer survey or mineral prospecting, and it is anticipated that the An-30 will be employed to obtain data on soil types, seasonal vegetation changes, flooding, ocean surface characteristics, etc.

Power Plant: *Two 2,820 e.h.p. Ivchenko AI-24VT turbo-props and one 1,764 lb (800 kg) Tumansky RU-19A-300 auxiliary turbojet.* ***Performance:*** *Max speed, 323 mph (520 km/h) at 19,685 ft (6 000 m); normal cruise, 264 mph (425 km/h); initial climb, 1,575 ft/min (8,0 m/sec); service ceiling, 27,230 ft (8 300 m), range, 1,616 mls (2 600 km); endurance, 6 hrs.* ***Weights:*** *Empty equipped, 32,408 lb (14 700 kg); max take-off, 50,706 lb (23 000 kg).* ***Dimensions:*** *Span, 95 ft 9½ in (29,20 m); length, 79 ft 7⅛ in (24,26 m); height, 27 ft 3½ in (8,32 m); wing area, 807·1 sq ft (74,98 m²).*

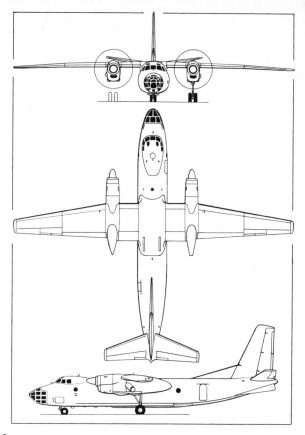

BERIEV BE-12 (MAIL)

The largest amphibian flying boat in military service over the past decade, the Be-12, known unofficially as the *Tchaika* (Gull) in the Soviet Union, was allegedly flown as a prototype for the first time in 1960. Intended as a successor to the Be-6 (see page 90) in the coastal and medium-range maritime patrol, ASW and submarine co-operation roles, the Be-6 entered service with the AV-MF during 1965–66.

Possessing a close family resemblance to the earlier Be-6 in both wing and tail configuration, the Be-12 is of conventional layout and construction, with a single-step hull and sharply-cranked, high-mounted wing, with non-retractable outboard stabilizing floats. The tailwheel undercarriage comprises single-wheel main units which retract upwards through 180 deg to lie flush within the sides of the hull and an aft-retracting tailwheel. A crew of five is apparently carried, consisting of two pilots, a navigator, a radar operator and a MAD (Magnetic Anomaly Detection) gear operator. There is a weapon bay in the hull aft of the step which may accommodate homing torpedoes, depth bombs,

mines, etc., and there is an external stores pylon under each outer wing panel presumably capable of carrying a guided ASM, homing torpedo or depth bomb, rails further outboard apparently being intended for unguided rockets.

The Be-12 is standard equipment with the Black Sea and

Currently the only large amphibian in extensive use anywhere in the world, the Be-12 (illustrated right and on following page) has been in service with the AV-MF for some 10 years, and succeeded the piston-engined Be-6 as standard medium-range anti-submarine warfare and maritime patrol equipment, primarily with the Northern and Black Sea fleets

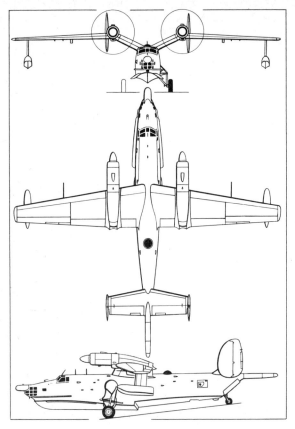

Northern fleets, and in four series of special flights in 1964, 1968, 1970 and 1973, this type has established a considerable number of international records in Class C.2 Group II and C.3 Group II which have been officially recognized by the FAI, these records being for altitude with and without payload, and closed-circuit speed and distance. The most recently announced (5 January 1974) of these records were a closed-circuit distance record of 1,592 miles (2 562 km) and a speed-with-load record over a 2 000-km (1,242·7-mile) closed circuit of 303·23 mph (488 km/h) with 11,055·7 lb (5 018,8 kg) for amphibians, and speed-with-load records over a 2 000-km closed circuit of 340·5 mph (548 km/h) with 4,441·2 lb (2 014,5 kg) and 297·6 mph (479 km/h) with 11,075 lb (5 023,7 kg) for flying boats.

The figures quoted in the following specification are estimated:

Power Plant: *Two 4,000 e.h.p. Ivchenko Al-20D turbo-props.* ***Performance:*** *Max speed, 380 mph (610 km/h) at 10 000 ft (3 050 m); typical patrol speed, 200 mph (320 km/h) at 985 ft (300 m); max range, 2,485 mls (4 000 km); initial climb, 3,000 ft/min (15,2 m/sec); service ceiling, 37,000 ft (11 280 m).* ***Weights:*** *Max take-off, 65,035 lb (29 500 kg).* ***Dimensions:*** *Span, 97 ft 6 in (29,70 m); length, 101 ft 11 in (32,90 m); height 22 ft 11½ in (7,00 m); wing area, 1,030 sq ft (95,69 m²).*

ILYUSHIN IL-14 (CRATE)

Essentially an outgrowth of the Il-12 (see page 42), the Il-14 was the first post-WW II design from the bureau led by Sergei V. Ilyushin to achieve production status and, by comparison with its predecessor, embodied a refined structure, improved aerodynamics and uprated engines. Flown in prototype form in 1952, the Il-14 entered production for both the V-VS and Aeroflot, the commercial version for the latter being designated Il-14P (*Passazhirskii*) and providing accommodation for 18–26 passengers. The military version featured a strengthened freight floor, double freight-loading doors in the port side of the fuselage and observation blisters aft of the flight deck for a paradrop controller. Both civil and military versions entered service in 1954, and some V-VS and Aeroflot Il-12s were subsequently reworked to Il-14 standard.

The Il-14P was manufactured under licence in East Germany, the first example from the German production line being flown in April 1956, and in Czechoslovakia at Prague–Letnany from where deliveries commenced during the fol-

(Above) An Avia-built Il-14 testing the Motorlet M 601 turboprop

Despite its obsolescence, a substantial number of Il-14s remain in military service, both with the V-VS V-TA and with smaller air arms, such as the Egyptian Arab Air Force, an example in the service of which is seen right. Some numbers of Il-14T commercial freighters are still utilized by Aeroflot, most being conversions of Il-14Ps and Il-14Ms

139

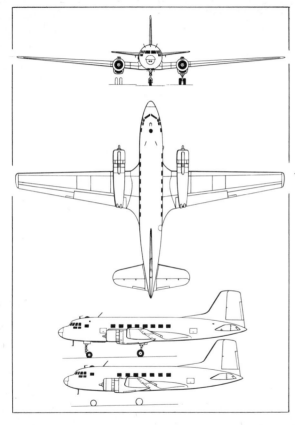

lowing year as the Avia 14 and Avia 14P, some Czechoslovak-built aircraft being exported to the Soviet Union. A 'stretched' variant, the Il-14M (*Modifikatsirovanny*), appeared in 1956, this having a 3 ft 4 in (1,0 m) additional section inserted in the forward fuselage and accommodation being increased to 24–28 passengers. A substantial number of Il-14P and Il-14M airliners in the inventory of Aeroflot were later adapted as freighters under the designation Il-14T (*Transportny*), and the Il-14 provided the backbone of the V-TA until supplemented by the An-12 from 1959.

Production of the Il-14 in the Soviet Union reportedly exceeded 3,500 aircraft, 80 were built by the VEB Flugzeugwerke in East Germany and approximately 80 Il-14Ps were manufactured in Czechoslovakia where production continued with the Il-14M in 32-passenger configuration as the Avia 14-32 and in freighter form as the Avia 14T, the latter having a single large loading door in the fuselage port side. A photographic survey model was designated Avia 14FG, and although production of the Il-14 series terminated in the Soviet Union in 1958, development continued in Czechoslovakia, where, in 1960, the 42-passenger Avia 14-42 was produced, this being a pressurized model with circular cabin windows.

The Il-14T remains in the Aeroflot inventory in some numbers, and other airlines that were still operating versions of the Il-14 mid-1974 were Balkan, CAAC, CSA, Cubana, Mongolian and Tarom. A substantial number of Il-14s remain in service with elements of the V-TA and other military examples continue in service with virtually all the Communist Bloc countries and in small numbers with the air forces of Afghanistan, Algeria, Cuba, Egypt, India, Iraq, Syria and Yugoslavia.

The following specification relates to the Il-14M:

Power Plant: *Two 1,900 h.p. Shvetsov ASh-82T 14-*

cylinder radial air-cooled engines. **Performance:** Max speed, 259 mph (417 km/h); high-speed cruise, 239 mph (385 km/h); long-range cruise, 193 mph (311 km/h); initial climb, 1,220 ft/min (6,2 m/sec); service ceiling, 22,000 ft (6 705 m); range with max payload, 810 mls (1 304 km), with max fuel, 1,988 mls (3 202 km). **Weights:** Operational equipped, 27,776 lb (12 600 kg); max take-off, 39,683 lb (18 000 kg). **Dimensions:** Span, 104 ft 0 in (31,69 m); length, 73 ft 2 in (22,30 m); height, 25 ft 11 in (7,90 m); wing area, 1,075 sq ft (99,70 m²).

(Above) The Avia 14-42 and (below) the Avia 14FG photographic survey aircraft, a number of such conversions having been built

ILYUSHIN IL-18 (COOT)

Numerically the second most important airliner in the current Aeroflot inventory, the Il-18 entered service with the Soviet carrier on 20 April 1959, and allegedly carried 60 million passengers by the spring of 1969, when it was being utilized on 800 international and domestic services. The prototype Il-18, which was known as the *Moskva*, was flown for the first time in July 1957, being followed by two pre-production examples, series production aircraft initially being delivered with accommodation for 75 passengers, the Kuznetsov NK-4 and Ivchenko AI-20 turboprops providing optional power plants. The 21st and subsequent aircraft standardized on the latter engine and the initial version was quickly supplanted by the Il-18B which had an increase in max take-off weight of 4,409 lb (2 000 kg) from 130,514 lb (59 200 kg) and accommodated 84 passengers.

Further development resulted in the Il-18V in 1961, with accommodation for 89–100 passengers, this being followed three years later, in 1964, by the Il-18I with 4,250 e.s.h.p. AI-20M turboprops in place of the 4,000 e.s.h.p. AI-20Ks of previous versions, accommodation for 110–122 passengers made possible by the lengthening of the pressurized section of the fuselage through deletion of the unpressurized tail cargo hold, and a 32 per cent increase in total fuel capacity as a result of the introduction of additional centre-section fuel tankage. Redesignated Il-18D, this model entered Aeroflot service in 1965, together with the Il-18Ye which was similar apart from having the same fuel capacity as the Il-18V. Both the Il-18D and Il-18Ye have a flight crew of five, and in their standard 110-seat high-density arrangement have 24 and 71 seats in six-abreast rows in the forward and main cabins respectively, and 15 seats five-abreast in the rear cabin.

Production of the Il-18 reportedly exceeded 800 aircraft of which more than 100 were exported for commercial and military use, foreign commercial operators including Air-Guinee, Air Mali, Air Mauritanie, Balkan, CAAC, CSA,

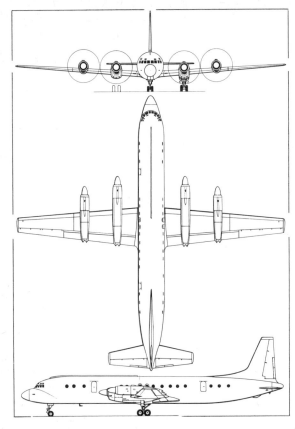

Both the general arrangement drawing (left) and the photograph above illustrate the Il-18D, the Polskie Linie Lotnicze aircraft at the foot of the page being an Il-18V

Cubana, Egyptair, Interflug, Lot, Malev, Tarom and Yemen Airways. The small number of examples in military service as personnel transports are operated by the air forces of Afghanistan, Algeria, Bulgaria, China, Czechoslovakia, Poland and Yugoslavia.

The following specification relates to the Il-18D:

Power Plant: *Four Ivchenko AI-20M turboprops each*

rated at 4,250 e.h.p. **Performance:** Max cruise (at max take-off weight), 419 mph (675 km/h); econ cruise, 388 mph (625 km/h); operating altitude, 26,250–32,800 ft (8 000–10 000 m); range (max payload and one hour's reserves), 2,300 mls (3 700 km), (max fuel and one hour's reserves), 4,040 mls (6 500 km). **Weights:** Empty equipped (90-seater), 77,160 lb (35 000 kg); max take-off, 141,000 lb (64 000 kg). **Dimensions:** Span, 122 ft 8½ in (37,40 m); length, 117 ft 9 in (35,90 m); height, 33 ft 4 in (10,17 m); wing area, 1,507 sq ft (140 m²).

ILYUSHIN IL-28 (BEAGLE)

in a fairing immediately aft of the nosewheel bay.

Although now obsolescent, the Il-28 three-seat light tactical bomber remains in service in some numbers with second-line elements of the *Frontovaya Aviatsiya*; is still standard Sino–Communist equipment and is included in the first-line combat aircraft inventories of Afghanistan, Algeria, North Korea and North Vietnam. It also serves in small numbers in non-operational roles with several Warsaw Pact air forces.

A straightforward design using proven aerodynamics, the Il-28 was nevertheless distinctive in combining an unswept wing with swept tail surfaces and, unlike contemporary western practice of omitting tail armament from combat aircraft in this category, Sergei Ilyushin's design bureau elected to provide an Il-K6 tail turret mounting twin 23-mm NR-23 cannon, two similar weapons being fixed to fire forward in the extreme fuselage nose and the pilot being provided with a gyro gunsight for use with the latter. Provision was made for an internal bomb load of 2,205 lb (1 000 kg); a total of 1,738 Imp gal (7 900 l) of fuel could be accommodated by five fuselage fuel tanks, integral wing tanks and auxiliary wingtip tanks; an AFA 33/20, 33/75-50 or 33/100 camera could be mounted beneath the rearmost forward fuselage tank and ground mapping radar was housed

(Above right) A standard production Il-28 tactical bomber while serving with the FA and (right) the Il-28U conversion trainer

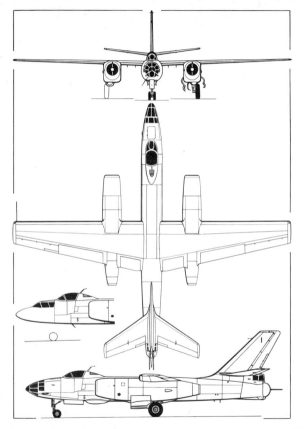

(Above) One of the pre-production Il-28s and (foot of page) an Il-28T torpedo-bomber while serving with the AV-MF

The first of three prototypes was flown on 8 August 1948, and 25 pre-production examples participated in the 1950 May Day celebrations, several thousand subsequently being built, variants including the Il-28U conversion trainer featuring a second cockpit for the trainee pilot ahead and

below the standard cockpit; the Il-28R tactical reconnaissance version with a combination of cameras and non-optical sensors and the Il-28T torpedo-bomber for the AV-MF, the last-mentioned model carrying two short torpedoes in a modified weapons bay. The following specification relates to the standard production model:

Power Plant: *Two 5,952 lb (2 700 kg) Klimov VK-1 turbojets.* **Performance:** *(At normal loaded weight) Max speed, 497 mph (800 km/h) at sea level, 559 mph (900 km/h) at 14,765 ft (4 000 m); initial climb, 2,953 ft/min (15,0 m/sec); ceiling, 40,355 ft (12 300 m); max fuel range, 1,355 mls (2 180 km) at 478 mph (770 km/h) at 32,810 ft (10 000 m).* **Weights:** *Empty equipped, 28,417 lb (12 890 kg); normal loaded, 40,565 lb (18 400 kg); max loaded, 46,297 lb (21 000 kg).* **Dimensions:** *Span (excluding tip tanks), 70 ft 4¾ in (21,45 m); length, 57 ft 10¾ in (17,65 m); wing area, 654·44 sq ft (60,8 m²).*

The Il-28, although remaining in some numbers with second-line elements of the FA, and seen below during its first-line service with the Polskie Wojska Lotnicze, now primarily performs ancillary roles such as target-towing (above right)

ILYUSHIN IL-38 (MAY)

The Il-38 long-range maritime patrol aircraft was evolved from the Il-18 commercial transport in a similar manner to

the development of the Lockheed P-3 Orion from the Electra. Apart from some strengthening, the wings, tail assembly and undercarriage are similar to those of the Il-18, these components having been married to an entirely new fuselage housing anti-submarine warfare systems, a tactical operations compartment and weapon bays. The fuselage terminates in a 'sting' fairing containing MAD (Magnetic Anomaly Detection) equipment and there are three internal bays for depth bombs, homing torpedoes, etc. It is believed that ASMs may be carried on four wing hardpoints. The normal crew appears to comprise 12 members of which four are on the flight deck and the remainder are housed by the tactical compartment above the weapon bays to operate sensors and indicators, and co-ordinate data flow to other aircraft and to ships. By comparison with the Il-18, the wing of the Il-38 is positioned further forward on the fuselage to compensate for the shift in the CG.

The Il-38 reportedly flew in prototype form during 1967—

Standard shore-based AV-MF maritime patrol equipment, the Il-38's derivation from the Il-18 commercial transport (see pages 141–3) is readily apparent from the photographs (above left and below), radome and MAD stinger being primary distinguishing features

1968, and entered service with the AV-MF early in 1970, having since been observed operating in the Mediterranean area and over the seas around the Soviet Union, apparently in a reconnaissance role monitoring the sea forces of the NATO countries. Examples were observed in service with Egyptian Air Force insignia during 1972, but these were apparently AV-MF aircraft temporarily deployed to Egyptian bases to facilitate the shadowing of NATO naval exercises in the Mediterranean.

An AV-MF II-38 photographed over the Mediterranean during 1972

The figures quoted in the following specification are estimated:

Power Plant: *Four 4,250 e.h.p. Ivchenko AI-20 M turbo-props.* **Performance:** *Max continuous cruise, 400 mph (645 km/h) at 15,000 ft (4 570 m); normal cruise, 370 mph (595 km/h) at 26,250 ft (8 000 m); patrol speed, 250 mph (400 km/h) at 2,000 ft (610 m); max range, 4,500 mls (7 240 km); loiter endurance, 12 hrs at 2,000 ft (610 m).* **Weights:** *Empty equipped, 80,000 lb (36,287 kg); max take-off, 140,000 lb (63 500 kg).* **Dimensions:** *Span, 122 ft 9 in (37,40 m); length, 131 ft 0 in (39,92 m); height, 33 ft 4 in (10,17 m); wing area, 1,507 sq ft (140,0 m²).*

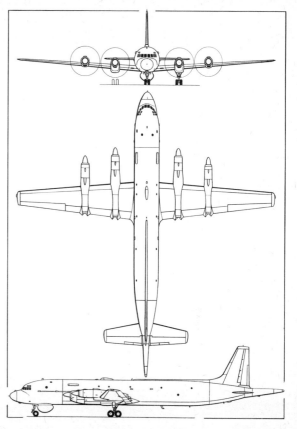

ILYUSHIN IL-62 (CLASSIC)

Entering service with Aeroflot on 15 September 1967, the Ilyushin Il-62 was the first long-range, four-engined jet transport developed in the Soviet Union for commercial use to achieve production status, and has become an essential component in the Aeroflot fleet in the 'seventies. The introduction into service—initially as a replacement for the Tupolev Tu-114 on the Moscow—Montreal transatlantic service—came almost exactly five years after the Il-62 had been publicly unveiled in Moscow, when the prototype was inspected as it neared completion by Soviet leaders including N. Khrushchov. In general configuration, the Il-62 closely resembles the BAC VC10, these being the only four-engined airliners to feature a rear-engined layout, although the former's wing has rather more sweepback—35 compared to 32·5 degrees.

The Il-62 has an all-manual flying control system, with a yaw damper in the rudder circuit, and an automatic flight control system that allows it to operate in weather minima similar to those defined as Cat II by ICAO standards.

(Above) Ilyushin Il-62s undergoing routine maintenance at the Domodedovo maintenance base and (below) an Il-62 of the East German operator Interflug which was operating a fleet of five aircraft of this type on long-distance services late 1974

Like many other aircraft with a rear-engined, high tail layout, the II-62 was found to have slender control margins at low speed, and an extensive flight test programme was undertaken to refine the wing design, resulting in the adoption of a fixed, drooped extension of the leading edge over approximately the outer half of each wing. The first flight was made in January 1963, and this prototype was fitted with 16,535 lb (7 500 kg) thrust Lyulka AL-7 turbojets pending the development of a new turbofan unit by the Kuznetsov engine design bureau. This new engine, the 23,150 lb (10,500 kg) s.t. NK-8-4, became available in time to power some of the later trials aircraft, comprising a second prototype and three pre-production examples. Cascade-type thrust reversers were fitted on the outer engines only.

With six-abreast seating and a central aisle, the II-62 accommodates 186 passengers in a high-density layout or 168 in a one-class tourist layout. A typical mixed-class layout has 20 seats four-abreast in the forward cabin and 102 six-abreast in the rear cabin, separated by a large galley amidship. There are two passenger doors, one immediately aft of the flight deck and the other just ahead of the wing leading edge. Other layouts have also been described in design bureau brochures but are not believed to have been adopted by any of the airlines using the II-62.

Aeroflot was believed to have over 100 II-62s in service by early 1974. Following its introduction on the Moscow–Montreal service, the II-62 went into service on the Moscow–New York prestige route in July 1968, and subsequently replaced Tu-114s and Tu-104s on many of the longer international routes as well as the trunk routes within the Soviet Union. The first user of the II-62 outside the USSR was Czechoslovakian Airlines CSA, which leased a single example from Aeroflot for its Prague–London service in May 1968. Subsequently CSA procured its own fleet of seven II-62s, and most of the East European bloc airlines followed suit, with Interflug putting the first of six into service in 1970, LOT ordering three in 1972 with a fourth being delivered mid-1974 when a fifth was on order, and Malev and Tarom acquiring two each. Under a 1970 trade agreement, China procured five examples for use by CAAC, and United Arab Airlines (later Egyptair) acquired seven.

During 1970, the Ilyushin design bureau evolved an improved version of the basic design with increased seating and more range. Known as the II-62M (and sometimes referred to as the II-62M-200), this new version is powered

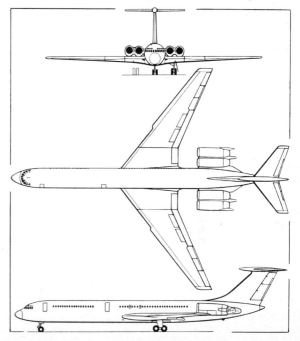

The early production Il-62 (above) featured a long antenna over the forward fuselage and a long dorsal spine, both features deleted from later production examples of this commercial transport responsible for virtually all Aeroflot long-range services

by four Soloviev D-30KU turbofans rated at 25,350 lb (11 500 kg) st each and with clamshell-type instead of cascade-type reversers on the outer engines. The extra power permits operation at a higher gross weight of 363,760 lb (165 000 kg) and additional fuel capacity is provided by a tank in the fin. These improvements give the Il-62M a better payload-range performance, the max range increasing to 6,400 mls (10 300 km); the max payload is unchanged, but internal redesign makes it possible to accommodate up to 198 passengers. The flight control system permits operation in Cat II weather minima and is capable of development for Cat III operation. Aeroflot introduced the Il-62M early 1974 and plans to standardize on this model for all its long-range subsonic operations, no examples being exported until Aeroflot's needs have been met.

The following specification relates to the standard Il-62:

Power Plant: *Four 23,150 lb (10 500 kg) s.t. Kuznetsov NK-8-4 turbofans.* **Performance:** *Typical cruising speed, 528–560 mph (850–900 km/h) at 33,000–39,400 ft (10 000–12 000 m); initial climb rate, 3,540 ft/min (18 m/sec); take-off distance required (FAR, SL, ISA, max weight) 10,660 ft (3 250 m); landing distance required (FAR, SL, ISA, max landing weight), 9,185 ft (2 800 m); range with max payload, and 1-hr fuel reserve, 4,160 mls (6 700 km); range with max fuel, 5,715 mls (9 200 km).* **Weights:** *Operating weight empty, 153,000 lb (69 400 kg); max payload, 50,700 lb (23 000 kg); max fuel load, 183,700 lb (83 325 kg); max take-off, 357,000 lb (162 000 kg); max landing, 232,000 lb (105 000 kg); max zero-fuel weight, 206,000 lb (93 500 kg).* **Dimensions:** *Span, 141 ft 9 in (43,20 m); length, 174 ft 3½ in (53,12 m); height, 40 ft 6¼ in (12,35 m); wing area, 3,010 sq ft (279,6 m²).*

ILYUSHIN IL-76 (CANDID)

Evolved primarily to meet a V-TA requirement and generally similar in concept to the Lockheed C-141A StarLifter, the Il-76 was flown for the first time on 25 March 1971, and it was anticipated that production deliveries to both the V-TA and to Aeroflot, which plans to standardize on the Il-76 for heavy freight haulage, would commence during the course of 1974.

Slightly larger, more powerful and heavier than the Star-Lifter, the Il-76 employs a mechanized cargo-handling system, a high flotation undercarriage—the main members of which each comprise four individual units of four parallel-mounted-wheels—and extensive high-lift devices to achieve short-field performance. Clamshell thrust reversers are fitted to all four power plants and straight-in freight loading is achieved through the rear fuselage which incorporates a loading ramp and clam-shell doors.

It may be assumed that the Il-76 will progressively supplant the An-12 in the V-TA, and an Aeroflot requirement

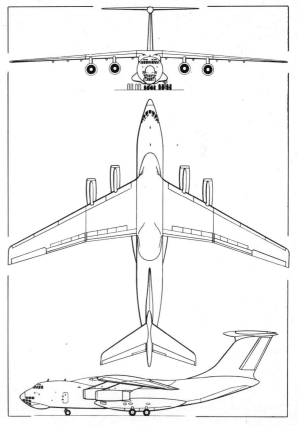

for 100 freighters of this type has been announced, Soviet statements indicating that Aeroflot will operate its Il-76s from short, unprepared strips in Siberia and other under-

developed areas of the Soviet Union during the period of the current five-year programme (1971–75). Six prototype and pre-production Il-76s were undergoing trials in the Soviet Union by early 1974, the second prototype being employed for commercial certification.

The Il-76 is operated by a flight crew of four, and the entire freight section, which includes a permanent station for the cargo master, is pressurized. The navigator's station is situated below and forward of the flight deck to facilitate visual selection of landing sites. The aircraft's internal crane system can accommodate universal or multi-mode containers, and each of two overhead cranes is of 5,000-lb (2 268-kg) capacity. It is anticipated that the production Il-76 will feature four such cranes.

Power Plant: *Four 26,455 lb (12 000 kg) thrust Soloviev D-30-KP turbofans.* **Performance:** *Max cruise, 528 mph (850 km/h) at 42,650 ft (13 000 m); range with max payload, 3,100 mls (5 000 km).* **Weights:** *Max payload, 88,185 lb (40 000 kg); max take-off, 346,122 lb (157 000 kg).* **Dimensions:** *Span, 165 ft 8½ in (50,50 m); length, 152 ft 10¼ in (46,59 m); height, 48 ft 5¼ in (14,76 m).*

Larger, more powerful and heavier than the C-141A StarLifter, the Il-76 will fulfil both military and civil roles. Six prototype and pre-production examples were flying by the beginning of 1974, and the first deliveries (to Aeroflot) were expected during the course of the year for operation in Siberia

ILYUSHIN IL-86

Following the introduction of wide-body large-capacity airliners of the 'airbus' type by Western manufacturers, Aeroflot indicated its interest in such a type to the Soviet design bureaux, primarily for use on the most-used medium-range routes within the Soviet Union. Designs were prepared by the three bureaux with the most experience of large transport aircraft development—those of Antonov, Tupolev and Ilyushin—and the proposal of the last-named team was selected for further definition. Within the Ilyushin bureau, initial design studies were conducted during 1970–71 under the bureau design number Il-86.

Early studies for the Il-86 were based on an extrapolation of the Il-62 configuration, using a new, large-diameter fuselage with substantially the same wing and tail unit, and a rear-engined layout. The weight penalty associated with such a layout proved to be unacceptable in so large an aircraft, however, and by the end of 1972 the Il-86 had been redesigned to have its engines in four underwing pods. Consequently, the Il-86 became the first Soviet airliner to follow what may fairly be called the classic 'Boeing' layout for jet transports.

First flight of the Il-86 is expected to take place in 1977, suggesting that entry into service with Aeroflot is unlikely much before the end of the present decade. The engines are expected to be derivatives of the Soloviev units that power the Il-62M, with clam-shell thrust reversers on each. Provision is being made for an advanced auto-pilot and flight control system to allow the Il-86 to operate down to ICAO Cat IIIA minima.

Within the 20-ft (6,08-m) diameter fuselage, the Il-86 has a cabin with a max width of approx 18 ft 9 in (5,70 m), sufficient for nine-abreast seating with two aisles. This makes it possible to accommodate 350 passengers in a one-class layout; alternatively, 28 passengers could be accommodated in a forward cabin six-abreast, and 206 eight-abreast (2+4+2) in the rear cabin in a typical mixed-class

layout. An unusual feature of the Il-86 is that passenger entrance doors are at the underfloor freight hold level, to

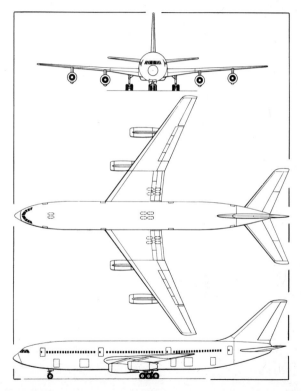

A model of the Il-86 wide-body 'airbus' type airliner which Aeroflot hopes to introduce towards the end of the present decade

avoid the need for special loading platforms at airports used by the new transport. One door near the nose and two aft of the wing each give access to a vestibule where coat stowage is provided; from each of these entrance lobbies, stairs lead up to the main cabin level. Underfloor freight holds, with their own access doors, will be able to accommodate standard LD-3 containers, or up to 16 pre-loaded baggage containers.

Power Plant: *Four 26,455 lb (12 000 kg) s.t. Soloviev D-30 KP turbofans.* **Performance:** *Typical cruising speed, 560–590 mph (900–950 km/h) at 30,000–33,000 ft (9 000–10 000 m); range with max payload and 1-hr reserve, 1,460 mls (2 350 km); range with 44,000-lb (20 000-kg) payload, 2,860 mls (4 600 km), range with max fuel, 3,420 mls (5 500 km).* **Weights:** *Max payload 88,185 lb (40 000 kg); max take-off weight, 414,470 lb (188 000 kg).* **Dimensions:** *Span, 158 ft 6 in (48,33 m); length, 191 ft 11 in (58,50 m), height, 51 ft 6 in (15,70 m); wing area, 3,444 sq ft (320 m²).*

KAMOV KA-25 (HORMONE)

In the late 'fifties, the AV-MF formulated a specification for a twin-turboshaft specialized anti-submarine warfare helicopter for both shore-based and shipboard use. To meet this requirement, Nikolai Kamov's bureau developed a helicopter with twin side-by-side turboshafts mounted above the cabin and driving three-bladed co-axial contra-rotating rotors. The prototype was demonstrated in public in July 1961 over Tushino, Moscow, (see *Harp*), but this type, the Ka-20, suffered protracted gestation and the developed version, the Ka-25, did not appear until 1967. It was subsequently developed both for the AV-MF (*Hormone-A*) and for commercial operation (Ka-25K).

The ASW version is currently deployed aboard various vessels of the Soviet Navy and, in particular, the anti-submarine cruisers *Moskva* and *Leningrad*, each of which has a complement of approximately 20 Ka-25s, and the *Kresta*-class cruisers. The Ka-25 has search radar in a large radome under the nose, dunking sonar, a towed magnetic anomaly detector, an electro-optical sensor and an internal weapons bay accommodating anti-submarine torpedoes or depth charges. Each member of the four-wheel undercarriage features an inflatable pontoon surmounted by inflation bottles to provide flotation in the event of an emergency water landing. The Ka-25 is extensively used by the AV-MF and it is expected that some 30 helicopters of this type will be embarked on the Soviet Navy's carrier *Kiev* in order that six Ka-25s can be kept aloft for sustained periods with at least two more ready on the flight deck for immediate launch.

A commercial counterpart, the Ka-25K, is basically a flying crane helicopter with a removable gondola for the crane operator replacing the undernose radome of the ASW model, the basic structure, overall dimensions and dynamic components of the two models being similar. The Ka-25K accommodates the crew of two side-by-side on the flight deck, one of the pilots occupying the gondola during loading

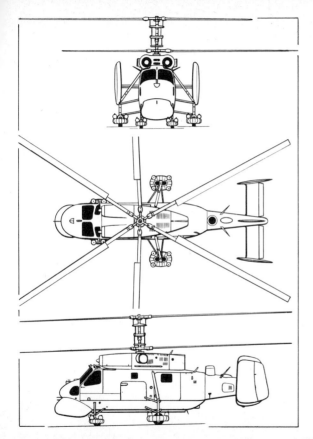

The general arrangement drawing (left) illustrates the ASW Ka-25 employed extensively by the AV-MF and the photographs (above and below) depict the civil Ka-25K, the dynamic components of the two models being similar

A Ka-25 ASW helicopter from the anti-submarine cruiser Leningrad photographed over the Mediterranean

and unloading while hovering, and the positioning of externally-slung cargoes. The rotors, transmission and engines of both versions of the Ka-25, together with their auxiliaries, form single self-contained assemblies which it is claimed can be removed within one hour. The current status of the commercial version is uncertain.

The following specification relates to the commercial Ka-25K, but it may be assumed that the ASW Ka-25 differs only in detail:

Power Plant: *Two 900 s.h.p. Glushenkov GTD-3 turboshafts.* **Performance:** *Max speed, 137 mph (220 km/h); normal cruise, 120 mph (193 km/h); service ceiling, 11,500 ft (3 500 m); range (standard fuel and reserves), 250 mls (400 km), (max fuel and reserves), 405 mls (650 km).* **Weights:** *Empty, 9,700 lb (4 400 kg); max take-off, 16,100 lb (7 300 kg).* **Dimensions:** *Rotor diam (each), 51 ft 8 in (15,74 m); overall length, 32 ft 3 in (9,83 m); height, 17 ft 7½ in (5,37 m).*

KAMOV KA-26 (HOODLUM)

Smallest of the helicopters currently in production in the Soviet Union, the Ka-26 was developed as an entirely original design to succeed the Ka-15 in the agricultural and general utility role. Flexibility of loading and the ability to carry various types of equipment were keynotes of the design, which was initiated in the early 'sixties, and to this end the Ka-26 was conceived as a lifting system, comprising power plant, rotor system, cockpit, undercarriage and a twin-boom tail unit. The rotor system follows Kamov tradition in being co-axial, the blades being of plastics construction.

The cockpit has two seats side-by-side although the Ka-26 is designed for safe operation by one pilot. Immediately behind the cabin and below the rotor head, a variety of payloads can be fitted, including a six-seat passenger cabin, a cargo pod, an open platform or a sling for bulky loads. For the primary agricultural use, a hopper can be fitted, or insecticide tanks and spray bars. Another version has been equipped for geophysical surveys, with an electromagnetic pulse generator in the cabin and a large circular antenna.

For fish-spotting duties from Soviet trawlers, Ka-26s are fitted with inflated pontoons for water operation. The type also operates from Soviet whalers and ice-breakers. In Siberia, Ka-26s have been used to carry fire-fighting teams to forest fires.

First flown in 1965, the Ka-26 is operated in the Soviet Union as a civil helicopter by Aeroflot, and several hundred have been built. Examples have been exported to Hungary, Bulgaria, East Germany and Rumania for agricultural and utility duties. Single examples were also sold to Sweden and Federal Germany.

The Ka-26 is seen (right top) equipped for geophysical survey with a large circular antenna for the electromagnetic pulse generator, and (right) equipped with chemical hopper and spreader bars for the agricultural role

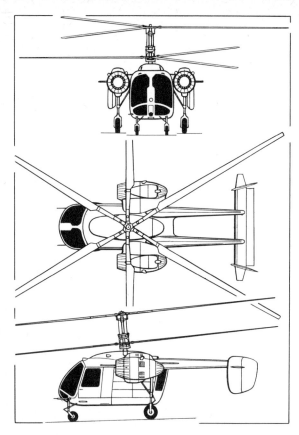

The Ka-26 is illustrated left and above fitted with the cargo/passenger pod that can accommodate up to six persons

Power Plant: Two 325 h.p. Vedeneev M-14V-26 radial air-cooled engines. **Performances:** Max speed, 105 mph (170 km/h); max cruising speed 93 mph (150 km/h); economical cruise, 56–68 mph (90–110 km/h); service ceiling, 9,840 ft (3 000 m); hovering ceiling (IGE), 4,265 ft (1 300 m); hovering ceiling (OGE), 2,625 ft (800 m); range with passenger pod ($\frac{1}{2}$-hr reserve), 248 mls (400 km); max range, auxiliary tanks, 745 mls (1 200 km). **Weights:** Empty (stripped), 4,300 lb (1 950 kg); empty (passenger pod) 4,630 lb (2 100 kg); max payload (transport), 1,985 lb (900 kg); max payload (crane), 2,425 lb (1 100 kg); max take-off, 7,165 lb (3 250 kg). **Dimensions:** Rotor diameter, 42 ft 8 in (13,00 m); fuselage length, 25 ft 5 in (7,75 m); height, 13 ft $3\frac{1}{2}$ in (4,05 m).

MIKOYAN-GUREVICH MIG-15UTI (MIDGET)

Derived from the MiG-15 (*Fagot*) single-seat fighter, which was phased out of service during the 'sixties by the V-VS and the various other air arms to which it had been supplied, the MiG-15UTI advanced trainer remains in service in numbers with the V-VS, all Warsaw Pact air forces, and the air arms of Afghanistan, Albania, Algeria, Cuba, Egypt, Guinea, Iraq, Khmer, Mali, Somalia, Southern Yemen, Sri Lanka, Syria, Pakistan, North Vietnam, North Yemen and the Chinese People's Republic.   It has been manufactured under licence in the last-mention country and in Czechoslovakia (as the CS 102) and Poland (as the SBLim-1).

The MiG-15UTI followed the trend established by most earlier Soviet two-seat derivatives of single-seat fighters in that overall length was held constant, obviating the need for an increase in the size of the vertical tail surfaces and minimizing the task of aerodynamic development.   The second seat was inserted aft of the standard cockpit at the expense of fuel tankage, which was reduced to 224 Imp gal (1 080 l)

The MiG-15UTI is currently the world's most widely-used advanced trainer and the accompanying photographs show this type in service with (top right) the V-VS, (centre right) the Pakistan Air Force and (immediately right) the Finnish air arm.   The Pakistani example was supplied by the Chinese People's Republic in which it has been licence built

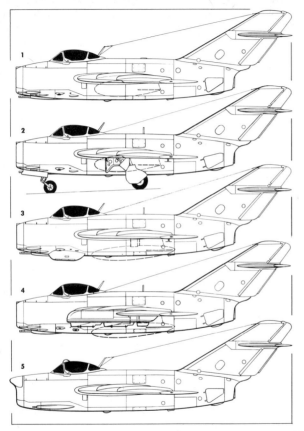

The side profiles (left) depict: (1) The initial production MiG-15; (2) The production MiG-15bis with undercarriage extended; (3) The MiG-15bisR fighter reconnaissance aircraft with camera pack below cannon magazines; (4) The MiG-15bis modified for ground attack with tandem stores stations on projecting pylons; (5) The MiG-15P all-weather interceptor with twin 23-mm cannon armament and early Izumrud AI radar. Further details of these MiG-15 versions are provided on pages 52–54, but apart from a few surviving examples of the MiG-15bis with smaller air forces, the MiG-15UTI two-seater is now the only MiG-15 variant in service

from 321 Imp gal (1 460 l), the rear seat being raised so that the instructor was afforded a measure of forward vision, and each seat being enclosed by an individual canopy, the forward canopy hinging to starboard and the rear canopy sliding aft. Largely as a result of poor canopy shape, the high-speed performance of the MiG-15UTI was markedly inferior to that of the single-seat fighter from which it was derived, but it simulated the combat aircraft's handling characteristics exactly. Training armament was normally fitted, this consisting of either a 12,7-mm UBK-E machine gun with 150 rounds or a 23-mm NS-23 cannon with 80 rounds, the single weapon being offset to port.

The initial production model of the MiG-15UTI was powered by an RD-45A turbojet rated at 4,850 lb (2 200 kg) thrust, but this gave place, in turn, to the RD-45FA rated at 5,005 lb (2 270 kg) and, in the definitive production model, the 5,952 lb (2 700 kg) Klimov VK-1. Some MiG-15UTI aircraft were modified as intercept radar trainers, these being fitted with the fixed-scan S-band Scan Fix (Izumrud) AI radar in an extended nose with a projecting upper intake lip and a cone housing on the intake splitter.

The MiG-15UTI is normally flown with auxiliary underwing tanks, a variety of which may be fitted, these including the 55 Imp gal (250 l) and 66 Imp gal (300 l) slipper-type tank and the 88 Imp gal (400 l) or 132 Imp gal (600 l) pylon-type tank. The following specification relates to the standard production model:

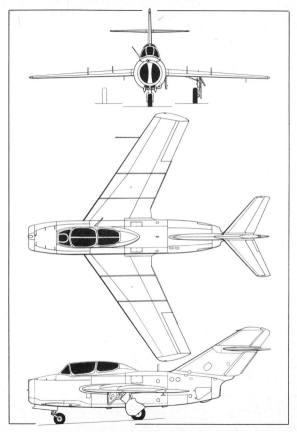

(Above, below and right) The standard two-seat MiG-15UTI trainer

Power Plant: *One 5,952 lb (2 700 kg) Klimov VK-1 turbojet.* **Performance:** *Max speed (clean), 630 mph (1 015 km/h) or M=0·826 at sea level, (with two 55 Imp gal/250 l slipper tanks), 559 mph (900 km/h) or M=0·73; initial climb, 10,235 ft/min (52 m/sec); time to 16,405 ft (5 000 m), 2·6 min, to 32,810 ft (10 000 m), 6·8 min; service ceiling, 47,980 ft (14 625 m); range at 16,405 ft (5 000 m), (clean) 422 mls (680 km), (with 55 Imp gal/ 250 l slipper tanks), 590 mls (950 km), at 32,810 ft (10 000 m), (clean) 590 mls (950 km), (with slipper tanks), 885 mls (1 424 km).* **Weights:** *Empty, 8,818 lb (4 000 kg); loaded (clean), 10,692 lb (4 850 kg); max take-off, 11,905 lb (5 400 kg).* **Dimensions:** *Span, 33 ft 0⅞ in (10,08 m); length, 32 ft 11¼ in (10,04 m); height, 12 ft 1⅝ in (3,70 m); wing area, 221·74 sq ft (20,6 m²).*

161

MIKOYAN-GUREVICH MIG-17 (FRESCO)

The MiG-17 was a thoroughgoing redesign of the basic MiG-15 (*Fagot*) intended to afford a marked improvement in transonic handling. The entire fuselage of the earlier fighter forward of the rear frame of the engine plenum chamber was retained virtually unchanged, but the rear fuselage was lengthened by 35·4 in (90 cm), permitting a finer taper aft from the maximum fuselage diameter of 4·81 ft (1,45 m). The vertical tail surfaces remained unchanged other than in detail but the leading and trailing edges of the fixed-incidence tailplane were given increased sweep angles and an entirely new wing was adopted, this being of thinner section swept 45 deg inboard and 42 deg outboard.

The initial production version of the MiG-17 (*Fresco-A*), which began to enter V-VS service in 1952, retained the same VK-1 engine as that of the MiG-15bis and a similar cannon armament to that of the late production versions of the earlier fighter (i.e., one 37-mm N-37 and two 23-mm NR-23 cannon), and a limited all-weather version, the MiG-17P (*Fresco-B*) was evolved, this differing from the clear-weather interceptor version primarily in having fixed-scan S-band *Scan Fix* AI radar, known as *Izumrud* (Emerald), with the ranging scanner housed by a lip extension above the engine air intake and a radome on the intake splitter accommodating the conical scan dish. The fuselage nose was marginally lengthened—by 5 in (12,7 cm) forward of the wing root—to provide the additional space necessary for the pilot display instrumentation, the windscreen being moved forward, increasing the rake angle from 50 to 60 degrees and the broader side panels being reinforced by horizontal frames.

Production of both variants quickly gave place to the MiG-17F and MiG-17PF (*Fresco-C* and *Fresco-D* respectively), these utilizing the VK-1F engine fitted with a short afterburner which boosted the maximum dry thrust from 5,732 lb (2 600 kg) to 7,452 lb (3 380 kg). The tail cone of the VK-1F-powered models was cut back, exposing the

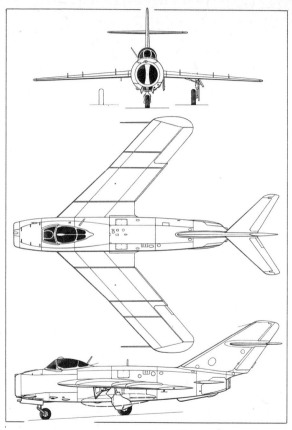

end of the afterburner nozzle, and shorter, deeper air brakes were introduced, the hydraulic jack fairings being raised to the fuselage centreline. The cannon armament for both models was standardized as three 23-mm NR-23s. The MiG-17PF was fitted with progressively improved versions of the *Scan Fix* AI radar, operating in both S-band and X-band, and with the availability of the first-generation AA-3 *Alkali* radar-homing AAM, all cannon armament was deleted and a quartet of the small beam-riders was pylon-mounted on launching rails ahead of the main undercarriage wells, this model being designated MiG-17PFU (*Fresco-E*).

The MiG-17F continued in production in parallel with the

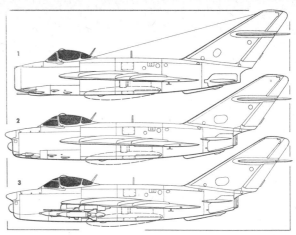

The general arrangement drawing (opposite page) illustrates the MiG-17F (Fresco–C) and the side profiles (right) depict: (1) The initial production version of the MiG-17 (Fresco–A) which retained the same VK-1 engine as the MiG-15bis; (2) The MiG-17PF (Fresco–D) with Izumrud AI radar; (3) The MiG-17PFU (Fresco–E) with cannon armament deleted and provision for four AAMs. The photograph below depicts a MiG-17F of the East German air arm

The MiG-17F remains in first-line service with a considerable number of air forces and was used operationally, particularly by the Syrian Arab Air Force, during the Middle East conflict of 1973. The example illustrated (immediately left) is seen in the markings of the DDR and that (lower left) in service with the air arm of Khmer (Cambodia)

large number of smaller air forces and is still employed by the V-VS and the Sino—Communist air arm, although, outmoded in the intercept role, it is now employed primarily as a ground attack fighter. Various arrangements of weapons pylons have been applied to MiG-17Fs serving in the ground attack role, the standard fuel tank-carrying pylons beneath the central wing fences being retained and most aircraft having additional pylons inboard of the inner wing fences and forward of the mainwheel wells, these normally carrying a 551-lb (250-kg) bomb or a UV-16-57 pod containing 16 55-mm S-5 rockets, and these are sometimes supplemented by racks outboard of the drop tanks carrying two 240-mm S-24 rockets beneath each wing.

limited all-weather models but in substantially larger quantities as, from the late 'fifties through the mid 'sixties, it was the most widely exported of Soviet combat aircraft and it was also licence-manufactured in Poland (as the LIM-5P) and China (as the F-4). Although the MiG-17PF and PFU were phased out of first-line service in the late 'sixties, the MiG-17F remains an important item in the inventories of a

The following specification relates to the standard MiG-17F day fighter:

Power Plant: *One 5,732 lb (2 600 kg) dry and 7,452 lb (3 380 kg) reheat Klimov VK-1F turbojet.* **Performance:** *Max speed (clean), 711 mph (1 145 km/h) or M=0·974 at 9,840 ft (3 000 m), 702 mph (1 130 km/h) or M=0·986*

at 16,400 ft (5 000 m), 626 mph (1 071 km/h) or M=0·93 at 32,810 ft (10 000 m); max climb rate, 12,795 ft/min (65 m/sec); ceiling (without reheat), 49,540 ft (15 000 m), (with reheat), 54,460 ft (16 600 m); range (internal fuel), 422 mls (680 km) at 16,400 ft (5 000 m), 603 mls (970 km) at 32,810 ft (10 000 m), (with two 88 Imp gal/400 l drop tanks), 640 mls (1 030 km) at 16,400 ft (5 000 m), 913 mls (1 470 km) at 32,810 ft (10 000 m). **Weights:** Loaded (clean), 11,733 lb (5 340 kg), (with two 88 Imp gal/400 l drop tanks), 13,380 lb (6 069 kg). **Dimensions:** Span, 31 ft 7⅛ in (9,63 m); length, 36 ft 4⅝ in (11,09 m); height, 12 ft 5⅝ in (3,80 m); wing area, 243·26 sq ft (22,6 m²).

(Right and below) A MiG-17PF limited all-weather fighter of the Československé vojenské letectvo. The ranging scanner was housed in the upper lip and the scan dish on the intake splitter

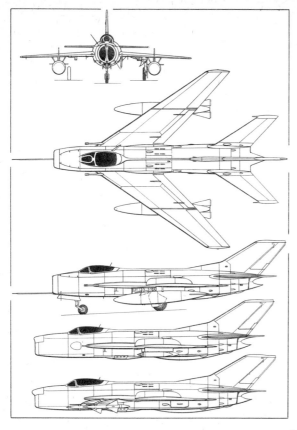

MIKOYAN MIG-19 (FARMER)

The first Soviet production fighter capable of attaining supersonic speed in level flight and a contemporary of the North American F-100 Super Sabre, the MiG-19 is no longer included in the first-line inventory of the Warsaw Pact air forces (apart from one squadron of MiG-19PMs that remained with the *Polskie Wojska Lotnicze* late in 1974), but remains in service in some numbers with the air forces of Cuba and Egypt, while a copy of the basic dual-role clear weather model, the MiG-19S, produced by the Chinese People's Republic as the F-6, has been supplied to Albania, North Vietnam and Pakistan, and is currently one of the principal combat aircraft of the Sino-Communist air arm.

The MiG-19 was designed to meet a requirement calling for a clear-weather single-seat interceptor capable of supersonic speed in level flight and possessing secondary ground attack capability, and the first prototype was flown in 1953, deliveries of the initial production model (*Farmer-A*) to the V-VS commencing early in 1955. Of relatively simple concept, the MiG-19 was powered by two small-diameter Mikulin AM-5 axial-flow turbojets mounted side-by-side in the rear fuselage and each offering a maximum dry thrust of 4,850 lb (2 200 kg) which was boosted by reheat to 6,700 lb (3 040 kg). The three-spar wing, swept 55 deg on the leading edge, carried large-area Fowler-type flaps which had a combat manoeuvre setting for use up to 495 mph (797 km/h) IAS; four fuselage fuel cells had a total capacity of 477 Imp gal (2 170 l) and could be supplemented by two 176 Imp gal (800 l) underwing drop tanks, and armament comprised one 37-mm N-37 in the starboard side of the forward fuselage and a 23-mm NR-23 in each wing.

At an early stage in the production life of the fighter, control problems, primarily related to elevator ineffectiveness, resulted in the replacement of the conventional elevators by a slab-type tailplane, the designation being changed to

The three upper views (left) illustrate the MiG-19S, the centre sideview shows the MiG-19PF and the bottom view the MiG-19PM

166

MiG-19S, the suffix letter indicating *Stabilizator*. Various modifications dictated by early service usage included the addition of spoilers to boost the ailerons and the provision of a ventral air brake to supplement the two lateral air brakes. Increased attention was given to flight safety, the hydraulic system being fully duplicated, automatic stick-to-tailplane gearing to give a near-constant rate of stick force per *g* was provided by means of an electro-mechanical linkage and an electrical system was provided to operate the slab tail for pitch control in the event of a hydraulic failure. All control runs were re-routed, those between the cockpit and the tail being inserted in a 'tunnel' which formed a dorsal spine and armament was changed to three 30-mm NR-30 cannon.

The MiG-19S began to appear in service in substantial numbers in the latter half of 1956, and for the secondary ground attack role two weapons stations were introduced beneath the wing aft and slightly inboard of the main under-carriage attachment points, these each carrying such loads as a UV-8-57 pod containing eight 55-mm S-5 rockets, a 551-lb (250-kg) bomb, or a 190-mm TRS-190 or 212-mm ARS-212 rocket. Further development resulted, in 1957, in the service appearance of the MiG-19SF (*Farmer-C*), the additional suffix letter indicating *forsirovanny* or *Forsazh*—

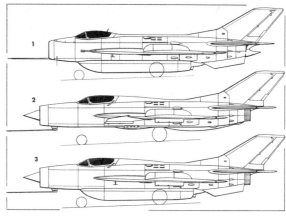

The side profiles above illustrate: (1) The rocket-boosted SM-50; (2) The RS-26-powered SM-12PM; (3) The rocket-boosted SM-12PMU. Details of these MiG-19 versions appear on page 62

Built in larger numbers than any other version of the MiG-19 and now the only model still serving in sub-stantial numbers, the MiG-19SF (right) has a secondary ground attack role and (apart from the Chinese-built version) is now largely confined to the V-VS FA and the air forces of Cuba and Egypt

literally 'boosted'—and signifying the replacement of the Mikulin engines by Tumansky RD-9Bs each offering a maximum dry thrust of 5,732 lb (2 600 kg) boosted to 7,165 lb (3 250 kg) with reheat and offering a very good thrust-to-weight ratio. In service, the 'F' suffix letter was usually discarded, the aircraft being known simply as the MiG-19S. A small number of examples of the MiG-19SF

were supplied to China prior to 1960, when ideological differences between the two countries resulted in the severance of relations, and both the MiG-19S airframe and its RD-9B-811 turbojet were subsequently manufactured in China without benefit of a licence agreement.

Although designed as a clear-weather fighter with a gyro gunsight and no radar ranging, some limited all-weather capability was given to the aircraft by the installation of the so-called *Scan Odd* radar, a dual-PRF (Pulse Repetition Frequency) X-band set for search and intercept with the conical scan dish housed in a central cone carried by the intake splitter and the range measurement antenna being incorporated in an enlarged intake upper lip. This variant was designated MiG-19PF (*Farmer-B*), the first suffix letter indicating *Perekhvatchik*, which, by this time, was a term being used in the all-weather intercept connotation. One further version of the fighter was to appear before the MiG-19 was phased out of production in the early 'sixties, this, the MiG-19PM (*Perekhvatchik Modifikatsirovanny*), being the second V-VS service fighter to discard gun armament in favour of AAMs. The MiG-19PM was equipped with four

Although supplanted by the MiG-21 in the DDR (top left), the MiG-19SF is numerically the most important fighter in the inventory of the Pakistan Air Force (left) which has been supplied with this type by China, others having been supplied to Albania and North Vietnam. A Chinese two-seat version is known as Farmer—F

The MiG-19PM (immediately right and below right) was the second V-VS fighter to discard cannon in favour of an all-missile armament and normally carried a quartette of first-generation AA-3 Alkali radar homing missiles. Limited all-weather capability was provided by X-band Scan Odd radar with range measurement antenna in an enlarged intake upper lip and a conical scan dish in a central cone on the intake splitter

first-generation AA-3 *Alkali* radar homing missiles carried by pylons projecting forward of the wing leading edge.

The following specification relates to the MiG-19S:

Power Plant: *Two 5,732 lb (2 600 kg) dry and 7,165 lb (3 250 kg) reheat Tumansky RD-9B turbojets.* **Performance:** *Max speed, 902 mph (1 452 km/h) or M=1·35 at 32,800 ft (10 000 m); range cruise, 590 mph (950 km/h) or M=0·827 at 32,800 ft (10 000 m); initial climb, 22,640 ft/min (115 m/sec); normal range, 864 mls (1 390 km) at 45,930 ft (14 000 m); max range (with two 176 Imp gal/ 800 l auxiliary tanks), 1,367 mls (2 200 km).* **Weights:** *Empty, 12,698 lb (5 760 kg); normal loaded, 16,755 lb (7 600 kg); max take-off, 19,180 lb (8 700 kg).* **Dimensions:** *Span, 29 ft 6⅓ in (9,00 m); length, 42 ft 11⅓ in (13,09 m); height, 13 ft 2¼ in (4,02 m); wing area, 269·1 sq ft (25,00 m²).*

MIKOYAN MIG-21 (FISHBED)

The basic MiG-21 design has been extensively developed since the initial production model (*Fishbed-C*) entered V-VS service during the last quarter of 1959, a somewhat complex genealogical process endowing the fighter, in its current versions, with limited all-weather and multi-role capability, whereas the original version was a relatively simple clear-weather point defence and air superiority aircraft. Evolved from the MiG-21F (*forsirovanny* or *forsazh*) was the MiG-21PF (*Perekhvatchik*) with a lengthened nose and substantially enlarged air intake to accommodate a conical centrebody housing R1L search and track radar, a modified canopy and a substantial aerodynamic aft fairing to improve wave drag, plus raised internal fuel capacity from 515 to 626 Imp gal (2 340 to 2 850 l), this being distributed between seven wing and fuselage tanks. The starboard cannon (retained by the MiG-21F) and the port cannon fairing were deleted, permitting simplification of the forward air brake design, and appreciably larger mainwheels were

introduced. The MiG-21PF (*Fishbed-D*) appeared for the first time over Tushino in 1961, and whereas the initial service version possessed similar vertical tail surfaces to those of the definitive MiG-21F, these were later to give place to a still broader fin, the leading edge of which was carried forward some 18 in (46 cm), thus eliminating the root fillet (*Fishbed-E*).

The MiG-21PF, like the MiG-21F, initially featured a braking chute compartment alongside the ventral fin. This was replaced by a bullet fairing at the base of the rudder, and other changes introduced progressively included attachment points for RATOG (Rocket Assisted Take-off Gear) flanking the ventral aft air brake and provision for a system of boundary layer flap blowing known as SPS (*sduva pogranichnovo sloya*) which reduced the landing speed by some 15 per cent, the use of SPS being indicated by the introduction of enlarged flap guide fairings which replaced the smaller guide fairings situated at the outer extremities of the Fowler-type flaps. These changes were introduced individually on various production batches before all were standardized on

(Left) MiG-21F clear-weather interceptors in service with the Hungarian air arm. The MiG-21F differed from the initial production MiG-21 in having a marginally uprated R-11 turbojet of 12,676 lb (5 750 kg) with full reheat and a tailfin of increased chord. Armament comprised a single 30-mm NR-30 cannon and two K-13A (Atoll) IR-homing AAMs

A MiG-21F clear-weather interceptor of the Finnish air arm (above) and MiG-21PFS limited all-weather fighters of the V-VS (below). The MiG-21PFS was an interim production model which introduced the SPS flap blowing system as standard

the model designated as MiG-21PFS.

The R1L search and track radar gave place to R2L (*Spin Scan*) with a reported lock-on range of 7–8 miles (11–13 km), and the uprated R-11-F2S-300 turbojet was standardized, this developing a static thrust of 8,598 lb (3 900 kg) boosted to 13,670 lb (6 200 kg) with reheat. The inadequacy of the armament of the MiG-21PF, which comprised two K-13A (*Atoll*) IR-homing missiles, resulted in provision being made for a GP-9 gun pack to be mounted on the fuselage centreline in place of the standard stores pylon. This pack housed a twin-barrelled 23-mm GSh-23 cannon together with its ammunition, and its introduction on the MiG-21PF was accompanied by a predictor sight and electrical ranging. One other addition to the equipment of the MiG-21PF made at this time was a radar 'sniffer' (informing the pilot when his aircraft was being painted by enemy radar) in an enlarged bullet fairing at the tip of the vertical surfaces.

A late production model of the MiG-21PF with broad-chord fin and bullet-type parabrake housing but lacking

provision for RATOG and SPS was adopted by the Indian government for licence manufacture by Hindustan Aeronautics in 1965, this being given the generic designation of MiG-21FL (*Forsazh Lokator* signifying that it was the 'boosted' version equipped with AI radar). A total of 196 MiG-21FLs had been delivered by Hindustan Aero-

The side profiles (left) illustrate: (1) The initial production MiG-21;
(2) The principal production series MiG-21F with broader chord
fin; (3) The principal production series MiG-21PF; (4) The late
series MiG-21PF with revised fin, GSh-23 gun pack and parabrake
in bullet fairing at the base of the fin

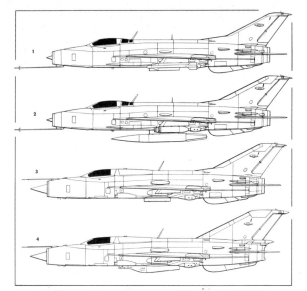

nautics (Indian-manufactured components being progressively introduced during the programme) when production
terminated in 1973 in favour of the MiG-21M, early aircraft
of this series being retroactively modified to provide inter-
changeability between the centreline pylon and the GP-9
gun pack.

The MiG-21PFS gave place to the MiG-21PFM (*Modifikatsirovanny*) which incorporated all the progressive changes
standardized by the PFS and introduced a conventional fixed
windscreen with quarterlights which were associated with
the provision of a simple ejection seat, the cockpit canopy
hinging to starboard. Previously, the canopy with integral
windscreen had tilted forward and remained attached to the
ejector seat to protect the pilot from blast effects.

The MiG-21PFM (*Fishbed-F*) was succeeded by the
MiG-21PFMA (*Fishbed-J*) which introduced further revision of the upper fuselage contours, the dorsal fairing
being enlarged so that the depth became virtually constant
back to the fin. An important innovation was the provision
of two additional wing pylons, the MiG-21PFMA thus being

(Left) A MiG-21PF
(SPS) taking-off with
the aid of RATOG.
It will be noted that
this interim model
featured the early-
standard tail fin
coupled with the
bullet-type parabrake
housing at the base of
the rudder

(Above) The first HAL production MiG-21MF and (below) a MiG-21PFMA of the Ceskslovenské vojenské letectvo

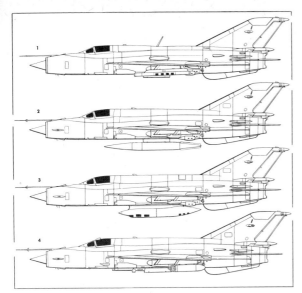

The side profiles (above) illustrate: (1) The MiG-21PFM with fixed windscreen and ECM pod on wing pylon; (2) The MiG-21PFMA with revised upper fuselage contours; (3) The MiG-21R reconnaissance version of the PFMA; (4) The MiG-21MF which standardized on the R-13 (SPS) engine and an internal GSh-23 twin-barrel 23-mm cannon

enabled to carry up to three 108 Imp gal (490 l) drop tanks and two K-13A IR-homing missiles, or a drop tank or GP-9 gun pack on the centreline and a K-13A on each wing pylon. The additional pylons endowed the PFMA with some additional (if rather limited) ground attack capability, typical offensive loads for the ground attack mission being four 240-mm S-24 ASMs, two 1,100-lb (500-kg) and two 550-lb (250-kg) bombs, or four UV-16-57 rocket pods, plus the centreline GP-9 gun pack. The PFMA was the first MiG-21 variant to feature a genuine zero-zero ejection seat,

173

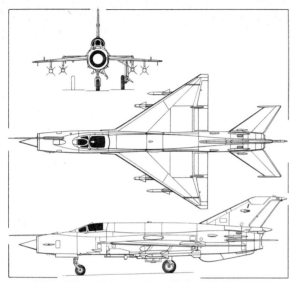

(Above) The 'third generation' MiG-21SMT (Fishbed–K)

and late production batches introduced an internal GSh-23 twin-barrel cannon between the twin forward air brakes. A tactical reconnaissance version, the MiG-21R (*Fishbed-H*), made provision for an interchangeable reconnaissance pod on the fuselage centreline housing a combination of cameras and fuel. Sensor pods or fuel tanks could be carried on the inboard wing pylons and a suppressed antenna was introduced in the dorsal spine. Wingtip ECM fairings were retroactively fitted to some examples of the MiG-21R.

The power-to-weight ratio of the MiG-21 had worsened with the PFMA version, the loaded weight of which, with two K-13As, three 108 Imp gal (490 l) drop tanks and the internal GSh-23 cannon, had risen to something of the order of 21,605 lb (9 800 kg), but a lighter and more powerful Tumansky turbojet, the R-13 (SPS) was introduced to result in the externally similar MiG-21MF and its tactical reconnaissance equivalent, the MiG-21RF. The R-13 turbojet makes extensive use of titanium in its construction and affords a dry thrust of 11,244 lb (5 100 kg) increasing to 14,550 lb (6 600 kg) with full reheat. The only noticeable external change between the PFMA and the MF was the provision on the latter of a small debris deflector plate beneath the suction relief door.

Licence production of a version of the MiG-21 approximating to the MF model is being undertaken in India as the MiG-21M. The first of three pre-series aircraft (retaining the R-11-F2S-300 engine) was handed over to the Indian Air Force on 14 February 1973, the fourth and subsequent aircraft standardizing on the R-13, and current planning calls for Hindustan Aeronautics to deliver approximately 150 MiG-21Ms by 1980, although it is anticipated that deliveries from late 1975 will be of a model equivalent to the MiG-21SMT.

The most recently introduced variant, the MiG-21SMT (*Fishbed-K*), is equipped with tail warning radar which overcomes the inability of earlier models to detect aft attack by aircraft or missiles. Associated with this new equipment is the rearward extension of the dorsal spine to the bullet at the base of the rudder, this modification endowing the variant with a very distinctive upper aft fuselage contour. The enlarged dorsal spine of the MiG-21SMT accommodates a saddle tank to increase fuel capacity which, with a single drop tank, endows this model with an endurance of 3·5 hours. In other respects the MiG-21SMT is similar to the basic MiG-21MF.

The following specification relates to the MiG-21MF:

Power Plant: *One 11,244 lb (5 100 kg) dry and 14,550 lb (6 600 kg) Tumansky R-13 (SPS) turbojet.* **Perfor-**

The first of the 'third generation' series of MiG-21 fighters, the MiG-21SMT (right) has a substantial 'saddle' tank which endows this model with an endurance of three-and-a-half hours. The aircraft illustrated carries an Advanced Atoll missile on the port outboard pylon

mance: Max speed (clean), 808 mph (1 300 km/h) or M=1·06 at 1,000 ft (305 m), 1,386 mph (2 230 km/h) or M=2·1 above 36,090 ft (11 000 m); range (internal fuel), 683 mls (1 100 km); ferry range (max external fuel), 1,118 mls (1 800 km); service ceiling, 59,055 ft (18 000 m). **Weights:** Normal take-off (with four K-13A AAMs), 18,078 lb (8 200 kg), (with two K-13As and two 108 Imp gal/490 l drop tanks), 19,731 lb (8 950 kg); max take-off (two K-13As and three drop tanks), 20,723 lb (9 400 kg). **Dimensions:** Span, 23 ft 5½ in (7,15 m); length (including probe), 51 ft 8½ in (15,76 m), (without probe), 44 ft 2 in (13,46 m); wing area, 247·57 sq ft (23,0 m²).

The MiG-21MF (right), the first version of the fighter to employ the Tumansky R-13 turbojet, may, together with its reconnaissance equivalent, be considered the last of the 'second generation' of MiG-21s. Apart from the semi-externally mounted cannon, the MiG-21MF differs externally from the PFMA only in having a deflector beneath the suction relief door

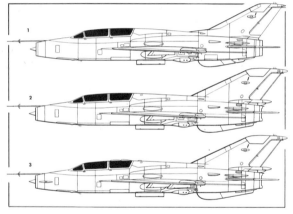

MIG-21U (MONGOL)

A two-seat operational training version of MiG-21 single-seat interceptor, the MiG-21U was initially thought to be a straightforward adaptation of the MiG-21F (*Fishbed-C*) with a second seat inserted behind the normal cockpit at some expense to fuel volume. However, while retaining the engine air intake of the MiG-21F, the MiG-21U had more in common with the MiG-21PF (*Fishbed-D*) airframe, featuring the enlarged main undercarriage members of the latter with the attendant blister fairings of increased size over the wheel wells protruding above the wing roots and on the wheel doors. A single-piece forward air brake was fitted, gun armament was deleted and a starboard-hinging double canopy enclosed the tandem cockpits.

The initial production series MiG-21U had the definitive MiG-21F-type vertical tail surfaces, but the principal production series had the bullet-type parabrake stowage and the definitive broader-chord MiG-21PF-type vertical surfaces. The introduction of the R-11(SPS) engine on the MiG-21PF providing a system of boundary layer flap blowing was followed by a similar modification to the tandem two-seater, this modified version receiving the designation MiG-21US. Almost simultaneously, tandem retractable mirrors appeared on the aft canopy section.

All production series of the tandem two-seater powered by the Tumansky R-11 or R-11(SPS) turbojet had a single fuselage centreline pylon and two wing pylons, typical external loads including a single 108 Imp gal (490 l) drop tank and two K-13A IR-homing missiles, but with the service phase-in of the R-13-powered MiG-21MF an equivalent two-seater, the MiG-21UM, entered production, this having two additional underwing pylons.

Single and two-seaters possess similar performances.

MIKOYAN MIG-23 (FLOGGER)

The multi-role MiG-23, which reportedly began to enter service with the V-VS in 1971 and which, since 1973, has been deployed with the Group of Soviet Forces in Germany in its strike version, is the first Soviet combat aircraft designed from the outset to utilize variable geometry to attain production and service status.   Presumably developed to meet a requirement framed in 1965 and comparable in size with the French Mirage G experimental v-g fighter, the MiG-23 appeared in prototype form over Domodedovo on 9 July 1967.   There are indications that the MiG-23 prototypes suffered CG problems, and by comparison with these the entire wing of the production model was set further forward, increasing the wing/tailplane gap, and the fixed wing glove was markedly reduced in chord.   Simultaneously, the folding ventral fin was repositioned forward.

The initial production version was apparently optimized for the intercept role with a pulse Doppler fire control system that has been compared with the Westinghouse AWG-10 installed in the US Navy's F-4J Phantom.   The strike version, the MiG-23B, has a built-in 23-mm twin-barrel GSh-23 cannon immediately aft of the nosewheel bay and may carry an auxiliary fuel tank on a centreline pylon aft of the cannon.   Various ordnance loads may be carried by four pylons, two side-by-side beneath the fuselage and two at the extremities of the small fixed wing centre section.

Fully forward the wings have leading-edge sweep of 21 deg and translate to the fully-swept position within approximately four seconds, leading-edge sweep in this position being 71 deg.   Slats occupy the outboard three-fifths of the leading-edge of the pivoting outer panel, plain flaps spanning the entire trailing-edge, and part of the ventral fin folds to starboard during take-off and landing in order to provide ground clearance.

A tandem two-seat version, the MiG-23U for transitioning pilots is known as the *Flogger-C*.   This variant of the aircraft possesses the same overall dimensions and combat

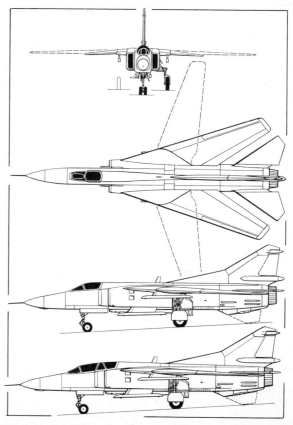

The general arrangement drawing (previous page) depicts the MiG-23B, the lower sideview and the photographs (left) illustrating the tandem two-seat MiG-23U (Flogger-C)

capability as the single-seater, internal fuel tankage having presumably been rearranged to provide for the second seat, which, situated aft of the standard cockpit, is mounted slightly higher, both cockpits being enclosed by a continuous canopy which fairs into raised aft decking. Each MiG-23 unit includes two or more two-seat MiG-23Us on strength.

A prototype MiG-23 which was demonstrated at Domodedovo in 1967

The figures quoted in the following specification are estimated:

Power Plant: *One 14,330 lb (6 500 kg) dry and 20,500 lb (9 300 kg) reheat turbojet.* **Performance:** *Max speed, 865 mph or M=1·2 at sea level, 1,520 mph (2 446 km/h) or M=2·3 at 39,370 ft (12 000 m), in high-drag configuration (e.g., centreline fuel tank, two AAMs of advanced Anab type on fuselage pylons and two AAMs on wing pylons), 1,120 mph or M=1·7; tactical radius (with centreline drop tank), 620 mls (1 000 km).* **Weights:** *Max loaded, 33,070 lb (15 000 kg).* **Dimensions:** *Span (max), 46 ft 9 in (14,25 m), (min), 26 ft 9½ in (8,17 m); length, 55 ft 1½ in (16,80 m).*

MIKOYAN MIG-25 (FOXBAT)

Designed primarily for the intercept mission at extreme altitudes and speeds but also serving in the high-altitude reconnaissance role, the MiG-25 was responsible for establishing a large number of FAI-homologated international records between March 1965 and July 1973 under the designation Ye-266 (see pages 19–20). Featuring a shoulder-mounted wing of cropped-delta form, huge rectangular air intake trunks into which the slim fuselage is blended and twin inclined vertical tail surfaces, the MiG-25 is a titanium aircraft.

The interceptor variant (*Foxbat-A*) has *Jay Bird* (J-band) radar for missile guidance and target location, and is equipped to receive signals from the *Markham* ground-to-air digital transmission system in which ground-based tracking radars feed information directly to the cockpit display. Four wing stations are provided for AAMs and these are believed to carry a mix of IR-homing and radar-homing AA-4 *Ash* missiles, or two AA-6 and two AA-2-2 *Atoll* missiles. There is a small weapons bay in the fore-part of each air intake trunk which is believed to be capable of accepting the 23-mm twin-barrel GSh-23 cannon. Approximately 25,000 lb (11 340 kg) of fuel is believed to be usually accommodated internally which is sufficient for a normal combat radius, depending on duration of the supersonic portion of the mission, of between 460 and 805 miles (740 and 1 300 km), but the MiG-25 has strictly limited conventional dogfighting capability at altitudes below 25,000–30,000 ft (7 620–9 145 m), having been optimized for operation at extreme altitudes and probably possessing a q limitation (dynamic force) equivalent to an airspeed of some 620 mph (1 000 km/h) at sea level. Possessing a short-period dash speed of M=3·2, or 2,100 mph (3 380 km/h), and a max sustained speed of about M=2·7, or 1,780 mph (2 865 km/h), at high altitudes and an operational ceiling of 80,000 ft (24 385 m), the MiG-25 has a speed and altitude capability superior to that of any operational

The photograph below depicts the reconnaissance version of the MiG-25 (Foxbat–B) with camera nose

military aircraft other than the Lockheed SR-71A strategic reconnaissance aircraft and is expected to possess full look-down shoot-down radar/missile capability during the second half of the present decade.

The high-altitude reconnaissance version of the MiG-25 (Foxbat-B) differs from the interceptor primarily in having a camera nose in place of the radome, and apparently the slim wingtip pods (which presumably accommodate ECM equipment on the interceptor model) are deleted.

The MiG-25 was presumably designed in the early 'sixties to counter high-altitude supersonic bombers, such as the North American XB-70 Valkyrie, and is believed to have flown in prototype form in 1963–64 with initial deliveries to the V-VS following in 1970–71. The figures quoted in the following specification are estimated:

The photograph (below) and the general arrangement drawing (right) illustrate the basic interceptor version of the MiG-25 (Foxbat–A) which has weapons bays in the air intake trunks

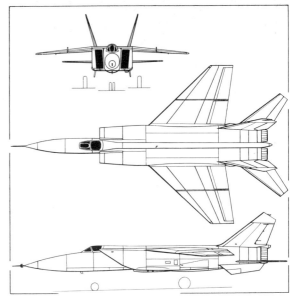

Power Plant: *Two 24,250 lb (11 000 kg) reheat Tumansky turbojets.* **Performance:** *Max speed (short-period dash), 2,100 mph (3 380 km/h) or M=3·2, (max sustained), 1,780 mph (2 865 km/h) or M=2·7; normal combat radius, 700 mls (1 125 km); time to 36,000 ft (10 970 m) with full reheat, 2·5 min, with full military power, 7·8 min; service ceiling, 80,000 ft (24 385 m).* **Weights:** *Empty equipped, 34,000 lb (15 420 kg); max take-off, 64,200 lb (29 120 kg).* **Dimensions:** *Span, 41 ft 0 in (12,50 m); length, 70 ft 0 in (21,33 m).*

MIL MI-1 (HARE)

The first helicopter to bear the name of Mikhail Mil, until his death in 1970 the doyen of Soviet rotary-winged aircraft designers, the Mi-1 was also the first helicopter to achieve major production and service status in the Soviet Union. Development began in the period immediately following the end of the war and the first of three prototypes flew in September 1948, with production deliveries commencing during 1951 to meet the then-urgent need of the V-VS for a general purpose helicopter.   In size and configuration, the Mi-1 was similar to western counterparts such as the Sikorsky S-51 and Bristol 171.   Powered by a 575 hp Ivchenko AI-26V piston radial engine, it was basically a four seater, but a later production series carried only the pilot and two passengers, plus additional operational equipment, and this type was designated the Mi-1T.   The Mi-1U was a training variant with dual controls.

After the initial needs of the armed forces had been met, accounting for the production of several hundred Mi-1s,

(Above right) A military Mi-1 equipped with 33 Imp gal (150 l) auxiliary fuel tanks, and (immediately right) an Mi-1 belonging to the DOSAAF organization which competed in the 2nd World Helicopter Championships held in the UK in July 1973. The Mi-1, particularly in its dual-control Mi-1U version, is widely employed in the training role in the Soviet Union

various civil rôles were developed for the helicopter, and Aeroflot began operating this type for mail-carrying, ambulance, whale-spotting, taxi and agricultural duties. With suitable equipment for various of these roles, and especially the agricultural one, a version designated Mi-1NKh was produced (NKh=*Narodnoye-khozyaistvenny*, or National Economy), and a more refined version for passenger carrying appeared in Aeroflot service in 1960 as the *Moskvich*, its special features including an all-metal rotor, sound-proofing for the cabin and night-flying instrumentation.

During 1956, an externally-similar variant with a four-blade (instead of three-blade) main rotor and improved weights and performance (sometimes erroneously referred to as the Mi-3) was evaluated. A radio compass was fitted and a small fairing under the tail housed new equipment. For ambulance use it carried an external, fully-enclosed pannier on each side of the fuselage; alternatively, insecticide hoppers, freight containers or fuel could be carried in the same position. In the event, no production of this version was undertaken.

Examples of the Mi-1 were exported to various countries having military or commercial links with the USSR, including Poland, Czechoslovakia, Rumania, Bulgaria, East Germany, China, Egypt, India, Cuba and Indonesia. A second production source was established in Poland in 1954, at the WSK-Swidnik factory, and production continued for some years after the Mi-1 had been superseded in the Soviet Union by the larger Mi-4. The basic Mi-1 entered production in Poland as the SM-1, the first examples being delivered from Swidnik in 1956, and several further variants were then developed. These comprised the SM-1S ambulance, with side panniers as developed for the 'Mi-3'; the SM-1W, with improvements similar to those introduced on the Moskvich, and the SM-1Z version with dusting or spraying equipment.

All Polish versions had the locally-produced Lit-3 engine, this being the AI-26V built under licence. Much of the Polish production was for export, to countries in the Soviet sphere of influence and elsewhere, including Finland, Brazil

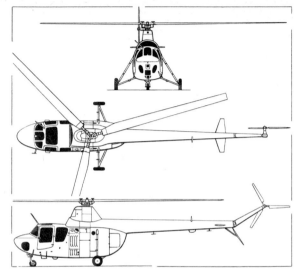

and Indonesia. The SM-1 was also the basis for development by WSK of a larger helicopter, the SM-2, with a longer front fuselage accommodating five persons.

The following specification refers to the SM-1W:

Power Plant: *One 575 h.p. Ivchenko AI-26V seven-cylinder radial engine.* ***Performance:*** *Max speed, 105 mph (170 km/h) at 6,560 ft (2 000 m); initial inclined climb rate, 886 ft/ min (4.5 m/sec); ceiling 9,840 ft (3 000 m); range, 360 mls (580 km).* ***Weights:*** *Empty, 4,142 lb (1 880 kg); loaded, 5,300 lb (2 404 kg).* ***Dimensions:*** *Rotor diameter, 46 ft 11 in (14,35 m); fuselage length, 39 ft 4¾ in (12,10 m); height, 10 ft 10 in (3,3 m).*

MIL MI-2 (HOPLITE)

To improve the performance of the Mi-1 helicopter, the Mil design bureau evolved a turbine-engined version in the late 'fifties, in parallel with a similar adaptation of the larger Mi-4. These turbine-engined versions appeared in 1961 as, respectively the Mi-2 and the Mi-8. In the case of the Mi-2, the Mi-1's three-bladed rotor and transmission system were retained, with two small Isotov turboshaft engines mounted above the cabin of a redesigned and enlarged fuselage.

Mi-2 prototypes were built in the Soviet Union and were used to complete certification by the end of 1963. As Soviet production facilities were then fully occupied with the Mi-8 and larger Mil helicopters, an agreement was concluded with the WSK-Swidnik works in Poland in January 1964 giving the latter exclusive production rights and permission to undertake further technical development. The Polish designation SM-3 was allocated but is seldom used, the Mi-2 designation being preferred.

The basic Mi-2 is a general purpose transport helicopter having a convertible cabin for eight passengers or 1,545 lb

Built exclusively by the Polish WSK-Swidnik works, the Mi-2 (right) has been under continuous refinement in Poland for some 10 years, prototypes of a new version, the Mi-2M, being under test early in 1975. The Mi-2M embodies improvements to the airframe, engine installation and instrumentation. One version will carry 11 passengers

engines. **Performance:** *Max speed, 130 mph (210 km/h); max cruise, 124 mph (200 km/h); economical cruise, 118 mph (190 km/h); max endurance speed, 62 mph (100 km/h); initial climb rate, 885 ft/min (4,5 m/sec); service ceiling, 13,755 ft (4 200 m); hovering ceiling IGE, 6,550 ft (2 000 m); hovering ceiling OGE. 3,275 ft (1 000 m); range with max load, 105 mls (170 km); range with max fuel, 360 mls (580 km).* **Weights:** *Empty, 5,213 lb (2 365 kg); max payload, 1,763 lb (800 kg); max take-off, 7,826 lb (3 550 kg).* **Dimensions:** *Rotor diameter, 47 ft 6¾ in (14,50 m); fuselage length, 38 ft 10 in (11,86 m); height, 12 ft 3½ in (3,75 m).*

(700 kg) of freight.   There is also a passenger-only version, and a freight version with sling for external loads of up to 1,765 lb (800 kg).   These versions usually have only one pilot's seat in the cabin, but a dual control trainer, with two seats side by side, has been developed by WSK.   There are also three special-purpose versions: an ambulance carrying four stretchers and an attendant; an agricultural version with spraying or dusting equipment and a search and rescue model with an external winch to lift survivors.   The agricultural version carries hoppers each side of the fuselage and/or a spray bar; an external fuel tank can also be carried each side of the cabin.

The WSK-Delta factory at Swidnik is currently engaged in developing a new series of Mi-2 helicopter known as the Mi-2M, this being under test in prototype form at the beginning of 1975.   Incorporating a revised fuselage capable of accommodating 11 passengers, the Mi-2M has rotor blades of plastics construction and a skid landing gear.

Power Plant: *Two 437 s.h.p. Isotov GTD-350 turboshaft*

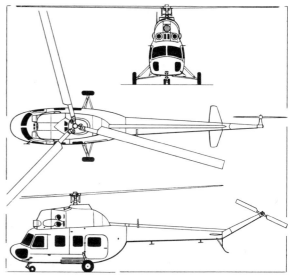

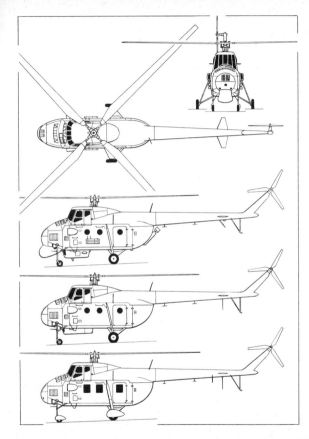

MIL MI-4 (HOUND)

The second Mil-designed helicopter to reach major production status, the Mi-4 has been built in larger quantities than any other Soviet helicopter to date, and continues in service in large numbers in various parts of the world although gradually being superseded by turbine-engined types.

The Mi-4, which serves with all the Warsaw Pact countries and has been widely exported, is seen below disembarking assault troops. The upper three views (left) illustrate the ASW Mi-4, the lower views showing the standard Mi-4 and the civil Mi-4P

(Above) The commercial Mi-4P with rectangular cabin windows and lacking the ventral gondola featured by other Mi-4 variants

common with its western counterpart, the Mi-4 was adapted for many different purposes, its roles falling into three broad categories—military, commercial passenger carrying and agricultural.

Publicly revealed in August 1953, the Mi-4 had entered production in 1952, with military requirements taking up all the output for the first few years. The basic military version had a crew of two pilots and provision for an observer in a gondola under the front fuselage. With the ASh-82V radial engine in the extreme nose, the main cabin was completely unobstructed, and could accommodate up to 14 equipped troops, 3,525-lb (1 600-kg) of freight or small vehicles, loaded through rear clam-shell doors. In this form, the Mi-4 was delivered in large quantities to serve with the various components of the V-VS, and in due course a close-support variant was developed with a single gun located in the front of the gondola and air-to-surface rockets pylon-mounted on each side of the fuselage.

The Mi-4 also entered service with the Soviet Naval Air Force, the AV-MF, for anti-submarine duties, in which role it carried a search radar under the gondola (ahead of the gondola), sonobuoys on the sides of the fuselage and a dipping sonar stowed behind the fuselage pod. Basic military

With the same overall configuration as the Mi-1, the Mi-4 represented a natural progression in size, and was comparable in most respects to the Sikorsky S-55 family. In

(Left) The anti-submarine warfare version of the Mi-4 was used extensively by the AV-MF but has now been largely supplanted by Ka-25 (see pages 154–6). The photograph shows sonobuoys on the starboard fuselage side, the search radar under the nose and dipping sonar behind the fuselage pod

Although progressively supplanted by the turbine-powered Mi-8 in recent years, the Mi-4 (seen above in Czechoslovak service) is still widely used

models were exported to virtually all the countries of the East European Bloc and to many other nations, including Afghanistan, Algeria, Cambodia, China, Cuba, Egypt, Finland, India, Indonesia, Iraq, North Korea, Mali, Mongolia, North Vietnam, Syria, the Yemen and Yugoslavia.

For freight carrying and general utility duties, a 'civil' version of the basic military Mi-4 was produced for Aeroflot, and this was followed by a more refined passenger-carrying version, the Mi-4P (*Passazhirskii*), which did not have the under-fuselage gondola, and had square instead of circular windows. Entering regular service with Aeroflot in November 1958, the Mi-4P carried up to 11 passengers, or, as an ambulance, eight stretchers and a medical attendant. The special agricultural version was designated Mi-4S, and had a container in the main cabin with a capacity of 2,200 lb (1 000 kg) of solid insecticide or 352 Imp gal (1 600 l) of liquid, plus suitable distribution equipment for either type of chemical. Civil versions went into service in most of the East European countries and elsewhere, although they were less widely used than the military models.

The following specification applies to the standard Mi-4:

Power Plant: *One 1,700 h.p. ASh-82V eighteen-cylinder radial engine.* **Performance:** *Max speed, 130 mph (210 km/h) at 4,920 ft (1 500 m); economical cruising speed, 99 mph (160 km/h); service ceiling, 18,000 ft (5 500 m); range with 11 passengers, 155 mls (250 km); max range, 370 mls (595 km).* **Weights:** *Empty, 11,650 lb (5 268 kg); max payload, 3,835 lb (1 740 kg); max take-off, 17,200 lb (7 800 kg).* **Dimensions:** *Rotor diameter, 68 ft 11 in (21,0 m); fuselage length, 55 ft 1 in (16,80 m); height, 17 ft 0 in (5,18 m).*

MIL MI-6 (HOOK)

Like the Mi-12 that was to follow it a decade later, the Mil

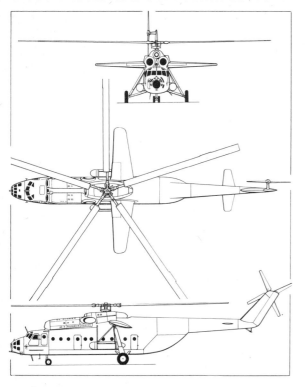

Mi-6 was, at the time of its appearance, the world's largest helicopter. Its development was undertaken in the first instance to meet military requirements, for a helicopter to complement the Antonov An-12 transport with the ability to ferry to the front line many items of equipment that could be transported in that aircraft. Although the cross section of the Mi-6 fuselage is a little less than that of the An-12, any outsize item can be lifted externally and two sorties by an Mi-6 can move the entire payload of an An-12. Rear loading doors and ramps facilitate the handling of vehicles and other items of freight in the helicopter, in conjunction with a built-in electric winch. Tip-up seats are fitted along each side of the cabin, and can be supplemented by seats down the centre, bringing trooping capacity to 65.

As an ambulance, the Mi-6 can carry 41 stretchers plus two attendants. A trolley-mounted APU is usually carried to provide engine starting without external aid, and full all-weather instrumentation is fitted. The Mi-6 can carry tactical SSMs, a group of three helicopters being able to handle two such missiles plus the necessary support equipment. A few examples have been armed with a 23-mm cannon in the nose for suppressive fire when landing close to enemy ground forces, and external fuel tanks are often carried to supplement the internal fuel load.

The Mi-6 was first revealed in the late summer of 1957, the helicopter having made its first flight earlier in that year. Five or six prototypes were used for flight development and some of these were flown initially without the wings that serve to off-load the rotor; wheel spats were also fitted at first. A number of record-breaking flights were made in 1957, 1959 and 1962, including a payload of 44,350 lb (20 117 kg) lifted to a height of 8,983 ft (2 738 m), and a speed of 186·64 mph (300,4 km/h) over a 1 000-km (620-ml) closed circuit.

Following the introduction of the Mi-6 into service with the V-VS, this type was also adopted by Aeroflot for the transportation of heavy loads in connection with various construction activities, including sections of oil pipe lines,

(Right) A Mil Mi-6 operated by Aeroflot by which it is used for forest fire-fighting (with auxiliary wings removed) and the transportation of heavy loads in connection with various construction activities. A version with airline-style interior and rectangular cabin windows, the Mi-6P, was developed

oil drilling rig assemblies, construction camp equipment and fire-fighting equipment and personnel. One version was also demonstrated as a water-bomber, with the ability to dump the entire load through a central hatch in the floor, or to spray it from nozzles. Production of the Mi-6 is reported to have exceeded 500, with the majority going into military service; none has been exported for commercial use but considerable quantities were supplied to the air forces of Egypt, Bulgaria and North Vietnam, and six to the Indonesian Air Force (which no longer uses them).

Power Plant: *Two 5,500 s.h.p. Soloviev D-25V turboshaft engines.* **Performance:** *Max speed, 186 mph (300 km/h); max cruise, 155 mph (250 km/h); operating ceiling, 14,750 ft (4 500 m); range with 13,228-lb (6 000-kg) internal payload, 404 mls (650 km); range with external tanks and 9,480-lb (4 300 kg) payload, 652 mls (1 050 km); max ferry range, 900 mls (1 450 km).* **Weights:** *Empty, 60,055 lb (27 240 kg); max internal payload, 26,450 lb (12 000 kg); max slung payload, 19,840 lb (9 000 kg); max take-off weight (vertical), 93,700 lb (42 500 kg); max take-off weight with slung load, 82,675 lb (37 500 kg); max internal fuel load, 13,920 lb (6 315 kg); max external*

The Mi-6 serves in some numbers with Aeroflot and helicopters of this type in the airline's inventory form a V-VS reserve

fuel load, 7,695 lb (3 490 kg). **Dimensions:** *Rotor diameter, 114 ft 10 in (35,00 m); fuselage length, 108 ft 10½ in (33,18 m); height, 32 ft 4 in (9,86 m); wing span, 50 ft 2 in (15,30 m).*

MIL MI-8 (HIP) AND MI-14

More than 1,000 examples of the Mil Mi-8 helicopter had been built by the end of 1973, of which 300 had been exported according to Soviet sources. Designed to supersede the Mi-4, the Mi-8, in common with other Soviet helicopters, has dual military and civil functions and its size makes it suitable for operation in a wide variety of roles. These range, in the civil version as operated by Aeroflot, from passenger transportation to air ambulance, air survey, ice reconnaissance and patrols (in the Arctic and Antarctic) and air-sea rescue operations. Military duties include troop and supply transport, in some cases carrying armament.

The Mi-8 (under its original V-8 designation) first appeared in public in 1961, the prototype then being powered

Currently the most widely-used of Soviet helicopters, the Mi-8 is seen (top left) in de luxe commercial transport form with rectangular cabin windows (illustrated with wheel spats at foot of opposite page) and (immediately left) in standard military transport form serving with the Czechoslovak air arm. The Mi-8 serves in a wide variety of roles and armed assault transport versions with pylon-mounted missiles and a mine-sweeping variant serve in numbers

by a single 2,700 s.h.p. Soloviev turboshaft engine driving a four-blade rotor derived from that used by the Mi-4. A second prototype, first flown on 17 September 1962, was powered by two 1,400 s.h.p. Isotov TV2 engines, this being the production configuration, but the now-standard five-blade rotor and uprated TV2-117A engines were introduced at later stages in the production run.

The Mi-8 cabin provides an uninterrupted length of 17 ft 6 in (5,34 m) with a cross-section of 7 ft 7 in (2,34 m) wide by 5 ft 11 in (1,82 m) high, excluding the space available in rear clam-shell doors. In the standard passenger version, a folding airstair is incorporated in these rear doors, and 28–32 seats can be fitted, four abreast, respectively with and without wardrobe space. These seats can be quickly removed for freight carrying, but a specialized utility version is also available as the Mi-8T, this having a winch and pully block to facilitate loading of large freight items through the rear doors, cargo tie-down rings in the floor, an external cargo sling system and 12 tip-up seats along each cabin wall. Either version can be converted to carry 12 stretchers and an attendant. A *de luxe* model has also been built in small numbers and is known as the Mi-8 *Salon*, with 11 seats and special facilities in the cabin. This version operates at the lower gross weight of 22,930 lb (10 400 kg) and has a range of 236 mls (380 km).

Comprehensive all-weather instrumentation is fitted, with provision for the special requirements of Polar flying, and some examples have Doppler navigation equipment in the tail boom. An automatic stabilization system is linked to the external cargo sling in the Mi-8T, to compensate for CG shifts. During 1973, a floatplane version of the Mi-8 was also successfully test flown, as the V-14, and was expected to enter production as the Mi-14 following certification. Operating at the same gross weight as the Mi-8, it has a reduced payload due to the extra weight of the floats.

Civil versions of the Mi-8 have six rectangular windows in each side of the cabin, but military versions have smaller, circular windows. Basically similar to the Mi-8T, the mili-

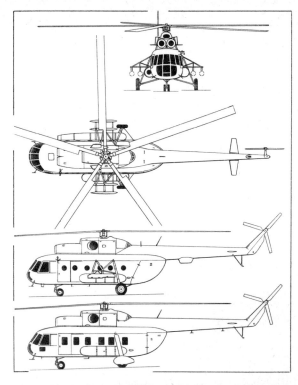

The upper three views (above) illustrate the standard V-VS assault transport Mi-8 with randome under tailboom and missile pod pylons. Bottom view shows de luxe Mi-8

tary version can carry small wheeled and tracked vehicles, equipped troops and miscellaneous supplies. Provision is made on later Mi-8s for rocket or gun pods or ASMs to be carried on racks strut-rigged from each side of the fuselage above the external fuel tanks. The standard installation has two racks each side, and this version of the Mi-8 was operational with the Egyptian Air Force during the Six-Day War, but there are also reports of versions operated by the Soviet Air Force with a total of 16 racks, eight each side in two rows of four, one above the other.

Many air forces have received Mi-8s, including those of Bulgaria, Czechoslovakia, Ethiopia, East Germany, Hungary, India, Iraq, Pakistan, Poland, Sudan and Syria.

Power Plant: Two 1,500 s.h.p. Isotov TV-2-117A turbo-shaft engines. **Performance:** Max speed, 137 mph (220 km/h) at max weight and 112 mph (180 km/h) with slung load; max cruise, 140 mph (225 km/h) at 24,470 lb (11 100 kg) gross weight; normal operating ceiling, 14,760 ft (4 500 m); hovering ceiling (IGE), 6,233 ft (1 900 m); hovering ceiling (OGE), 2,625 ft (800 m); range with 28 passengers ($\frac{1}{4}$-hr reserve), 232 mls (375 km); range with 8,820-lb (4 000 kg) payload, 62 mls (100 km); ferry range, 745 mls (1 200 km). **Weights:** Empty (passenger version), 16,007 lb (7 261 kg); max payload, 8,820 lb (4 000 kg) internal or 6,614 lb (3 000 kg) external; max take-off weight, 26,455 lb (12 000 kg). **Dimensions:** Rotor diameter, 69 ft 10$\frac{1}{4}$ in (21,29 m); fuselage length, 60 ft 0$\frac{3}{4}$ in (18,31 m); height, 18 ft 6$\frac{1}{2}$ in (5,65 m).

MIL MI-10 (HARKE)

This large helicopter is a variant of the Mi-6 previously described, being a special purpose adaptation to carry outsize loads beneath, rather than in, the fuselage. First flown early in 1960, it has the same power plant/transmission/rotor system as the Mi-6 but the fuselage is 'slenderized', no wings are fitted and the undercarriage is modified so that items up to about 19 ft (5,79 m) in width can be carried. The overall height is unchanged, but the reduction in fuselage depth gives a ground clearance of over 12 ft (3,65 m).

Several types of load and loading technique have been demonstrated by Mi-10s, which often have a pre-loaded platform slung beneath the fuselage and between the undercarriage legs. Alternatively, the helicopter can taxi into position over a load such as a prefabricated house, and Mi-10s have also been used to carry complete wing assemblies of the Tu-144 between factories. Originally, a retractable 'dustbin' was located in the nose to allow an observer to watch the slung load during lift-off and touchdown, but a closed-circuit TV system was subsequently introduced. The Mi-10 can carry up to 28 passengers in tip-up seats in the fuselage, or additional freight. Examples are in service both with Aeroflot and with the Soviet armed forces, and one example was exported to Petroleum

A standard Mi-10 (top right) with a 28-seat bus on the cargo platform (centre right) and the special short-legged Mi-10 (immediately right) which was used to establish a series of records with payload in May 1965

193

Helicopters in the United States.

Power Plant: *Two 5,500 s.h.p. Soloviev D-25V turboshaft engines.* ***Performance:*** *Max speed, 124 mph (200 km/h); cruising speed, 112 mph (180 km/h); max operating* ceiling, 9,850 ft (3 000 m); range with payload of 26,455 lb (12 000 kg) on platform, 155 mls (250 km). ***Weights:*** *Empty, 60,185 lb (27 300 kg); max payload, 33,070 lb (15 000 kg); max internal fuel load, 13,980 lb (6 340 kg); max external fuel load, 4,230 lb (1 920 kg); max take-off weight, 96,340 lb (43 700 kg).* ***Dimensions:*** *Rotor diameter, 114 ft 10 in (35,00 m); fuselage length, 107 ft 9¾ in (32,86 m); height, 32 ft 2 in (9,80 m).*

MIL MI-10K

A further derivation of the Mi-6/Mi-10 formula, the Mi-10K, first publicly displayed in March 1966, is, like the Mi-10, a flying crane, but adapted to carry different types of external load. The major change concerns the undercarriage, which is shorter and simpler, with a significant saving in airframe weight and improvement in payload. Consequently, the Mi-10K is not able to carry very large loads on a platform or close-coupled under the fuselage, as does the Mi-10. Instead, it is a true 'flying crane', its load being slung beneath the fuselage from the winch-controlled cable.

To permit precise positioning of such slung loads without

(Above left) The Mi-10 employs an essentially similar fuselage to that of the Mi-10K (below and opposite page, top left)

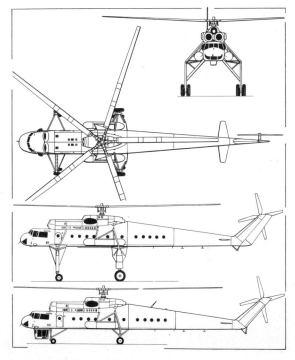

kg); max fuel load, 19,114 lb (8 670 kg); max take-off weight, with slung cargo, 83,776 lb (38 000 kg). **Dimensions:** Rotor diameter, 114 ft 10 in (35,00 m); fuselage length, 107 ft 9¾ in (32,86 m); height, 25 ft 7 in (7,80 m).

aid from the ground, the Mi-10K also is provided with a rearwards-facing control gondola beneath the nose, from which a pilot can control the helicopter through the whole flying range while watching the unloading (or loading) operation. Like the Mi-10, the Mi-10K can carry up to 28 passengers in the fuselage, or small-size cargo items, and an APU is carried to give independence from external supplies.

Among several record flights made by Mi-10K, was a flight to 23,461 ft (7 151 m) with a 11,023-lb (5 000 kg) payload, and a climb to 9,318 ft (2 840 m) with a payload of 55,347 lb (25 105 kg). A small number of Mi-10Ks is used by Aeroflot on special tasks but the type is not known to be in military service. A version with 6,500 s.h.p. D-25VF engine is reported to be under development, in which variant a payload of 30,865 lb (14 000 kg) is expected to be achieved.

Power Plant: *Two 5,500 s.h.p. Soloviev D-25V turboshaft engines.* **Performance:** *Max cruising speed, 155 mph (250 km/h); cruising speed with slung load, 125 mph (200 km/h); max operating ceiling, 9,850 ft (3 000 m); max ferry range, 484 mls (795 km).* **Weights:** *Empty, 54,410 lb (24 680 kg); max slung load, 24,250 lb (11 000*

MIL MI-12 (HOMER)

With the Mi-12, first flown in 1968, the Soviet Union maintained its world lead in the construction of outsize helicopters, this rotorcraft having the capability of lifting more than the fully-loaded weight of the largest helicopter

built to date outside the USSR. This capability was demonstrated early in the flight testing of the prototype Mi-12, when a load of 68,410 lb (31 030 kg) was lifted to a height of 9,682 ft (2 951 m), an average rate of climb of 600 ft/min (3,0 m/sec) being achieved on the way. Some six months later, in August 1969, a load of 88,636 lb (40 204,5 kg) was lifted to a height of 7,398 ft (2 255 m), again setting new world records.

Design of the Mi-12 (usually referred to as the V-12 in the Soviet Union) was initiated in 1965, primarily to meet a military requirement for a transport helicopter compatible with the Antonov An-22, and capable of transferring to the battlefield front line any loads carried into rear airfields by the latter aircraft. This requirement could only be met by a twin-rotor helicopter if the size of the rotors was to be kept within practical limits, and a side-by-side rotor arrangement was adopted by the Mil design bureau, rather than the more obvious tandem layout, so that the complete power plant/transmission/rotor system of the Mi-6/Mi-10 helicopter could be used with little or no modification, one such

(Left and opposite page) One of the Mil Mi-12 prototypes that have been under test since 1968. Designed as a transport helicopter compatible with the An-22, the Mi-12 is expected to be used by both the V-VS and Aeroflot but production status was uncertain at the beginning of 1975. The Mi-12 has established a number of international records

package being mounted at each extremity of a fixed, inversely-tapered wing.

The Mi-12 has a large, completely enclosed fuselage, with a rear loading ramp giving access to the unobstructed cargo hold. In the standard arrangement, about 50 fold-up seats are provided along the cabin sides for troops or loaders. An APU is installed for independent engine starting and an automatic stabilization system is fitted as standard.

Testing of the Mi-12 is reported to have suffered a setback in 1969 when the prototype crashed, but two more prototypes were flying by 1971, and production of a somewhat refined model was reported to be under way in 1974 to meet both military and Aeroflot requirements. Commercial uses will include support of oil and natural gas production within the Soviet Union and ferrying heavy loads in the more remote areas of the USSR.

Power Plant: *Four 6,500 s.h.p. Soloviev D-25VF turboshafts.* ***Performance:*** *Max speed, 161 mph (260 km/h); max cruising speed, 150 mph (240 km/h); service ceiling, 11,500 ft (3 500 m); range with 78,000-lb (35 400-kg) payload, 310 mls (500 km).* ***Weights:*** *Payload, 55,000 lb (25 000 kg) for VTOL, 66,000 lb (30 000 kg) or more for STOL operation; max take-off weight, 231,500 lb (105 000 kg).* ***Dimensions:*** *Main rotor diameter, 114 ft 10 in (35,00 m) each; span over rotor tips, 219 ft 10 in (67,00 m); length, 121 ft 4½ in (37,00 m); height, 41 ft 0 in (12,50 m).*

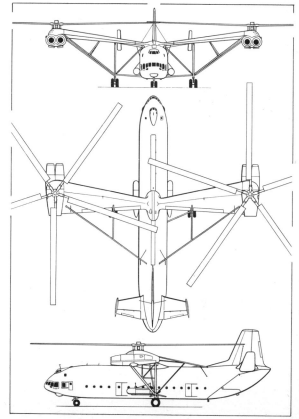

(Left and top right) The Hind–A version of the Mi-24 gunship and assault transport helicopter and (bottom right) the Hind–B with vertical extensions at the tips of the auxiliary wings. The lower three views of the general arrangement drawing on the opposite page depict the Hind–A, the upper head-on view illustrating the Hind–B

MIL MI-24 (HIND)

The first combined gunship and assault transport helicopter to enter service with the V-VS, the Mi-24 first appeared on the strength of the Group of Soviet Forces in Germany early in 1973, and is now employed in considerable numbers. Utilizing similar power plant, gearboxes, drive shafts and controls to those of the Mi-8 (see pages 190–2), the Mi-24 has appeared in two versions which differ in the type of auxiliary wings fitted. One version (*Hind-A*) has three weapons stations on each auxiliary wing, the two inboard stations each carrying a UV-32-57 pod containing 32 S-5 55-mm rockets and the third station, taking the form of a vertical extension of the wingtip, having a double carrier for two *Swatter* wire-guided anti-tank missiles. The other version (*Hind-B*) does not have the vertical extensions at the tips of the auxiliary wings, each of which has only two stations for rocket pods or other ordnance. The auxiliary wings of both versions are set at a substantial angle of incidence to alleviate wing/rotor interaction problems and, as

well as providing ordnance load-carrying stations, offload the rotor in forward flight. The wings of the *Swatter*-carrying variant have a pronounced anhedral angle and the tail rotor pylon of both versions is canted to starboard on the longitudinal axis.

Both versions of the Mi-24 have a 12,7-mm UBK machine gun in the extreme nose, armour protection for the flight crew and accommodation for 8–10 assault troops with a large door aft of the flight deck on each side enabling them to exit rapidly.

The figures quoted in the following specification are estimated:

Power Plant: *Two 1,500 s.h.p. Isotov TV-2-117A turboshafts.* ***Performance:*** *Max speed, 160 mph (257 km/h); max cruise, 140 mph (225 km/h); hovering ceiling (in ground effect), 6,000 ft (1 830 m), (out of ground effect), 1,600 ft (790 m); normal range, 300 mls (480 km).* ***Weights:*** *Normal loaded, 25,000 lb (11 340 kg).* ***Dimensions:*** *Rotor diam, 60 ft 0 in (18,30 m); fuselage length, 55 ft 0 in (16.76 m); height, 20 ft 6 in (6,25 m).*

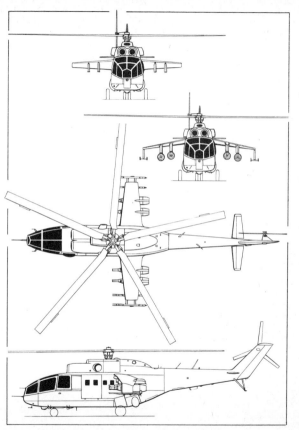

MYASISHCHEV M-4 (BISON)

(Above and below) The initial maritime M-4 (Bison—B)

Flown in prototype form for the first time in 1953 and displayed publicly for the first time over Moscow in May 1954, the M-4 was the Soviet Union's first long-range strategic jet bomber and a contemporary of the Boeing B-52 Stratofortress. Designed by a team headed by Chief Designer (later General Designer) Vladimir M Myasischev and known unofficially as the *Molot* (Hammer) when it first entered service with the strategic component of the V-VS, the ADD, in 1955—56, the M-4 in its initial service form (*Bison-A*) was powered by four Mikulin AM-3M turbojets each rated at 19,180 lb (8 700 kg) buried in the wing roots and fed via canted intakes. It was allegedly capable of carrying a 10,000-lb (4 500-kg) load of nuclear or conventional free-fall bombs at a speed of 520 mph (835 km/h) at 39,370—42,650 ft (12 000—13 000 m) over a tactical radius of 3,500 miles (5 630 km) on internal fuel. This fell

(Below) The definitive production version of the M-4 (Bison-C) switched to Soloviev turbofans and featured revised nose design with a centrally-mounted refuelling probe and optically-flat transparent panels

somewhat short of the 4,500-mile (7 240 km) radius needed to cover Los Angeles, Chicago and New York at a time when the ADD had still to develop a flight refuelling capability, limiting production of the M-4. Nevertheless, the development of the M-4 was continued but by the early 'sixties, when a version of the bomber entered service with appreciably more powerful and more economical D-15 turbofans and by which time flight refuelling tanker support was available, the ADD was already diminishing in importance with the growth of the Strategic Rocket Forces, and the M-4 had since served primarily in the long-range maritime reconnaissance role with the AV-MF.

The initial model (*Bison-A*) had a wing span of 165 ft $7\frac{3}{8}$ in (50,48 m) and an overall length of 154 ft $10\frac{1}{4}$ in (47,20 m), maximum take-off weight being 363,760 lb (165 000 kg). A crew of six was carried and defensive armament comprised two 23-mm NR-23 cannon in each of four remotely-controlled gun barbettes (two above and two beneath the fuselage fore and aft of the wing). Adaptation for the maritime role (*Bison-B*) in the early 'sixties included the replacement of the hemispherical glazed nose by a radome, the provision of a large refuelling probe superimposed above the nose, the deletion of the aft upper and lower cannon barbettes, the bulging of the forward portion of the centre weapons bay doors and the introduction of numerous bulges and antennae for specialized electronic equipment. All M-4s converted for the maritime role can serve as refuelling tankers with fuel tanks occupying the weapons bays, the bulged portion of the centre weapons bay doors enclosing the refuelling drogue cable drum.

The definitive D-15-powered version (*Bison-C*) is generally similar to the preceding version but has a redesigned fuselage nose of improved form with a centrally-mounted refuelling probe and incorporating an observation station with optically-flat transparent panels aft of the nose

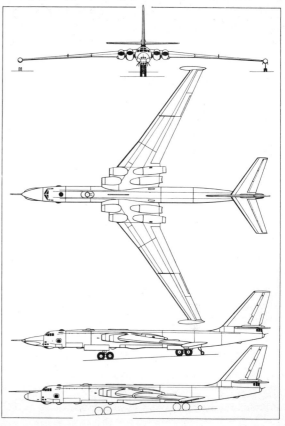

The upper three views (right) depict the D-15-powered M-4 (Bison-C), the lower sideview illustrating the Bison-B

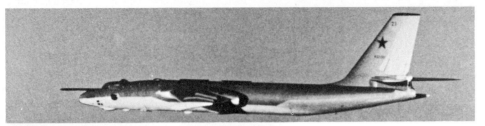

The Bison—B maritime version of the M-4 (left and below left) has a secondary tanker role, a bulged portion of the centre weapons bay doors enclosing the refuelling drogue cable drum, tanks occupying the weapons bays

search radar housing. Overall wing span has been marginally increased as a result of the slightly broader engine-housing centre section; the forward upper and lower twin-cannon barbettes and the twin-cannon tail position are retained, and current AV-MF M-4s are equipped with X-band *Puff Ball* search radar which is able to control surface-to-surface missile launches, the PPI display showing target location and SSM launch site and the presentation being data-linked to the missile site. Other equipment includes four-PRF (Pulse Repetition Frequency) range J-band *Short Horn* circular and sector scan bombing and navigation radar, and *Bee Hind* I-band tail warning radar which searches with a four-degree wide beam for tail threats through a 90-degree solid angle centred at the aircraft fuselage centreline.

The figures quoted in the following specification for the D-15-powered M-4 (*Bison-C*) maritime reconnaissance/tanker aircraft are estimated:

Power Plant: *Four 28,660 lb (13 000 kg) Soloviev D-15 turbofans.* **Performance:** *Max speed, 625 mph (1 060 km/h) or M=0·85 at 9,840 ft (3 000 m), 594 mph (955 km/h) or M=0·9 at 39,370 ft (12 000 m); typical range cruise, 520 mph (835 km/h) or M=0·78 at 39,370 ft (12 000 m); ceiling, 51,180 ft (15 600 m); max endurance, 15 hr.* **Weights:** *Max take-off, 363,760 lb (165 000 kg).* **Dimensions:** *Span, 170 ft 0 in (51,82 m); length, 162 ft 0 in (49,38 m).*

SUKHOI SU-7 (FITTER-A)

Currently the standard ground attack fighter of the FA component of the V-VS and included in the first-line inventories of the Czechoslovak, East German, Egyptian, Hungarian, Indian, Iraqi, Polish and Syrian air arms, the Su-7 (*Fitter-A*) has been in continuous production for 16 years, several thousand having been manufactured. A large aeroplane powered by a massive Lyulka turbojet, the Su-7 first appeared as an aerodynamic prototype over Tushino in June 1956, and since its service introduction by the V-VS in 1959 has been produced in progressively improved versions.

Initially, the Su-7 possessed some commonality with the Su-11 (*Fishpot-B*) all-weather interceptor, employing an essentially similar fuselage and tail assembly but discarding the 57 deg delta wing in favour of a 62 deg (leading edge) swept wing to enable higher lift coefficients to be achieved at subsonic speeds without buffeting, although the highly swept wing undoubtedly proved something of an embarrassment in catering for adequate external stores flexibi-

lity. Cannon armament comprised two 30-mm NR-30 weapons in the wing roots with 70 rpg and four stores pylons were provided, two side-by-side beneath the fuselage and one beneath each wing, immediately outboard of the main-wheel wells. These four pylons were each capable of

The Su-7BMK (above right and immediately right) is currently the standard ground attack fighter of the V-VS FA, most Warsaw Pact air forces and the air forces of India, Egypt, Iraq and Syria. This type suffers rather high drag rise, particularly in manoeuvring flight, an overly modest radius of action and rather poor ordnance capability

203

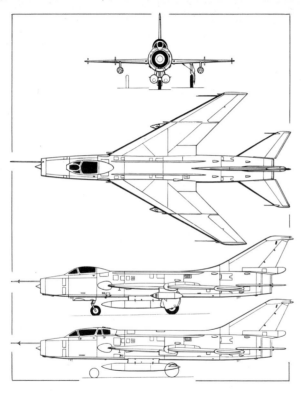

The upper three views of the general arrangement drawing above depict the Su-7BMK, the lower sideview illustrating the Su-7U

lifting a 132 Imp gal (600 l) drop tank to supplement the (approx) 910 Imp gal (4 140 l) max internal fuel capacity, alternative loads capable of being lifted by each pylon being a 551-lb (250-kg) or 1,102-lb (500-kg) bomb, a 240-mm S-24 rocket or a UV-16-57 pod housing 16 55-mm S-5 rockets.

There is some evidence to suggest that the initial production model assigned to the FA was officially designated Su-7B, progressive improvement resulting in the Su-7BM, this featuring an uprated Lyulka AL-7F turbojet and various modifications, including a changed parabrake arrangement, the original single-chute housing in the rear fuselage being replaced by a clamshell-type fairing at the base of the vertical tail surfaces deploying twin ribbon-type chutes. Improved short-field capability, including RATOG attachment points, a low-pressure nosewheel accompanied by bulged nose-wheel doors and revised mainwheel flaps, resulted in the Su-7BMK, 150 examples of this model being supplied to the Indian Air Force, the first 100 being delivered in 1968 with the remaining 50 following late in 1971. The Su-7BMK saw extensive operational use with the IAF during the Indo—Pakistan conflict of 8–17 December 1971, during which it revealed a number of shortcomings, including an overly modest radius of action with a worthwhile ordnance load and vulnerability to groundfire. The AL-7F engine of the Su-7BMK has a specific fuel consumption in maximum dry thrust at low altitude of 0·817 lb/lb thrust/hour at which maximum speed is of the order of 540 mph (870 km/h). Drag rise is high, particularly when manoeuvring and the extra power derived from the afterburner increases the SFC to 2·2 lb/lb thrust/hour at sea level, endurance with full reheat on internal fuel thus being barely more than eight minutes. Conversely, the IAF has commented favourably on the handling characteristics, reliability, and ease and simplicity of servicing the Su-7BMK under operational conditions.

Tail warning radar is reportedly being fitted retroactively to Su-7s, and two additional wing pylons are being fitted to some aircraft (notably those serving with the Polish air arm),

The Su-7BMK has good short-field capability and may be equipped with RATOG (with which it is seen taking-off below right) and has twin ribbon-type braking chutes and low-pressure tyres. The Su-7BMK is normally equipped with four external stores pylons but some aircraft have two additional pylons outboard

these being mounted outboard of the main wing fences and usually carrying a UV-16-57 rocket pod.

A tandem two-seat transitional training version, the Su-7U (*Moujik*), has the second cockpit for the instructor inserted aft of the standard cockpit fairing into a prominent dorsal spine extending to the base of the tail fin. The two occupants have separate aft-hinging canopies (the canopy of the single-seater slides aft) and the second ejector seat is raised slightly to afford the instructor a measure of forward view. The second seat has been inserted at some cost to internal fuel capacity and this has reportedly been compensated for in part by the use for tankage of part of the capacity of the dorsal spine as a saddle tank.

The following specification relates to the standard single-seat Su-7BMK:

Power Plant: *One 14,200 lb (6 440 kg) dry and 22,046 lb (10 000 kg) reheat Lyulka AL-7F-1 turbojet.* **Performance:** *Max speed (clean), 1,188 mph (1 910 km/h) or M=1·8 at 39,370 ft (12 000 m), high-drag configuration: e.g., side-by-side drop tanks on fuselage stations and two rocket pods), 790 mph (1 270 km/h) or M=1·2,*

(clean with full reheat), 720 mph (1 160 km/h) or M=0·95 at 1,000 ft (305 m), (clean with max dry thrust), 540 mph (870 km/h) or M=0·72 at 1,000 ft (305 m); initial climb, 30,000 ft/min (152,4 m/sec); service ceiling, 49,200 ft (15 000 m); tactical radius (hi-lo-hi), 285 mls (460 km). **Weights:** *Empty, 19,000 lb (8 620 kg); normal loaded, 26,455 lb (12 000 kg); max take-off, 29,600 lb (13 425 kg).* **Dimensions:** *Span, 29 ft 3½ in (8,93 m); length (including probe), 57 ft 0 in (17,37 m); height, 15 ft 5 in (4,70 m).*

The Su-11 all-weather interceptors illustrated immediately left and below left are of the early production version (Fishpot—B) equipped with S-band R1L (Spin Scan) search and track radar and normally carrying a quartette of first-generation AA-3 Alkali radar-guided missiles. This model has now been replaced in IAP-VO Strany formations by the more advanced version known as Fishpot—C (opposite)

SUKHOI SU-11 (FISHPOT-C)

The first single-seat all-weather interceptor to enter service with the IAP-VO *Strany* was a clean tailed-delta evolved by the Sukhoi bureau to complement the Artem Mikoyan bureau's smaller and lighter clear weather fighter (MiG-21) which was being developed contemporaneously. Aerodynamic prototypes of the Sukhoi fighter, which was to enter service as the Su-11, were demonstrated over Tushino during the 1956 Aviation Day display. The initial production model (*Fishpot-B*), which attained service with the IAP-VO *Strany* in 1961, was equipped with S-band R1L (*Spin Scan*) search and track radar with a rotating scan and an effective range of about 12 miles (19 km) and carried a quartette of first-generation AA-3 *Alkali* radar-guided AAMs on pylons projecting forward from the wing leading edges outboard of the main undercarriage wells.

During the mid 'sixties, the availability of the appreciably more effective and larger AA-6 *Anab* AAM with alternative IR-homing and semi-active radar homing guidance systems resulted in the application of this missile to the Su-11. Simultaneously, the small variable centrebody in the engine air intake was replaced by an appreciably larger cone and the lip diameter of the air intake increased, these changes signifying the introduction of an upgraded version of the *Spin Scan* radar and an uprated Lyulka AL-7F engine (*Fishpot-C*), this entering service with the IAP-VO *Strany* in 1966–67 and

(Left and above) The Sukhoi Su-11 (Fishpot–C) interceptor

subsequently being delivered in substantial quantities until finally supplanted in production by the Su-15. A tandem two-seat version for transitioning pilots and retaining the smaller engine air intake is currently in service and has been assigned the ASCC reporting name *Maiden*. The cockpit arrangement of this aircraft is essentially similar to that of the Su-7U (*Moujik*).

The figures quoted in the following specification are estimated and relate to the standard Su-11 (*Fishpot-C*) single-seat all-weather interceptor:

Power Plant: *One 14,200 lb (6 440 kg) dry and 22,046 lb (10 000 kg) reheat Lyulka AL-7F-1 turbojet.* **Performance:** *Max speed (clean), 720 mph or M=0·95 at 1,000 ft (305 m), 1,190 mph (1 915 km/h) or M=1·8 at 39,370 ft (12 000 m), (high-drag configuration: e.g., side-by-side drop tanks on fuselage stations and two Anab AAMs), 790 mph (1 270 km/h) or M=1·2; initial climb, 27,000 ft/min (137 m/sec); service ceiling, 55,000 ft (16 765 m).* **Weights:** *Empty, 20,000 lb (9 072 kg); normal loaded, 27,000 lb (12 247 kg); max take-off, 30,000 lb (13 608 kg).* **Dimensions:** *Span, 27 ft 0 in (8,23 m); length (including probe), 57 ft 0 in (17,37 m); height, 16 ft 0 in (4,88 m); wing area, 425 sq ft (39,48 m²).*

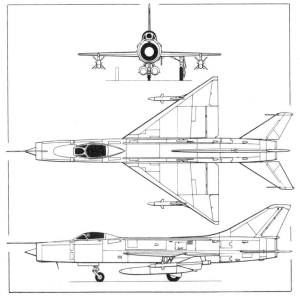

The Sukhoi Su-15 (above and below left) is probably now numerically the most important all-weather interceptor employed by the IAP-VO Strany. A successor to the Su-11 (see previous page), the Su-15 possesses an essentially similar delta wing

SUKHOI SU-15 (FLAGON)

Intended as a successor to the Su-11 (*Fishpot-C*) single-seat all-weather interceptor and possessing an essentially similar delta wing to that of its predecessor, the Su-15 was apparently flown in prototype form during 1964–65 and first entered service with the IAP-VO *Strany* in 1969, being, by mid-1974, numerically probably the most important all-

weather fighter in the inventory of that component of the V-VS.

The Su-15 (*Flagon-A*) has a mid-mounted wing swept 57 deg on the leading edge and incorporating a weapons pylon beneath each outer panel, this normally carrying an AA-6-2 advanced *Anab* AAM which is guided by *Skip Spin* X-band radar which has an effective range of some 25 miles (40 km). Side-by-side fuselage pylons normally carry two 132 Imp gal (600 l) drop tanks and some aircraft are apparently fitted with a 23-mm twin-barrel GSh-23 cannon forward of these pylons.

The Su-15 equips IAP-VO *Strany* elements responsible for the air defence of Moscow and other major Soviet centres, and during 1971 was deployed in small numbers to Egypt for the air defence of Cairo but was withdrawn during the following year. A tandem two-seat version for transitioning pilots (*Flagon-C*) is in service, and a STOL (Short-Take-Off-and-Landing) version (*Flagon-B*) was demonstrated

The Su-15 (Flagon–A), illustrated in its standard form by the general arrangement drawing (right), has also been developed in a STOL version (Flagon–B)—see pages 69–70—but the status of this version was uncertain at the time of closing for press

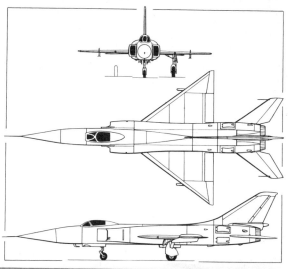

publicly at Domodedovo in July 1967 (see pages 69–70). The latter, which may have been purely a technology development aircraft, featured three lift jets mounted vertically in the centre fuselage and wings of extended span with compound sweep, this latter feature also being utilized by the *Flagon-D* and *-E* service versions.

The figures quoted in the specification, which refers to the standard fighter model (*Flagon-A*), are estimated:

Power Plant: *Two 17,195 lb (7 800 kg) dry and 24,700 lb (11 200 kg) reheat Lyulka AL-21F-3 turbojets.* **Performance:** *Max speed (clean), 1,650 mph (2 655 km/h), or M=2·5, (high drag configuration: e.g., side-by-side drop tanks on fuselage stations and AAMs on wing stations), 1,120 mph or M=1·7; tactical radius, 450 mls (725 km); range at subsonic cruise (with max external fuel), 1,500 mls (2 415 km).* **Weights:** *Normal take-off, 35,000 lb (15 876 kg).* **Dimensions:** *Span, 31 ft 3 in (9,50 m); length, 70 ft 6 in (21,50 m); height, 16 ft 6 in (5,00 m).*

The Su-15 (right) represented a major upgrading in the all-weather intercept capability of the IAP-VO Strany when phased into service during 1969–70. Armament normally comprises a pair of AA-6-2 advanced Anab AAMs plus a twin-barrel GSh-23 cannon

SUKHOI SU-20 (FITTER-B)

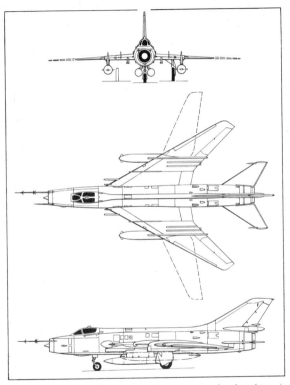

In order to improve on the modest tactical radius of the standard Su-7 (*Fitter-A*) and to afford better weapons-carrying and short-field characteristics, the Sukhoi design bureau adapted the basic design to incorporate pivoting outer wing panels, a more powerful engine and a small increase in internal fuel capacity. A prototype of the variable-geometry version of the Su-7 was demonstrated publicly at Domodedovo in July 1967, this aircraft embodying only the pivoting wing panels and being otherwise similar to the fixed-wing Su-7. Referred to as the *Fitter-B* in the West, this aircraft was subsequently developed for the strike role as the Su-20 and entered service with the FA in 1972.

The Su-20 has a Lyulka AL-21F-3 turbojet in place of the AL-7F-1 of the Su-7 and the overall dimensions of the two aircraft are similar with the wings of the former at maximum sweep angle, the span of the Su-20 increasing to approximately 45 ft (13,70 m) with outboard panels at minimum sweep. The deep dorsal spine, which first appeared on the tandem two-seat Su-7U (*Moujik*) is employed by the Su-20 to raise internal fuel capacity by a small amount to 1,000 Imp gal (4 550 l) and this tankage may be supplemented by twin 132 Imp gal (600 l) drop tanks carried side-by-side on fuselage pylons. The built-in armament is similar to that of the Su-7, comprising two 30-mm NR-30 cannon in the wing roots with 70 rpg, and four underwing weapons pylons are provided, the inboard pylons projecting forward of the wing leading edges to avoid the mainwheel wells and the outboard pylons being situated at the extremities of the fixed-wing centre section. A maximum ordnance load of 7,716 lb (3 500 kg) may be lifted for relatively short-range missions, typical external stores including UV-16-57 or UV-32-57 rocket pods containing 16 and 32 55-mm S-5 rockets respectively, 240-mm S-24 rockets, or 550-lb (250-kg) or 1,100-lb (500-kg) bombs.

The Su-20, being a comparatively simple adaptation of a type that has been in continuous production for 16 years and

The Su-20, illustrated by the general arrangement drawing above, is unique among current service combat aircraft in being a variable-geometry derivative of an existing fixed-geometry aircraft

utilizing much of the jigging and tooling for that type, represents an economical means of upgrading the capabilities of a standard combat aircraft.

Power Plant: *One 17,195 lb (7 800 kg) dry and 24,700 lb (11 200 kg) reheat Lyulka AL-21F-3 turbojet.* **Performance:** *Max speed (clean), 808 mph (1 300 km/h) or M=1·06 at sea level, 1,430 mph (2 300 km/h) or M=2·17 at 39,370 ft (12 000 m); combat radius (lo-lo-lo mission profile), 260 mls (420 km), (hi-lo-hi), 373 mls (600 km); range with 2,205-lb (1 000-kg) weapon load and auxiliary fuel, 1,415 mls (2 280 km); service ceiling, 57,415 ft (17 500 m).* **Weights:** *Max take-off, 39,022 lb (17 700 kg).* **Dimensions:** *Approximate span (max sweep), 29 ft 3¼ in (8,93 m); length (including probe), 57 ft 0 in (17,37 m); height, 15 ft 5 in (4,70 m).*

(Above right) The variable-geometry adaptation of the Su-7 being demonstrated publicly at Domodedovo in July 1967, and (below) the production development which is now serving in some numbers with the FA and the Polish air arm

Now employed primarily by the AV-MF, the Tu-16 is seen above in its Badger-E version which has a camera fit in the weapon bay and, below left, in Badger-B anti-shipping missile-carrying form

TUPOLEV TU-16 (BADGER)

Now serving primarily with the AV-MF, the Tu-16 provided the ADD with an aircraft broadly comparable in both role and performance with the B-47 Stratojet finally phased out of service with the USAF's Strategic Air Command in February 1966. Flown for the first time in prototype form (as the Tu-88) in 1952, the Tu-16 remained in production in the Soviet Union until the mid 'sixties, by which time approximately 2,000 examples had been built, and during its production life the Tu-16 was fitted with progressively more powerful turbojets, the principal of which was the AM-3M (RD-3M) of 19,290 lb (8 750 kg) thrust.

The initial production version of the Tu-16 (*Badger-A*) was phased into service with the ADD as a medium-range strategic bomber in 1954–55, and was capable of carrying a maximum internal load of 19,800 lb (9 000 kg) of free-falling weapons with which tactical radius was approximately

The upper three views (right) depict the Badger–F version of the Tu-16, the bottom side profile illustrating the Badger–D

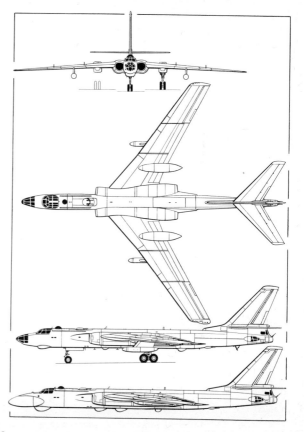

1,500 mls (2 415 km). The flight crew comprised either five or six members and defensive armament consisted of six 23-mm NR-23 cannon in pairs in dorsal, ventral and tail turrets with a seventh NR-23 fixed to fire forward from the starboard side of the front fuselage.

Now confined almost exclusively to maritime tasks with the AV-MF, the Tu-16 has served with that component of the V-VS since the late 'fifties and the appearance of an anti-shipping missile-carrying variant (*Badger-B*). This model was fitted with underwing pylons for carrying two AS-1 *Kennel* ASMs, target acquisition being provided by I-band *Komet* 3 radar. A relatively unsophisticated turbojet-driven missile, the *Kennel* possessed a range of the order of 63 miles (100 km) at a speed of M=0·9, but this weapon has now been supplanted as a Tu-16-launched anti-shipping missile by the AS-5 *Kelt*. A second missile-carrying version for anti-shipping use (*Badger-C*), first seen in 1961, featured a broad or duck-billed radar nose which supplanted the glazed nose of preceding models. The fixed forward-firing 23-mm cannon was discarded and provision was made for an AS-2 *Kipper* ASM to be mounted beneath the forward portion of the weapon bay. This turbojet-driven missile cruised at speeds of the order of M=1·2 over a range of approximately 130 miles (210 km).

For maritime surveillance and electronic intelligence missions the AV-MF currently makes extensive use of a version of the Tu-16 possessing a similar duck-billed radar nose to that of the *Kipper*-launching variant, a longer under-nose fairing for the *Short Horn* navigation radar and a series of three blister fairings in tandem under the centre fuselage (*Badger-D*). Two other maritime versions employed for reconnaissance and surveillance are the *Badger-E* and *Badger-F*, both of which revert to the original glazed nose, the former having a camera fit in the weapon bay and only two blister fairings under the centre fuselage, and the latter

being similar apart from an electronic pod on a pylon beneath each wing. These aircraft usually operate in pairs, a *Badger-F* normally performing its mission with a *Badger-D* or *-E*. A

(Below) An example of the Badger–F version of the Tu-16 with electronic pods on underwing pylons. The Badger–F usually operates as a team with another variant of the Tu-16 (e.g., Badger–D)

wingtip-to-wingtip 'buddy' system of in-flight refuelling is employed, some Tu-16s fulfilling the tanker role with weapon-bay fuel tanks.

For the anti-shipping mission some Tu-16s are equipped to carry the rocket-propelled AS-5 *Kelt* ASM which, possessing a close external similarity to the *Kennel*, is believed to have a range of some 200 miles (320 km). Known as *Badger-C*, the *Kelt*-launching version is generally similar to the *Badger-B* and has basically similar underwing pylons.

The following specification applies to the basic Tu-16:

Power Plant: *Two 19,290 lb (8 750 kg) Mikulin AM-3M turbojets.* **Performance:** *Max speed, 596 mph (960 km/h) or M=0·9 at 36,090 ft (11 000 m); range with max fuel, 4,536 mls (7 300 km), with 6,600-lb (3 000-kg) bomb load, 3,975 mls (6 400 km); service ceiling, 42,650 ft (13 000 m).* **Weights:** *Empty, 88,185 lb (40 000 kg); normal loaded, 115,742 lb (52 500 kg); max take-off, 169,756 lb (77 000 kg).* **Dimensions:** *Span, 108 ft 0½ in (32,93 m); length, 114 ft 2 in (34,80 m); wing area, 1,772·28 sq ft (164,65 m²).*

TUPOLEV TU-20 (BEAR)

The Tu-20 long-range heavy strategic bomber was the final product of a long process of evolution begun when the Soviet Union placed in production a pirated copy of the Boeing B-29 Superfortress as the Tu-4, and it was unique in being the only turboprop-driven strategic bomber ever to attain first line service with any air arm.   Flight testing of the

(Right) The Bear—D and (below) the Bear—C maritime versions of the Tu-20 currently operated by the AV-MF.   The former is distinguished by the undernose radar scanner and very large underbelly radome, while the latter has a wide undernose radome similar to that of the ASM-carrying Bear—B

first prototype (under the design bureau designation Tu-95)
was initiated in the late summer of 1954, and the ADD began
to phase the Tu-20 into service during the second half of
1956. The initial version (*Bear-A*) possessed a radius of
action of some 4,500 miles (7 240 km) with a 11,000-lb
(5 000-kg) load of free-falling weapons, maximum bomb
load being about 25,000 lb (11 340 kg) and defensive
armament comprising three pairs of 23-mm NR-23 cannon
in remotely-controlled dorsal and ventral barbettes and a
manned tail position, the barbettes being controlled from
either a station aft of the flight deck or a position beneath the
tailplane featuring glazed side blisters for sighting purposes.

The Tu-20 (*Bear-A*) provided the backbone of the heavy
bomber component of the ADD until the mid 'sixties, together with a missile-carrying variant (*Bear-B*) featuring an
extensively modified nose with a large duck-billed radome
surmounted by a large flight refuelling probe and a modified
weapon bay capable of carrying semi-externally a single
AS-3 *Kangaroo* ASM with a range of 400 miles (650 km)
and a speed of M=2·0. Subsequently, the Tu-20 was progressively phased out of ADD service, assuming new tasks
with the AV-MF, first appearing in service with the naval air

Illustrated above and right is the Tu-20 in its so-called Bear–D version which can fulfil an anti-shipping missile control role

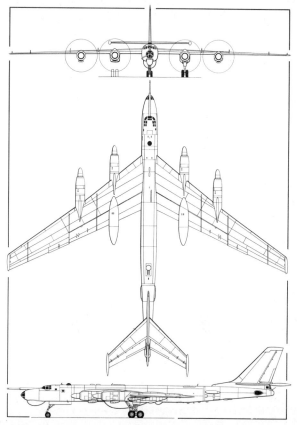

arm during the early 'sixties, the initial AV-MF model (*Bear-C*) making its debut in the maritime surveillance role during the NATO naval exercise *Teamwork* in September 1964. The *Bear-C* was externally similar to the *Kangaroo*-carrying variant apart from additional streamlined blister

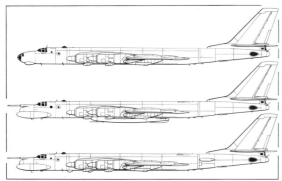

the launching aircraft or site, the Tu-20 thus serving as an intermediate control station ensuring precise terminal guidance. The *Bear-D* has a generally similar glazed nose to that of the *Bear-A* but features large undernose and very large ventral radomes, a variety of other blisters and antennae, and a nose flight refuelling probe. The *Bear-E* has a generally similar external configuration to that of the *Bear-A*, a nose refuelling probe, aft-fuselage blister fairings similar to those of the *Bear-C* and six camera windows in the forward portion of the weapon bay. One further version, the *Bear-F*, has enlarged fairings aft of the inboard engine nacelles.

The following specification is estimated and is generally applicable to all versions of the Tu-20:

Power Plant: *Four 14,795 e.hp. Kuznetsov NK-12 MV turboprops.* **Performance:** *Max speed (at normal loaded weight), 530 mph (853 km/h), or M=0·755 at 29,530 ft (9 000 m), 500 mph (805 km/h) or M=0·76 at 41,000 ft (12 500 m); max continuous cruise, 440 mph (708 km/h) or M=0·67 at 36,090 ft (11 000 m); max unrefuelled range (with 25,000 lb/11 340 kg weapons load), 7,800 mls (12 550 km); service ceiling, 44,290 ft (13 500 m).* **Weights:** *Max take-off, 340,000 lb (154 220 kg).* **Dimensions:** *Span, 159 ft 0 in (48,50 m); length, 155 ft 10 in (47,50 m) wing area, 3,150 sq ft (292,6 m²).*

fairings on the aft fuselage.

The Tu-20 was subsequently employed increasingly for 'ferret' missions with various optical and non-optical sensors and also for anti-shipping missile control. For the latter role (*Bear-D*), X-band *Puff Ball* search radar is carried, this being able to control air-to-surface and surface-to-surface missile launches, the PPI display showing the target location and

TUPOLEV TU-22 (BLINDER)

Evolved as a successor to the subsonic Tu-16 and apparently flown in prototype form in 1959–60, the Tu-22 currently provides the medium bomber backbone of the ADD and some 50 aircraft of this type also serve with the AV-MF in the anti-shipping strike role, operational status having been attained in 1964–65. Aerodynamically one of the most sophisticated of Soviet warplanes at the time of its service introduction and possessing several unusual design features, not least of which being the unique positioning of the turbojets in relatively short pods above the aft fuselage to offer minimum wetted area, keep the intakes clear of wing wake and leave the fuselage free to accommodate a useful load. The ring-type lip of each engine pod is extended forward by means of jacks during take-off, air injected through the resultant annular slot supplementing air entering the ram intake. The wing, which is set low on the area-ruled fuselage, features compound taper, leading-edge sweepback varying from 45 deg on the outer panels through

(Above right) The Tu-22U (Blinder-D) trainer version of the supersonic Tu-22 reconnaissance-bomber and (below) the standard service version of the Tu-22 (Blinder-A). A heavy long-range interceptor variant of the basic Tu-22 has now entered service

(Left and below) The Blinder—C maritime reconnaissance version of the Tu-22 has a battery of six cameras in the weapons bay, and nosecone and dielectric panel modifications suggest an electronic intelligence capability. The AV-MF is believed to include a force of some 50 Tu-22s for the maritime role

50 deg on the inner panels to 70 deg at the extreme root. The wide-track four-wheel bogie-type main undercarriage units retract into aft-projecting wing trailing-edge fairings, and two of the three crew members have downward-ejecting seats, the pilot having an orthodox upward-ejecting seat.

The first version of the Tu-22 (*Blinder-A*) was a reconnaissance-bomber, six cameras normally being mounted in the forward weapon bay and defensive armament comprising a single 23-mm NR-23 cannon in a tail barbette directed by I-band *Bee Hind* radar. This model apparently achieved only limited service with the ADD, the principal version of the Tu-22 supplied to this component of the V-VS being equipped to carry a single AS-4 *Kitchen* stand-off missile (*Blinder-B*), featuring a larger nose-mounted radar and having a partially-retractable flight refuelling probe in the nose. The *Kitchen* ASM, which is carried semi-recessed under the centre fuselage, is some 36 ft (10,97 m) in length and has a range of some 460 miles (740 km).

The variant of the Tu-22 serving with the AV-MF (*Blinder-C*) has a modified nose cone, numerous dielectric panels which suggest an ELINT role in addition to the primary maritime reconnaissance/anti-shipping strike task for which six cameras are mounted in the forward weapon bay and free-fall weapons are accommodated in the aft bay. A further service version (*Blinder-D*) has a raised rear cockpit with dual controls for an instructor behind the standard pilot's cockpit and replacing the radar observer's position.

During the latter half of 1974, a long-range heavy interceptor version of the Tu-22 was being phased into service as a successor to the ageing Tu-28P. The Tu-22 interceptor, which carries a mix of infra-red homing and semi-active or active radar homing missiles, is primarily intended to fulfil standing patrol missions over the large sections of the Soviet periphery unprotected by SAM screens.

The figures quoted in the following specification are estimated and are applicable to the *Blinder-B* but also apply in general to other service versions.

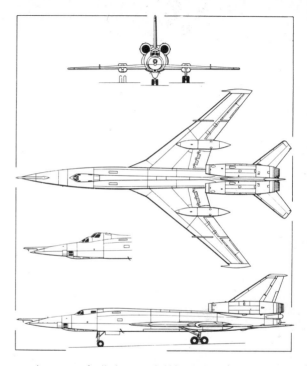

Power Plant: *Two 27,000 lb (12 250 kg) reheat turbojets.*
Performance: *Max speed (clean), 720 mph (1 160 km/h) or M=0·95 at 1,000 ft (305 m), 990 mph (1 590 km/h) or M=1·5 at 39,370 ft (12 000 m); normal range cruise, 595 mph (960 km/h) or M=0·9 at 39,370 ft (12 000 m);* maximum unrefuelled range, 1,400 mls (2 250 km); service ceiling, 60,000 ft (18 290 m). **Weights:** *Max take-off, 185,000 lb (84 000 kg).* **Dimensions:** *Span, 91 ft 0 in (27,74 m); length, 133 ft 0 in (40,50 m); height, 17 ft 0 in (5,18 m); wing area, 2,030 sq ft (188,6 m².)*

(Left) The standard Tu-28P long-range heavy interceptor, which patrols areas of Soviet periphery unprotected by SAM screens, normally carries two infra-red and two semi-active or active radar homing missiles, but when first revealed it was seen to carry a large ventral pack presumably housing early warning radar (below left) and only two AAMs under wing. The Tu-28P is now being supplanted by an intercept version of the Tu-22

TUPOLEV TU-28P (FIDDLER)

The largest and heaviest interceptor in operational service

until the début in late 1974 of its successor, the interceptor version of the Tu-22, the Tu-28 is believed to have been evolved originally to fulfil a requirement for a long-range reconnaissance-strike aircraft and its design was biased towards economical high-altitude operation. A sole example was seen with a ventral pack that was presumed to house early warning radar, this pack being accompanied by two AA-4 *Ash* AAMs mounted on pylons outboard of the bulged housings for the four-wheel main undercarriage bogies. There was subsequently no evidence of the service introduction of this version, nor that of the reconnaissance-strike model which was probably intended to have an internal weapons bay in place of the ventral radar pack. However, the Tu-28P interceptor is known to have entered service with the V-VS in the early 'sixties, having apparently flown in prototype form in 1957, and is apparently employed to patrol the sections of the periphery of the Soviet Union unprotected by SAM screens.

Now approaching obsolescence, the Tu-28P (above and right) is expected to be phased out during 1975–76

$M = 1.65$ at 39,370 ft (12 000 m), (high drag configuration—four *Ash* AA Ms), 925 mph (1 490 km/h) or $M = 1.4$; tactical radius (high-altitude patrol mission), 900–1,000 mls (1 450–1 770 km). **Weights:** Normal loaded, 78,000 lb (35 380 kg); max take-off, 96,000 lb (43 545 kg). **Dimensions:** Span, 65 ft 0 in (19,80 m); length, 90 ft 0 in (27,43 m).

The Tu-28P possibly operates in conjunction with the *Moss* AWACS aircraft and armament consists of two infra-red and two semi-active or active radar homing AA-4 *Ash* AAMs. Despite its extreme size, the Tu-28P possesses a crew comprising only two members. The normal endurance in the patrol interceptor role is believed to be some 3·5 hours and possibly exceeds 5·5 hours with overload tanks. This very large fighter was apparently phased out of production during the late 'sixties but is believed to have undergone progressive updating of its intercept and missile guidance radar, and may also have been re-engined with more powerful Lyulka units, such as the AL-21F-3 which possesses similar overall dimensions to those of the AL-7 around which the Tu-28P was designed. From late 1974, the Tu-28P was being phased out of service in favour of an interceptor version of the Tu-22.

The figures quoted in the following specification are estimated:

Power Plant: Two 14,200 lb (6 440 kg) dry and 22,046 lb (10 000 kg) reheat Lyulka AL-7F turbojets. **Performance:** Max speed (clean), 1,085 mph (1 745 km/h) or

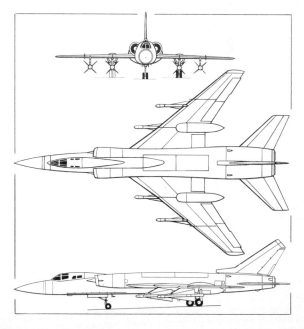

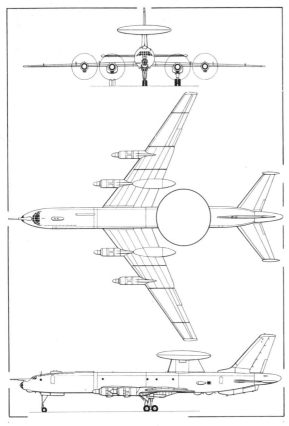

TUPOLEV MOSS

Essentially an adaptation of the Tu-114 commercial transport (see page 41) for the AWACS (Airborne Early Warning and Control System) aircraft role, the *Moss* (the Soviet designation of which was unknown at the time of closing for press) apparently retains the wings, tail surfaces, power plant and undercarriage of the earlier aircraft which have been married to a new fuselage of similar cross section surmounted by a saucer-shaped early warning scanner housing with a diameter of approximately 37·5 ft (11,4 m). In converting the Tu-114 for the AWACS task provision was made for in-flight refuelling, the probe being above the nose, just ahead of the windscreen, and to avoid major structural and system redesign in the front fuselage, the fuel line was carried from the probe along the starboard side of the fuselage to the wing leading edge and thus to the integral wing tanks.

The existence of *Moss* first became known to Western intelligence agencies in the mid 'sixties and the AWACS aircraft first appeared in service with the V-VS in 1970. It has since been encountered on numerous occasions over the seas around the UK, the US and Japan, and over the Mediterranean. It apparently possesses a flight crew of four and a systems operation crew of about 10–12, plus provision for relief and maintenance crews. The *Moss* is primarily intended to locate low-flying intruders and to vector interceptors towards them but apart from its fighter control task it may be assumed that this aircraft will also be employed in enabling strike aircraft to elude interceptors. A more advanced AWACS aircraft with look-down capability over land as well as water is expected to supplant *Moss* during the late 'seventies.

The figures quoted in the following specification are estimated:

Power Plant: *Four 14,795 e.h.p. Kuznetsov NK-12 MV turboprops.* **Performance:** *Max continuous cruise, 460 mph (740 km/h) at 25,000 ft (7 620 m); max unrefuelled range, 4,000 mls plus (6 440 km plus); service ceiling,*

The Tupolev Moss AWACS aircraft (illustrated above and on the opposite page) possesses look-down capability over water and is primarily used to patrol sections of the Soviet periphery unprotected by SAM screens

40,000 ft (12 190 m). **Weights:** *Max take-off, 360,000 lb (163 290 kg).* **Dimensions:** *Span, 168 ft 0 in (51,20 m); length, 188 ft 0 in (57,30 m); height, 51 ft 0 in (15,50 m); wing area, 3,349 sq ft (311,10 m²).*

TUPOLEV BACKFIRE

Development of a variable-geometry strategic bomber in the Soviet Union is believed to have started in the mid 'sixties, the first reported sighting of a prototype taking place in July 1970 at an airfield near the Tupolev plant at Kazan in Central Asia. This and subsequent sightings of the variable-geometry combat aircraft, assigned the reporting name *Backfire* by the Air Standards Co-ordinating Committee, were the result of reconnaissance satellite monitoring of Soviet activity, and by the beginning of 1974, western intelligence agencies believed this type to have attained initial service status with the ADD.

The *Backfire*, reported by some sources to be designated Tu-26 in V-VS service, is the first Soviet strategic bomber

combining supersonic capability with sufficient range to hit targets in Continental US, either with small nuclear missiles delivered in a low-altitude supersonic dash or using an ASM-6 stand-off missile launched some distance from the borders. The ASM-6, which is a solid-propellant missile with a range of approximately 460 miles (740 km), is believed to be the primary attack armament of *Backfire*, one ASM of this type normally being carried semi-internally.

Development of the variable-geometry *Backfire* was allegedly pursued in competition with a foreplane-equipped fixed delta-wing bomber attributed to Pavel Sukhoi's design team. Work on the latter, reportedly in the 300,000-lb (136 080-kg) weight class, apparently progressed no further than the prototype flight test stage. Two versions of the Tupolev v-g bomber are apparently in production or under

(Above and left) Provisional illustrations of the Backfire—A

development, the *Backfire-A* (illustrated) and the *Backfire-B*, the latter having modified wing configuration and a revised undercarriage arrangement, the main bogies being transferred from fairings on the wing trailing edges to the fuselage.

At the time of closing for press the power plants installed in the *Backfire* had not been positively identified, but it has been suggested that these may be uprated military derivatives of the reheated Kuznetsov turbofans employed by the Tu-144 commercial transport. The *Backfire* is comparable from some aspects with the USAF's Rockwell B-1 variable-geometry strategic bomber and its assumed performance matches that of the US bomber in key areas. After one observed flight refuelling, an early *Backfire* is alleged to have remained airborne for a further 10 hours.

The figures quoted in the following specification should be considered as provisional estimates:

Power Plant: *Two 40,000 lb (18 144 kg) reheat turbofans.* **Performance:** *Max speed (clean), 975 mph (1 570 km/h) or M=1·3 at 3,280 ft (1 000 m), (with semi-internally mounted ASM-6 stand-off missile), 1,450–1,650 mph (2 330–2 655 km/h) or M=2·2 to 2·5 at 36,090 ft (11 000 m); max unrefuelled range, 4,500 mls (7 240 km) plus at 39,370 ft (12 000 m); operational ceiling, 50,000 ft (15 240 m) plus.* **Weights:** *Normal loaded, 275,000 lb (124 740 kg).* **Dimensions:** *No details available.*

TUPOLEV TU-124 (COOKPOT)

Of the various Soviet aircraft design bureaux, that originally headed by the late Andrei Tupolev, and still bearing his name, has played the most significant role in the modernization of Aeroflot. This process began in 1956 when the Tu-104 entered service, becoming only the second jet airliner in the world to achieve this status (after the Comet). As the Soviet Union's first jet transport the Tu-104 (see page 46) was of historic importance; five other commercial Tupolev designs have followed with '1 × 4' designations, making this bureau the nearest thing in the USSR to the Boeing Company with its '7×7' series of airliners.

Second of the Tupolev jet transports was the Tu-124 (the Tu-114 being turboprop-powered—see page 40). Although the Tu-124 was very similar in overall appearance to the Tu-104, which was essentially a derivative of the Tu-16 bomber, it was some 25 per cent smaller and consequently was a completely new design insofar as structural detail was concerned. As part of an overall plan to introduce modern equipment on Soviet air services during the 'fifties, the Tu-124 was intended primarily for the shorter and less-used routes, replacing piston-engined Il-14s then in use. Like most Soviet airliners, it was designed to have very good field performance and the ability to operate from unprepared surfaces: to this end, a rugged undercarriage was provided, retracting into nacelles on the wing as in the Tu-104, and the wing incorporated double-slotted flaps and combined spoiler/lift dumper/air brakes.

The first Tu-124 was flown in June 1960, and following flight trials with a small number of prototypes, production was initiated in time for deliveries to be made to Aeroflot in mid-1962. The first commercial service was flown on the Moscow–Tallinn route on 2 October 1962, this being the first use anywhere in the world of an airliner with turbofan engines—specially developed by the Soloviev engine bureau. Originally, the Tu-124 was designed to carry 44 passengers in three separate cabins, this arrangement being necessary because the floor level was interrupted by the wing centre section passing through the fuselage; seating was increased to 56, however, in the standard Aeroflot version, designated the Tu-124V, with 12 seats each in the forward and centre cabin, and 32 in the rear cabin.

Production of the Tu-124 is believed to have ended with fewer than 200 examples built, primarily because the Tu-134 proved to be a more economic aircraft for similar operations. Apart from Aeroflot, only two airlines operated the Tu-124, CSA Czechoslovakian Airlines having acquired three and

One of the two foreign civil operators to acquire the Tu-124 was CSA Czechoslovakian Airlines. Illustrated right is one of the three aircraft of this type included in the CSA fleet. The other foreign operator is Interflug of the DDR

East Germany's Interflug, two. In addition, the Indian Air Force received three for use as VIP transports, and the air forces of East Germany and Iraq received one or two examples.

Two VIP interior layouts were developed for the Tu-124. In the Tu-124K, the forward cabin had only four seats, plus tables, desks and other amenities; the centre and rear cabins retained, respectively, the eight and 24-seat arrangements of the original Tu-124. In the Tu-124K2, the centre cabin contained only two seats plus a divan, and the rear cabin held eight pairs of seats, making a total of 22. Examples of these VIP models are believed to be used within the Soviet Union to carry senior officials and members of the government.

Power Plant: *Two 11,905 lb (5 400 kg) Soloviev D-20P turbofans.* **Performance:** *Max speed, 603 mph (970 km/h); max cruising speed, 540 mph (870 km/h); economical cruising speed, 497 mph (800 km/h) at 33,000 ft (10 000 m) at a mean weight of 58,000 lb (26 300 kg); typical take-off run, 3,380 ft (1 030 m); typical landing run, 3,050 ft (930 m); range with max payload and 1-hr reserve, 760 mls (1 220 km); range with max fuel and 7,715-lb (3 500-kg) payload, 1,305 mls (2 100 km).* **Weights:** *Empty, 49,600 lb (22 500 kg); max payload, 13,228 lb (6 000 kg); max take-off weight, 83,775 lb (38 000 kg); max landing weight, 77,160 lb (35 000 kg); max zero-fuel weight, 52,400 lb (23 770 kg).* **Dimensions:** *Span, 83 ft 9½ in (25,55 m); length, 100 ft 4 in (30,58 m); height,*

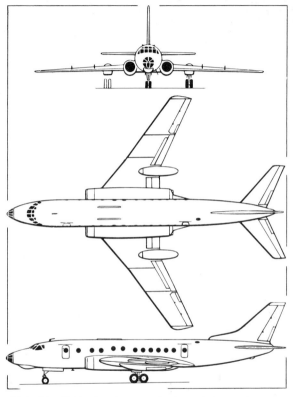

26 ft 6 in (8,08 m); wing area, 1,281 sq ft (119 m²).

TUPOLEV TU-134 (CRUSTY)

With the Tu-104 and the Tu-124, the Tupolev design bureau allowed Aeroflot to take a major step forward and to enter the jet age, but in a number of respects both these types lagged behind the standards being established by contemporary products of western companies. Recognizing the need to overcome these discrepancies and to match the standards of the equipment of other airlines in all respects, Aeroflot established a new requirement for a short-haul medium capacity airliner almost as soon as the Tu-124 had entered service, and to meet this requirement the Tupolev bureau evolved the Tu-134. The design was undertaken at the time that 'compact jets' such as the Caravelle, One-Eleven and DC-9 were receiving much publicity, and Tupolev adopted a similar rear-engined, T-tail layout.

Tu-134s of Malev (right) and Polskie Linie Lotnicze LOT (below). This short-haul medium-capacity airliner has enjoyed some success on the export market and a number are used for governmental transportation tasks in military markings (e.g., Poland, Czechoslovakia)

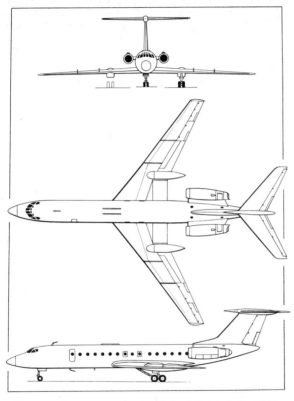

The general arrangement drawing (below) depicts the Tu-134A

Initially, an attempt was made to use the Tu-124 fuselage with minimum change, and the designation Tu-124A was applied, but a complete redesign was eventually found to be required, and the designation was then changed. The Tu-134 did retain, however, the short-field and rough-field capabilities of the Tu-124, with a similar undercarriage and high-lift features. Avionics and flight control system were suitable for operation in conditions approximately equivalent to those of ICAO Cat II, and an airbrake was fitted beneath the fuselage to permit steeper approaches to be flown.

Prototype testing began in late 1962, and the test programme used a total of six aircraft. Production was launched in 1964 at the Kharkov factory where the Tu-104 had also been built, and early production aircraft underwent a series of proving flights over Aeroflot routes before full commercial services were launched in September 1967, on the Moscow–Stockholm route. In its standard version, the Tu-134 seats 72, four-abreast in a single-class layout, alternative arrangements seat 68 one-class or 64 (eight first-class and 56 tourist). A 37-seat VIP transport version has also been designed by the Tupolev bureau.

In the second half of 1970, Aeroflot introduced the Tu-134A into service, this version differing from the Tu-134 in having the fuselage 'stretched' by 6 ft $10\frac{1}{2}$ in (2,10 m) and being fitted with Soloviev D-30 *Seriiny II* engines and an APU. The standard layout in this version seats 76, with up to 80 seats at reduced pitch or 68 in a mixed-class layout (12 first class and 56 tourist). Although all early Tu-134s and some Tu-134As had the distinctive glazed nose of earlier Tupolev designs, containing a navigator's station, some later examples dispense with this crew position and have a 'solid' nose fairing containing radar.

The Tu-134 and Tu-134A have proved to be among the most popular of Soviet airliners for export, matching the earlier success of the Il-18, which in many instances the Tu-134 has been purchased to replace. Among the operators in addition to Aeroflot are CSA, with 11 Tu-134s and Tu-134As; Interflug, with 11 Tu-134s; Balkan Bulgarian,

(Above) A Tu-134A utilized by the Yugoslav operator Aviogenex and (below right) a Tu-134A serving with the Hungarian government. The Aviogenex aircraft lacks the distinctive glazed nose of most Tu-134s and 134As, the navigational radar being housed in the nose

with six Tu-134s and three Tu-134As; LOT, with eight Tu-134s; Malev, with six Tu-134s and two Tu-134As; Iraqi Airways, with one Tu-134; Aviogenex, with three Tu-134s and four Tu-134As and Egyptair, with four Tu-134As. Aeroflot is believed to have about 150 of the two types in service. Examples of the Tu-134 are also operated by the V-VS, and the Czechoslovak, Hungarian and Polish Air Forces.

The following specification refers to the Tu-134:

Power Plant: *Two 14,990 lb (6 800 kg) s.t. Soloviev D-30 turbofans.* **Performance:** *Max cruising speed, 559 mph (900 km/h) at 28,000 ft (8 500 m); economical cruise, 466 mph (750 km/h) at 36,000 ft (11 000 m); initial climb rate, 2,913 ft (14,8 m/sec); normal operating ceiling, 39,370 ft (12 000 m); take-off field length (FAR, SL, ISA, max weight), 7,152 ft (2 180 m); landing field length (FAR, max landing weight), 6,726 ft (2 050 m); range with 1-hr reserve, 1,490 mls (2 400 km) with 15,430-lb (7 000-kg) payload and 2,175 mls (3 500 km)* with 6,600 lb (3 000 kg) payload. **Weights:** *Operating weight empty, 60,627 lb (27 500 kg); max payload, 16,975 lb (7 700 kg); max fuel, 28,660 lb (13 000 kg); max take-off, 98,105 lb (44 500 kg); max landing, 88,185 lb (40 000 kg); max zero fuel, 77,600 lb (35 200 kg).* **Dimensions:** *Span, 95 ft 1¾ in (29,00 m); length, 112 ft 8¼ in (34,35 m); height, 29 ft 7 in (9,02 m); wing area, 1,370·3 sq ft (127,3 m²).*

TUPOLEV TU-144 (CHARGER)

Holding a secure place in history as the World's first supersonic airliner to fly, the Tupolev Tu-144 has often been described in the popular press as the 'Soviet Concorde' or the 'Concordskii'—an appellation that underlines the similarity of the two types.　There is little doubt that Aeroflot was led to initiate design of an SST by the launching of the Concorde by Britain and France in 1963, and the Tupolev design bureau, having been selected to undertake this prestigious programme, reached similar design conclusions to those of the Concorde's designers.　The first public indication of the Tu-144's appearance came in May 1965, when a model was exhibited in Paris, revealing that it was a large ogival-wing transport with provision, like the Concorde, for the nose and visor to be hinged down ahead of the cockpit to improve the forward view in the nose-high approach angle.　Unlike Concorde, the chosen engines were turbofans rather than turbojets, and were arranged side by side across the underside of the fuselage in a single large nacelle; the overall dimensions were also somewhat greater than those of its western counterpart and the design cruising speed a little higher, at M=2·2 to 2·3.

The first of three prototypes of the Tu-144 to be assembled at the Zhukovsky works, near Moscow, made its first flight on 31 December 1968, and supersonic speed was achieved for the first time on 5 June 1969, followed by the first excursion beyond M=2·0 on 26 May 1970.　All these three events were World 'firsts', but the rate of flight testing with the prototypes was relatively slow with only about 200 hrs

The second pre-production Tu-144 shown (above left) with nose drooped, visor retracted and noseplanes extended, and (left) in high-speed configuration with nose and visor raised, and noseplanes retracted. This particular aircraft crashed during a demonstration at Le Bourget, Paris, in June 1973

achieved in the first $3\frac{1}{2}$ years after initial flight. During this period, and based on early flight test results, a major redesign of the Tu-144 was in hand, the production configuration appearing early in 1973 in the Soviet Union and in May 1973 at Paris. Compared with the prototypes, this production model had larger overall dimensions; a new wing; relocated engine nacelles; uprated engines; a new undercarriage and retractable noseplanes for improved slow-speed handling.

The wing of the Tu-144 has been changed from the original ogival form (with curved leading edges) to a compound delta, with straight leading edges and sweepback angles of about 76 deg on the inboard portions and 57 deg on the outer panels. The whole wing incorporates complex camber from leading to trailing edge, with anhedral towards the tips, and the main control surfaces comprise eight separate elevons across the wing, each with two hydraulic actuators. The rudder is similarly divided into two sections each with two actuators.

Addition of noseplanes to the production Tu-144 is an indication of the difficulties of achieving acceptable low-speed control, since they provide unwanted drag and weight penalties in cruising flight. The noseplanes, similar in aerodynamic function to the 'moustaches' developed by Dassault for the Milan delta-wing fighter, are stowed in the upper fuselage just behind the flight deck, pivoting to open to an overall span of about 20 ft (6,1 m); they have anhedral when open, and incorporate fixed double leading edge slots plus double slotted trailing edge flaps. The undercarriage comprises a very long nosewheel leg with twin wheels, retracting forwards into the fuselage, and main eight-wheel bogies that retract forwards and up, whilst also pivoting through 90 deg, to lie in wells in the engine nacelles between the ducts.

Each pair of engines is housed in an individual nacelle (unlike the prototype arrangement). The engines, specially developed for the Tu-144 by the Kuznetsov bureau, carry the NK-144 designation, and have been improved since first being flown in the prototype and now have a dry thrust rating

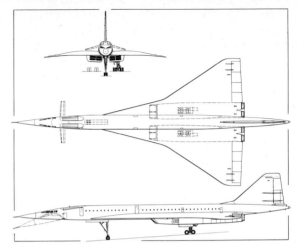

of 33,000 lb.s.t. (15 000 kgp) and an afterburner thrust of 44,000 lb.s.t. (20 000 kg). The cruising technique calls for about 35 per cent of maximum reheat boost to be maintained throughout the supersonic cruise, and the intakes incorporate fully-automatic movable ramps.

The Tu-144 is designed to be operated by a crew of three (two pilots and an engineer) and can carry up to 140 passengers. Separated from the flight deck by a narrow corridor between the wells into which the noseplanes retract, and by toilet and cloakroom areas, the cabin is usually divided into three, although movable bulkheads make other arrangements possible. Typically, the forward cabin seats 11 at first-class standards and the centre and rear compartments, separated by galleys, toilets and cloakrooms, seat 30 and 99 passengers at tourist class standards, basi-

cally five abreast. There are no under-floor freight or baggage holds, but provision is made for containerized baggage in a compartment behind the cabin.

The first production Tu-144 is believed to have flown towards the end of 1972, but flight testing suffered a severe set-back when the second example crashed during a demonstration in Paris in June 1973. By mid-1974, four production models and two prototypes were reported to be under test, with four examples engaged on route proving trials, carrying freight between Moscow, Tyumen and Vladivostok. Introduction into passenger service by Aeroflot—initially on routes within the Soviet Union—was expected during 1975.

The photographs above illustrate the second pre-production Tu-144 with noseplanes (immediately behind the flight deck) extended and with nose and visor hinged down

Power Plant: *Four 44,000 lb (20 000 kg) s.t. with reheat Kuznetsov NK-144 turbofans.* **Performance:** *Max cruising speed, up to M=2·35 (1,550 mph/2 500 km/h) at altitudes up to 59,000 ft (18 000 m); normal cruise, M=2·2 (1,430 mph/2 300 km/h); typical take-off speed, 216 mph (348 km/h); typical landing speed, 150 mph (241 km/h); balanced field length (ISA, sl, max take-off weight), 9,845 ft (3 000 m); landing run, 8,530 ft (2 600 m); max range with full 140-passenger payload, 4,030 mls (6 500 km) at an average speed of M=1·9 (1,243 mph/ 2 000 km/h).* **Weights:** *Operating weight empty, 187,400 lb (85 000 kg); max payload, 30,865 lb (14 000 kg); max fuel load, 209,440 lb (95 000 kg); max take-off weight, 396,830 lb (180 000 kg); max landing weight, 264,550 lb (120 000 kg); max zero fuel weight, 220,460 lb (100 000 kg).* **Dimensions:** *Span, 94 ft 6 in (28,80 m); length overall, 215 ft 6½ in (65,70 m); height (wheels up), 42 ft 2 in (12,85 m); wing area, 4,714·5 sq ft (438 m²).*

TUPOLEV TU-154 (CARELESS)

The sixth and latest of the Tupolev bureau's commercial airliners, the Tu-154 can be considered as a direct counterpart of the Boeing 727-200/HS Trident Three transports, having a similar three-engined T-tail layout. Compared with its western contemporaries, however, the Tu-154 has a higher power-to-weight ratio, giving it a better take-off performance, and a heavy duty undercarriage suitable for use from Class 2 airfields with surfaces of gravel or packed earth. These features are common to most Soviet transports and indicate the importance of air transport in the Union's remoter areas, where airfield facilities are minimal. Lacking the characteristic glazed nose of the earlier Tupolev transports, the Tu-154 nevertheless retains the wing pods for main undercarriage stowage that are a feature of all the Tupolev series except the Tu-144.

First flight of the Tu-154 was made on 4 October 1968, and six prototype/pre-production models were used for flight development. Production was launched soon after first flight, the Tu-154 having been selected by Aeroflot as a replacement for the Tu-104, Il-18 and An-10 on domestic and international routes of medium length, in partnership with the Il-62 and Il-62M on longer stages. The first delivery was made to Aeroflot early in 1971 and there followed the customary period of route proving with freight and mail, plus a few passenger services on an *ad hoc* basis, from May 1971 onwards, but full commercial exploitation began only on 9 February 1972, initially on the route from Moscow to Mineralnye Vady. First international services were flown August 1972, between Moscow and Prague.

The Tu-154, the first pre-production example of which is illustrated above right, is the first Aeroflot transport to be equipped with wing leading-edge high-lift devices, and more than 100 aircraft of this type were reportedly in service with this operator by mid-1974 on domestic and international routes

The Tu-154 is normally laid out to accommodate 158 or 164 passengers in a single-class layout, six abreast in two cabins separated by the galley. If a mixed-class layout is required, 24 seats can be provided four abreast in the forward cabin, with 104 tourist class seats in the rear cabin. Maximum high density seating is for 167. Standard avionics and flight control system permit operation to Cat II levels, with projected future development for fully automatic landings (Cat III). A 'stretched' version, the Tu-154M, is reported to be under development, with up to 220 seats and powered by 25,350 lb (11 500 kg) D-30KU engines.

Although the needs of Aeroflot in 1974 led to a temporary interruption in the export of Tu-154s during 1974, the type had already been specified by several airlines in the Soviet Bloc, with deliveries being made during 1973 and early 1974. These included CSA, with seven; Balkan Bulgarian, two; Malev, three and Egyptair, eight. The Tu-154s for the last-mentioned company were fitted with Rumbold seats in the UK before delivery but were withdrawn from service late in 1974. Over 100 Tu-154s had been delivered to Aeroflot by mid-1974.

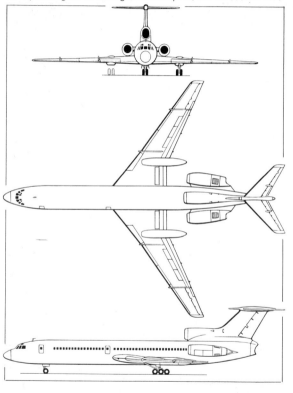

Power Plant: *Three 20,950 lb (9 500 kg) s.t. Kuznetsov NK-8-2 turbofans.* ***Performance:*** *Max cruising speed, 605 mph (975 km/h) at 31,150 ft (9 500 m); best-cost cruise, 560 mph (900 km/h); long-range cruise 528 mph (850 km/h); balanced take-off distance (FAR, ISA, SL, max take-off weight), 6,890 ft (2 100 m); landing field length (FAR, ISA, SL, max landing weight), 6,758 ft (2 060 m); range with max payload and 1-hr reserve, 2,150 mls (3 460 km); range with max fuel and 30,100-lb (13 650-kg) payload, 3,280 mls (5 280 km).* ***Weights:*** *Operating weight empty, 95,900 lb (43 500 kg); max payload, 44,090 lb (20 000 kg); max fuel load, 73,085 lb (33 150 kg); max take-off weight, 198,416 lb (90 000 kg); max landing weight, 176,370 lb (80 000 kg); max zero fuel weight, 139,994 lb (63 500 kg).* ***Dimensions:*** *Span, 123 ft 2½ in (37,55 m); length, 157 ft 1¾ in (47,90 m); height, 37 ft 4¾ in (11,40 m); wing area, 2,169 sq ft (201,45 m²).*

(Right) The Yak-18PM single-seater was evolved specifically for the 1966 aerobatic championships, and the Yak-18T (below right) four-seater appeared in 1967, offering max and cruise speeds of 183 mph (295 km/h) and 155 mph (250 km/h), and a range of 559 mls (900 km). Max take-off weight is 3,638 lb (1 650 kg)

YAKOVLEV YAK-18 (MAX)

The most widely-used primary training, club and sporting aircraft in the Soviet Union, the Yak-18 was flown for the first time in 1946 as a potential successor for the UT-2 (see page 93), being introduced into the elementary training schools of the V-VS in 1947, and rapidly supplanting older types in both military and civil training organizations. The initial production model was powered by the simple, robust M-11-FR five-cylinder radial engine rated at 160 h.p. Fully aerobatic, it had a maximum speed of 153 mph (248 km/h) at sea level and maximum cruise and stalling speeds of 133 mph (215 km/h) and 53 mph (85 km/h) respectively. Initial climb was 689 ft/min (3,5 m/sec), and empty and loaded weights were 1,799 lb (816 kg) and 4,469 lb (1 120 kg).

The Yak-18 was widely exported, rapidly becoming the standard primary trainer of all Soviet Bloc air forces, and the first modified version to achieve production status was the Yak-18U which made its debut in 1955. Whereas the initial model had employed a tailwheel undercarriage, the Yak-18U introduced an aft-retracting nosewheel, the mainwheel legs being transferred from the front to the rear spar for CG

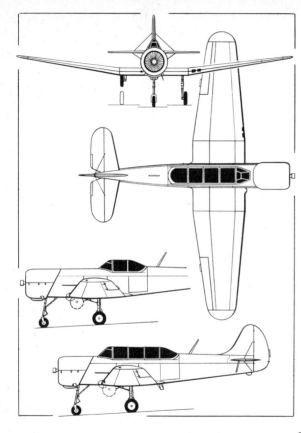

reasons.   These changes were accompanied by some aerodynamic refinement of the engine cowling featuring less prominent cylinder-head helmets.   The Yak-18U was somewhat heavier than its predecessor, with empty and loaded weights of 1,949 lb (884 kg) and 2,584 lb (1 172 kg) respectively, performance being commensurately reduced, including a maximum speed of 143 mph (230 km/h) and an initial climb rate of 472 ft/min (2,4 m/sec).   However, the Yak-18U was essentially an interim development and built in small numbers to provide nosewheel experience pending the availability from 1957 of a re-engined and modernized model, the Yak-18A.

The major change from the Yak-18U introduced by the Yak-18A was the replacement of the Shvetsov-designed M-11 engine by the nine-cylinder AI-14R rated at 260 h.p. for take-off and developed by the Ivchenko bureau.   Apart from some local structural strengthening, a slight increase in vertical tail surface area and the provision of a larger canopy over the tandem cockpits, the Yak-18A differed little from the Yak-18U and served as the basis for production over the next dozen years.   Developed in parallel with the Yak-18A was the single-seat Yak-18P intended primarily for competition flying, this entering production in 1961 and two models being produced: one with the cockpit positioned over the wing and having inward-retracting mainwheels and the other with the cockpit aft of the wing and featuring forward-retracting mainwheels similar to those of the two-seater. The single-seaters introduced longer-span ailerons.

A further single-seat variant evolved specifically for the 1966 aerobatic championships was the Yak-18PM, this having a 300 h.p. AI-14RF engine (which had supplanted the AI-14R during the course of production of the Yak-18A), a two-degree reduction in wing dihedral and the cockpit moved aft slightly (by comparison with the aft-cockpit version of the Yak-18P) to produce a 4·5 per cent rear

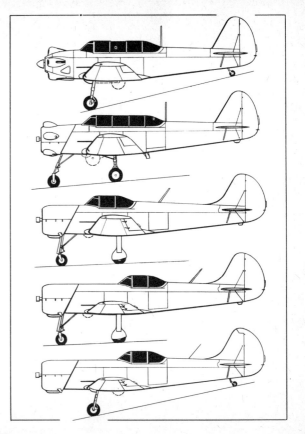

movement of the CG.   The Yak-18PS was similar to the PM apart from having a tailwheel undercarriage, the mainwheel legs reverting to the forward spar.

Still further development of the basic design resulted in the appearance in 1967 of the Yak-18T, a four-seat tourer with an entirely new all-metal semi-monocoque fuselage of square section and an extended constant-chord wing centre section.   The enclosed cabin provided two side-by-side pairs of seats, access being via a large forward-hinged door in each side of the cabin, and dual controls were standard. The rear seats could be removed to provide space for freight and in the aeromedical role, the Yak-18T could accommodate pilot, stretcher patient and medical attendant.   Like the definitive production two-seat and single-seat models, the Yak-18T is powered by the AI-14RF engine, and is currently serving (15 aircraft) as a basic trainer at Aeroflot's Sasovo flying school.   Development was continuing late 1974.

The Yak-18, of which 6,760 of all versions had been manufactured by the beginning of 1968, is extensively employed for *ab initio* training in both para-military and civil schools in the Soviet Union and Soviet Bloc countries before student pilots progress to the L 29 basic trainer.

The following specification relates to the most widely-used model, the Yak-18A:

Power Plant: *One 300 h.p. Ivchenko AI-14RF nine-cylinder radial air-cooled engine.* **Performance:** *Max speed, 186 mph (300 km/h); cruise, 161 mph (259 km/h); initial climb, 1,575 ft/min (8,0 m/sec); service ceiling, 16,600 ft (5 060 m); range with max fuel, 435 mls (700 km).* **Weights:** *Empty, 2,259 lb (1 025 kg); max take-off, 2,910 lb (1 320 kg).* **Dimensions:** *Span, 34 ft 9¼ in (10,60 m); length, 27 ft 4¾ in (8,35 m); height, 11 ft 0 in (3,35 m); wing area, 183 sq ft (17,0 m²).*

Broadly comparable with the Lockheed U-2, the Yak-26 (left and below) retained substantial proportions of the airframe of the Yak-25 (Flashlight—A) and, although obsolescent, is reportedly still used for occasional clandestine reconnaissance missions and for various high-altitude tasks

YAKOVLEV YAK-26 (MANDRAKE)

The Yakovlev high-altitude strategic reconnaissance aircraft believed designated Yak-26 was evolved by marrying the centre and aft fuselage, tail surfaces, power plant and zero-track tricycle undercarriage of the Yak-25 to a new forward fuselage and long-span high aspect ratio wing.   The result was an aircraft capable of operating at what, in the late 'fifties and early 'sixties, were considered to be extreme altitudes.   Cruise is probably commenced at approximately 56,000 ft (17 070 m) with the aircraft drifting up to 65,000 ft (19 800 m) as fuel is burned off.   It may be assumed that the Yak-26 has a 'wet wing' and equipment is believed to include J-band *Short Horn* navigation radar, a long focus camera for horizon-to-horizon photography and electronic sensing devices to pick up and record radio and radar transmissions.

This aircraft has not seen extensive use in the European theatre but has been employed for clandestine reconnaissance flights over China, India and Pakistan in recent years.   The figures quoted in the following specification are estimated:

Power Plant: *Two 5,730 lb (2 600 kg) Tumansky RD-9 turbojets.* **Performance:** *Max speed, 470 mph (756 km/h) at 45,930 ft (14 000 m), 300 mph (483 km/h) at sea level; range cruise, 400 mph (644 km/h); normal operational ceiling, 65,000 ft (19 800 m); maximum ceiling, 70,000 ft (21 335 m); operational radius, 1,200 mls (1 930 km); max range, 2,500 mls (4 000 km).* **Weights:** *Normal loaded, 21,000 lb.* **Dimensions:** *Span, 71 ft 0 in (21,64 m); length, 51 ft 0 in (15,54 m).*

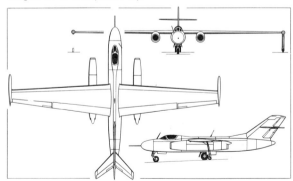

YAKOVLEV YAK-27R (MANGROVE)

The progressive development of the Yak-25R (*Flashlight-B*) tactical reconnaissance aircraft (see page 71), which was, itself, a derivative of the Yak-25 (*Flashlight-A*) all-weather interceptor, resulted in the Yak-27R optimized for the Tac-R role but possessing some limited secondary tactical strike capability. The forward fuselage of the Yak-27R was essentially similar to that introduced by the Yak-25R and, apart from some structural strengthening, the airframe was similar to that of the basic Yak-25. Changes included provision of a sharply-swept (63 deg) extension of the leading-edge wing root, inset rather than wingtip outriggers and the adoption of an afterburning version of the Tumansky RD-9.

Developed in parallel was an all-weather fighter version, the Yak-27P (*Flashlight-C*), embodying similar aerodynamic refinements and afterburners but providing tandem seating for the two crew members similar to that of the basic Yak-25, this combination being coupled with a sharply pointed nose radome to lessen drag and rain erosion. Production of the Yak-27P appears to have been strictly limited, possibly owing to the relatively marginal increase in performance that it offered over the Yak-25, and the type was phased out of service with the IAP-VO *Strany* during the mid-60s. The Yak-27P was equipped with similar X-band *Scan Three* search and track radar to that of the Yak-25, this employing three scan techniques and having a very high PRF (Pulse Repetition Frequency). Armament was similar to that of the Yak-25 in comprising a belly pack containing two 37-mm N-37 AAMs and provision for two AAMs on pylons.

Prototypes of the Yak-27R were apparently flown in 1956–57, with initial deliveries to the V-VS commencing in 1959. Armament comprises a single 30-mm NR-30 cannon in the starboard side of the forward fuselage, *Bee Hind* tail warning radar is installed, a camera pack is accommodated by a bay between the members of the zero-track tricycle undercarriage and various ECM, radio and IR sensor pods may be carried by two wing pylons. From the late '60s,

most RD-9-powered aircraft were phased out of first-line V-VS service and any remaining aircraft undoubtedly perform second-line roles.

The figures quoted in the following specification for the Yak-27R are estimated:

Power Plant: *Two 5,730 lb (2 600 kg) dry and 7,275 lb (3 300 kg) reheat Tumansky RD-9 turbojets.* **Performance:** *Max speed (clean), 686 mph (1 104 km/h) or M=0·95 at 36,090 ft (11 000 m); low-altitude cruise, 570 mph (917 km/h) or M=0·75; tactical radius (clean), 200 mls (320 km) at 1,000 ft (305 m), 500 mls (805 km) at*

(Below) The Yak-27R (Mangrove) tactical reconnaissance aircraft

36,090 ft (11 000 m); initial climb, 18,000 ft/min (91,4 m/ sec); service ceiling, 50,000 ft (15 250 m). **Weights:** *Normal loaded, 22,000 lb (9 980 kg); max take-off, 25,000 lb (11 340 kg).* **Dimensions:** *Span, 36 ft 1 in (11,00 m); length, 55 ft 0 in (16,76 m); height, 12 ft 6 in (3,80 m); wing area, 323 sq ft (30,0 m²).*

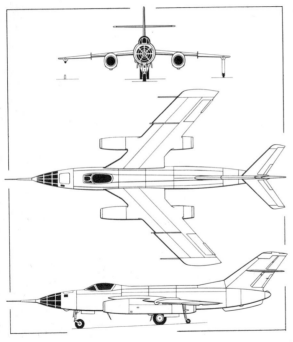

(Left) The Yak-27R (Mangrove) and (above) The Yak-28I (Brewer—C)

YAKOVLEV YAK-28 (BREWER)

Essentially a multi-purpose design suitable, with various degrees of modification, for the tactical strike, tactical reconnaissance, electronic countermeasures, all-weather intercept and advanced operational conversion training roles, the Yak-28 may be considered as a third-generation derivative of the Yak-25 two-seat all-weather fighter. Extensively employed in its multifarious forms by the V-VS, the Yak-28 possesses, in fact, only a superficial family resemblance to the earlier Yakovlev twin-jet two-seaters, and in its tactical strike form was intended primarily as a successor to the Ilyushin Il-28 in service with the FA.

Flown in prototype form in 1960, with production deliveries to the V-VS commencing 1963–64, the tactical strike model of the Yak-28 featured an internal weapon bay positioned well aft of the CG and apparently intended to accommodate quite modest loads, such as a small nuclear store or a pair of 1,100-lb (500-kg) bombs. Differing from the Yak-25 and Yak-27 in having a shoulder- rather than mid-mounted wing, this having a straight trailing edge between the fuselage and the engine nacelles and markedly increased sweep-back on the leading edges inboard of the nacelles, gross area being increased by some 60 sq ft (5,57 m²), the Yak-28 also displayed larger vertical tail surfaces, a more sharply swept tailplane and a widely-spaced 'bicycle' undercarriage in place of the 'zero-track' tricycle gear of its predecessors, the aircraft's weight being divided between the two twin-wheel fuselage-mounted units.

Two tactical strike versions of the Yak-28 were apparently phased into FA service simultaneously, one version (*Brewer-A*) having no ventral radome and the other, the Yak-28L (*Brewer-B*), having a ventral radome just aft of the forward undercarriage bay, this housing the *Short Horn* bombing and navigation circular and sector scan radar.   Both versions had a single 30-mm NR-30 cannon mounted in the starboard side of the forward fuselage, and a single stores point was provided immediately outboard of each engine nacelle, these normally carrying auxiliary fuel tanks which, mounted flush with the wing undersurfaces, projected well forward of the wing leading edges.   Provision for additional stores was apparently made between the engine nacelles and the fuse-lage, the inboard stations presumably carrying UV-16-57 or UV-32-57 pods each housing 16 and 32 55-mm S-5 rockets, or clusters of 240-mm S-24 rockets.

Further development of the tactical strike model resulted in the Yak-28I (*Brewer-C*) with a lengthened fuselage and longer engine nacelles and wingtip probes uniform with those of the all-weather interceptor Yak-28P (*Firebar*) that was being manufactured in parallel.   The forward fuselage of the Yak-28I was lengthened by approximately 2·5 ft/ 76 cm, and whereas the shorter engine nacelles of early pro-duction Yak-28s had prominent intake cones, the appre-ciably longer intakes subsequently introduced resulted in only the tips of the cones protruding.   These changes were accompanied by the lengthening of the probes extending

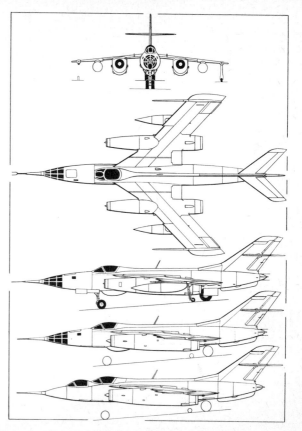

Illustrated above is the advanced operational conversion training variant of the Yak-28 (Maestro) based on the original Tac-R and strike model (Brewer–A), and below, the Yak-28R (Brewer–D) is seen with a recce pod beneath the fuselage

from the outrigger wheel housings near to the wingtips. The Yak-28I retained the ventral radome of the Yak-28L. A parallel version for the tactical reconnaissance role, the Yak-28R (*Brewer-D*), apparently had the weapon bay deleted, the space thus available being occupied by additional fuel tankage, and (like the *Brewer-A*) had no ventral radome. An external station was provided beneath the rear fuselage for a reconnaissance pod containing a number of sensors (probably including infrared linescanner and cameras providing horizon-to-horizon and forward-looking capability) and external antennae indicated the provision of other non-optical sensors and countermeasures equipment in the fuselage. An electronic reconnaissance (*Brewer-E*) variant features various external sensor housings and antennae.

The advanced operational conversion training model, the Yak-28U (*Maestro*) was based on the original tactical strike model (*Brewer-A*), retaining the shorter fuselage and engine nacelles. The nose glazing was deleted and a second cockpit for the pupil pilot was inserted ahead of the standard cockpit. An individual canopy was provided for each cockpit, the forward canopy hinging to starboard and the rear canopy sliding aft.

The figures quoted in the following specification for the tactical strike version of the Yak-28 are estimated:

Power Plant: *Two 10,140 lb (4 600 kg) dry and 13,670 lb (6 200 kg) reheat Tumansky R-11 turbojets.* ***Performance:*** *Max speed, 725 mph (1 167 km/h) or M=0·95 at sea level, 760 mph (1 225 km/h) or M=1·15 at 39,370 ft (12 000 m); tactical radius (lo-lo-lo mission profile), 230 mls (370 km/h) at 630 mph (1 015 km/h), (hi-lo-hi), 310 mls (500 km); range with two 220 Imp gal (1 000 l) auxiliary tanks, 1,100 mls (1 770 km) at 570 mph (917 km/h) at 36,090 ft (11 000 m); initial climb, 28,000 ft/min (142,2 m/sec); service ceiling, 55,000 ft (16 765 m).* ***Weights:*** *Loaded, 35,000 lb (15 876 kg); max take-off 41,890 lb (19 000 kg).* ***Dimensions:*** *Span, 41 ft 0 in (12,50 m); length, 70 ft 0 in (21,34 m); height, 13 ft 0 in (3,96 m).*

YAKOVLEV YAK-28P (FIREBAR)

Evolved in parallel with the Yak-28 (*Brewer-A*) tactical strike aircraft from which it differed primarily in having a dielectric nose cone, tandem seating for the two crew members with windscreen (and twin-wheel forward member of the 'bicycle' undercarriage) approximately 2·5 ft (76 cm) further

forward and internal weapons bay deleted, the Yak-28P all-weather interceptor fighter was flown as a prototype in 1960 with production deliveries to the IAP-VO *Strany* commencing some three–four years later. The Yak-28P has served with the V-VS for some 10 years and remains one of the primary interceptors of the IAP-VO *Strany*, the standard armament throughout having comprised a pair of AA-6 *Anab* (or AA-6-2 advanced *Anab*) AAMs with alternative infrared or semi-active radar homing heads, and X-band *Skip Spin* radar having been used for missile guidance and intercept.

An example of the Yak-28P exhibited at Domodedovo in 1967 featured a much longer and more pointed dielectric nosecone than that then standard on operational aircraft and also displayed four wing stores stations accommodating one *Anab* and one *Atoll* AAM beneath each wing. The lengthened nosecone, presumably adopted to lessen drag and reduce rain erosion but not indicating any increase in

(Above and below) The Yak-28P with the original short dielectric nose cone which has since been replaced by a much longer and more pointed cone (see page 246) which may be presumed to reduce drag and rain erosion

(Above, below and general arrangement drawing) The Yak-28P with the current lengthened dielectric nose cone and twin AAM pylons

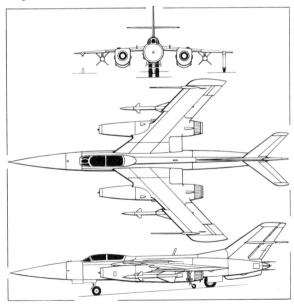

mance: Max speed (clean), 760 mph (1 225 km/h) or M=1·15 at 39,370 ft (12 000 m), (with two Anab AAMs), 695 mph (1 120 km/h) or M=1·05; max continuous cruise, 560 mph (900 km/h) or M=0·9; tactical radius (high-altitude patrol mission), 550 mls (885 km/h); initial climb, 28,000 ft/min (142,2 m/sec); service ceiling, 55,000 ft (16,765 m). **Weights:** Normal loaded, 37,480 lb (17 000 kg); max take-off, 40,785 lb (18 500 kg). **Dimensions:** Span, 41 ft 0 in (12,50 m); length, 72 ft 0 in (21,95 m); height, 13 ft 0 in (3,96 m).

radar capability, was subsequently standardized and fitted retroactively to operational Yak-28Ps but the standard twin-*Anab* armament appears to have been retained. The longer fuselage (and, in consequence, lengthened wheelbase) of the Yak-28P was eventually standardized for all versions of the Yak-28 (see *Brewer*), together with the longer air intakes and wingtip probes featured by the Yak-28P from the outset.

The figures quoted in the following specification are estimated:

Power Plant: Two 10,140 lb (4 600 kg) dry and 13,670 lb (6 200 kg) reheat Tumansky R-11 turbojets. **Perfor-**

246

YAKOVLEV YAK-40 (CODLING)

First flown on 21 October 1966, the Yak-40 marked the first venture of the Yakovlev design bureau into the civil transport field, although several light transport designs had previously been produced under the Yakovlev banner in addition to its better-known fighters and trainers. The task confronting the bureau was to evolve a small, economic short-haul transport that could replace many of the Lisunov Li-2 (DC-3) transports still being used in the Soviet Union, and this requirement meant that the new aircraft had to be able to operate at Class 5 airfields, with grass runways.

The emphasis on good field performance led the design team to adopt a three-engined layout rather than the usual twin-engined configuration for aircraft of this size; this meant that take-off weights and runway lengths could be calculated on the basis of losing only one-third, and not one-half, of total power in the case of an engine failure. The 3,300-lb (1 500-kg) turbofan engines were specially developed for the Yak-40 at the Ivchenko engine bureau, and the high thrust-to-weight ratio that they bestow on the aircraft is especially beneficial for operations at high-altitude airfields, of which there are many in the remoter regions of the USSR. The standard range of avionics and flight control system provides for operation down to Cat II standards, and future development for Cat III is projected.

The basic Yak-40 was designed as a 27-passenger short-haul feeder-liner, seating being three abreast (2+1) with an off-set aisle. A variety of alternative layouts has been evolved by the design bureau, including one with 33 seats at reduced pitch, mixed-class arrangements with 16 or 20 seats, and an executive model with 11 seats in two separate cabins. All versions have a ventral airstair as the main access to the cabin, and an APU is mounted above the rear fuselage, primarily for engine starting.

The Yak-40 (above right and immediately right) has been the subject of a major Aviaexport sales campaign and, by the beginning of 1975, had been exported to more than a dozen countries. The 500th Yak-40 was completed at Yakovlev's Saratov facility on 15 February 1974

Following construction of a batch of five prototypes, production of the Yak-40 was launched at a factory at

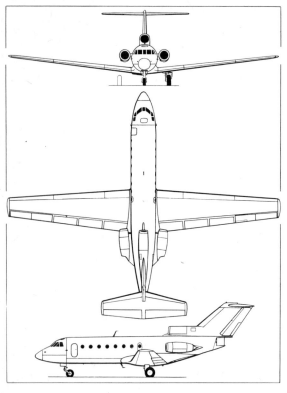

Saratov, some 300 miles (500 km) SE of Moscow, in 1967 and deliveries to Aeroflot began during the following year. Regular operations on scheduled services began on 30 September 1968, and production increased to eight a month by 1973 to meet the very large domestic demand. Between 500 and 600 Yak-40s have been built and the type has been the subject of a major export campaign by Aviaexport, the Soviet state aircraft marketing organization. To facilitate overseas sale, the Yak-40 has undergone full certification to western standards in Italy and Federal Germany, and a version with Collins avionics is available as the Yak-40EC. Among the users of the Yak-40 are Aertirrena in Italy; General-Air of Hamburg; Bakhtar Afghan; Air Calypso; Lloyd Aereo Boliviano; Balkan Bulgarian; CSA and its internal subsidiary Slovair, and Egyptair. Other examples are used by the government agencies and air forces.

Since the Yak-40 entered service, it has undergone some modifications, the most noticeable of which are the addition of a clam-shell thrust reverser on the centre engine, and deletion of the acorn fairing at the fin/tailplane leading-edge junction. During 1970, a version with a lengthened fuselage was projected as the Yak-40M, to carry 40 passengers, but this apparently did not proceed. During 1974, the Yak-40V became available for export, this having 3,858 lb (1 750 kg) s.t. AI-25T engines and fuel capacity increased from 6,614 lb (3 000 kg) to 8,820 lb (4 000 kg). This increased power permits the gross weight to be raised from 32,410 lb (14 700 kg) for the original 27-seater to 35,274 lb (16 000 kg) with a similar layout or 36,376 lb (16 500 kg) with a 32-seat high-density layout, when the payload is 6,000 lb (2 720 kg).

The following specification refers to the standard 27-seat Yak-40 with AI-25 engines:

Power Plant: *Three 3,300 lb (1 500 kg) s.t. Ivchenko AI-25 turbofans.* ***Performance:*** *Max speed, 373 mph (600 km/h) at sea level; max cruising speed, 342 mph (550 km/h) at 19,685 ft (6 000 m); initial climb rate,*

The Yak-40 has been progressively developed during the eight years that have elapsed since production was initiated, the most noticeable external change being the addition of a clam-shell thrust reverser on the centre engine and removal of the acorn fairing at the junction of the fin and tailplane

1,575 ft/min (8,0 m/sec); typical take-off run, 1,968 ft (600 m); typical landing roll, 1,804 ft (500 m); range with max fuel, 45-min reserve, 590 mls (950 km) at max cruise speed; max range, no reserves, 900 mls (1 450 km) at 261 mph (420 km/h) at 26,247 ft (8 000 m). **Weights:** Empty, 20,140 lb (9 135 kg); max payload, 5,070 lb (2 300 kg); max fuel load, 6,614 lb (3 000 kg); max take-off and landing weight, 32,410 lb (14 700 kg). **Dimensions:** Span, 82 ft 0¼ in (25,0 m); length, 66 ft 9½ in (20,36 m); height, 21 ft 4 in (6,50 m); wing area, 753·5 sq ft (70,0 m²).

The following specification relates to the 34-seat Yak-40V, with AI-25T engines; dimensions are as above:

Power Plant: Three 3,858 lb (1 750 kg) s.t. AI-25T turbofans. **Performance:** Max cruising speed, 342 mph (550 km/h) at 19,685 ft (6 000 m); typical take-off run, 2,625 ft (800 m); typical landing roll, 1,968 ft (600 m); range with max fuel, 45 min reserves, 810 mls (1 300 km) at max cruising speed; range with max fuel, no reserves, 1,210 mls (1 950 km) at 261 mph (420 km/h) at 26,247 ft (8 000 m). **Weights:** Empty, 20,955 lb (9 505 kg); max payload, 6,000 lb (2 720 kg); max fuel load, 8,820 lb (4 000 kg); max take-off and landing weight, 33,376 lb (16 500 kg).

YAKOVLEV YAK-42

In appearance an enlarged, swept-surface version of the Yak-40, the Yak-42 is in fact a completely new design, although it has many of the same design objectives— simplicity of operation, ability to fly into and out of restricted airfields with poor surfaces and minimum facilities, and good economy. Aeroflot, which drew up the requirement for an aircraft of Yak-42 size in the early 'seventies, is said to need up to 2,000 such transports in the 1980–90 timescale, primarily to help open up the remoter areas of the Soviet Union to the north and south of the main trunk air routes across the country.

The Yak-42 has the same configuration as the Yak-40, as indicated by model photographs and a mock-up completed in Moscow during 1973, but a more advanced standard of avionics is planned and leading-edge slats will be used on the wing to enhance the field performance. The basic layout is expected to provide 120 seats six-abreast, with a mixed-class version seating 40 first-class and 60 tourist-class passengers. Two-crew operation is planned, and access to the cabin will be through a ventral airstair and a

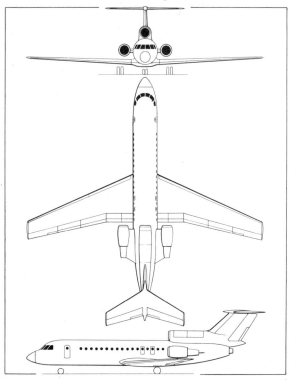

fuselage-side door aft of the flight deck.

To power the Yak-42, a new turbofan engine was under development by Vladimir Lotarev at the Azporozhyne engine works, with the best possible noise and smoke emission characteristics in order to meet the international requirements expected to apply in the next decade. Three prototypes of the Yak-42 are reported to be under construction, with the first flight to be made late in 1975. The following specification is provisional:

Power Plant: *Three 14,200 lb (6 440 kg) s.t. Lotarev D-36 turbofans.* **Performance:** *Cruising speed, 497 mph (800 km/h) at 26,250 ft (8 000 m); take-off run (all engines), 2,625 ft (800 m); range with max payload, 1,118 mls (1 800 km); range with max fuel, 1,740 mls (2 800 km).* **Weights:** *Max payload, 30,850 lb (14 000 kg); max take-off weight, 110,230 lb (50 000 kg).* **Dimensions:** *Span, 114 ft 10 in (35,00 m); length, 114 ft 10 in (35,00 m).*

INDEX OF AIRCRAFT TYPES

The parenthesized letters following some page numbers indicate photograph or photographs (p), general arrangement drawing (ga) or side elevation drawing (dr). Page numbers in **bold** type signify the primary entry relating to the type concerned.